UT campus and Texas state capitol looking south from the Main Building. *Prints and Photographs Collection, Dolph Briscoe Center for American History, di_06961.*

Horns of a Dilemma

Coping with Politics at the University of Texas

Kenneth Ashworth

Foreword by **Robert M. Berdahl**

Dolph Briscoe Center for American History
The University of Texas at Austin
Austin, Texas

A man can stand a lot as long as he can stand himself.

—**Alex Munthe,** *The Story of San Michele*

It is not so much knowledge of what you can do. It is knowledge of what you can stand, or better still, what you cannot stand.

—**T. V. Smith,** *A Non-Existent Man*

For Emily

Contents

Foreword

Shortly before leaving the University of Illinois in Urbana-Champaign to assume the presidency of the University of Texas at Austin, I had a conversation with Illinois's Arts and Sciences Dean Larry Faulkner, a native Texan who had spent time on the faculty at Texas, and who later succeeded me both as provost at Illinois and as president at Texas. "What can you tell me about Texas?" I asked. "Texas is an amazing combination of the ridiculous and the sublime," he replied. This book by Kenneth Ashworth, a memoir of his years in the offices of the University of Texas System, documents the truth of Faulkner's observation.

After receiving his bachelor's degree from the University of Texas in 1958, and a master's in public administration from Syracuse in 1959, Ashworth worked for various government agencies before returning to Texas to work for the Texas Higher Education Coordinating Board while completing his Ph.D. in the history and philosophy of education at UT Austin in 1969. Then, following seven years in several positions at the University of Texas System, he returned to the Texas Higher Education Coordinating Board as Commissioner of Higher Education in 1976, a position he held until 1997. To have occupied a position that put him squarely in the no-man's land of crossfire between the Texas legislature and the state's several university systems for twenty-one years indicates that Ashworth had considerable ability as a public servant and remarkable survival skills as a politician. He has documented some of those skills with his advice to aspiring public servants in his delightful book of monthly letters to an imaginary niece/nephew, entitled *Caught Between the Dog and the Fireplug, or How to Survive Public Service.*

The years Ashworth writes about here in *Horns of a Dilemma* were a tumultuous time on university campuses. The student rebellion against the Vietnam War became a broad rejection of authority and institutions, and spread across the country. While the University of Texas did not become one of the centers of revolt, it did not escape the conflict. Ashworth describes a tense encounter in which John Kenneth Galbraith, invited to lecture on the campus shortly after the Kent State massacre, was cornered by student leaders to address a crowd of demonstrators. Fortunately, he succeeded in defusing an explosive situation.

But much of the tumult on the Austin campus in these years resulted from politics within the university. At the center of the maelstrom of action was the chairman of the university's board of regents, Frank Erwin. Erwin was a hard-driving, hard-drinking, well-connected political operator who made the University of Texas his passion. He tolerated no opposition to his plans, cutting down his opponents and critics as relentlessly as he cut down the cypress trees and their student defenders that stood in the way of the expansion of the Texas football stadium.

In many fundamental ways, Frank Erwin ran the campus. He set up his office in the main building and roamed the campus as his domain, making his wishes known to compliant administrators. He held late-night drinking soirées with students, favored faculty, and select administrators. He despised liberal faculty and believed that the academic freedom they exercised in speaking out on the issues of the day damaged the university and interfered with his effort to secure resources from the legislature. His imperious involvement in the operations of the university undermined the authority of those charged to administer it. He was often contemptuous of university administrators. Ashworth relates a conversation with Erwin in which he pointedly asked Erwin whether he worried that his interference in university administration might weaken administrators. Erwin replied, with a grin, "You ever hear that old saw about when the emperor's in the field all his generals become lieutenants? Hell, all I have to deal with is corporals."

Two events central to Ashworth's narrative illustrate Erwin's impact on the campus. One is the meeting of the Board of Regents in May 1970. With the Kent State shootings earlier in the month, Erwin concluded that the university needed an administration that would take a harder line toward student demonstrations and that leadership changes needed to be made. In the course of one secret meeting, the regents undertook a Texas-sized bloodletting; they sidelined Harry Ransom, the chancellor who, while president of UT Austin, had built its reputation, and replaced him with Charles "Mickey" LeMaistre, a move that even mystified some of the regents. They sacked two vice chancellors and appointed Bryce Jordan interim president at UT Austin, replacing President Norman Hackerman, who was leaving for Rice. Ashworth, one year out of his Ph.D., with plans to leave his post as staff assistant to the executive vice chancellor for a position at UT Arlington, was appointed vice chancellor for academic affairs. Ashworth confesses that he had few qualifications for this appointment, but a regent liked him, so he got the job.

The second is the story of the firing of John Silber. As dean of the College of Arts and Sciences, John Silber presided over by far the largest portion of the university, a college with twenty-seven departments. Silber had built a significant power base within the college and among alumni throughout the state. Possessing a powerful intellect, Silber was also extremely ambitious, ruthless, and, like Erwin, luxuriated in the exercise of power. Also like Erwin, Silber relished confrontation. Erwin decided to break up Silber's academic empire by dividing the College of Arts and Sciences into four smaller colleges. Although openly angling to be named president of UT Austin, Silber nevertheless defended his position by opposing Erwin's plans for the reorganization of his college. In a meeting that has become part of university lore, Erwin fired him.

The aftermath of these events resulted in a number of the university's most well-known faculty deciding to leave for positions elsewhere. Erwin greeted each departure with caustic, personal attacks on the departing faculty. When Ashworth asked Erwin why he persisted in these public attacks, Erwin responded, "It's no fun to hate somebody if you can't hate 'em in public."

Regental and political interference in public universities is not unique to Texas. One need only recall that Ronald Reagan campaigned for governor with the promise to "clean up the mess in

Berkeley," and that one of his first acts as governor was to instigate the firing of UC President Clark Kerr. As Ashworth observes, political and regental intrusion in the University of Texas is less common today than in the period described here. But it is well recognized among academics that political intrusion still happens in Texas universities more often than elsewhere. Such intrusion both weakens the continuity of leadership and undermines the role of faculty governance that has been essential to the success of American universities. This may explain why the University of Texas at Austin has had twenty-eight presidents, including interim presidents, in 115 years, while Harvard has had thirty-three in 373 years. Public universities are one of the few institutions in our society capable of long-term thinking; their freedom is fundamental to American freedom, for they must serve both as sources of innovation and as critics of the status quo. As public institutions, they are accountable to the public, but they are too important to be made the sinecures for political favorites or to be subject to the short-term political whims or ambitions of governors or legislators.

The turbulence created by Erwin could easily have been avoided. His confrontations were largely about power, rarely about principle. Did it ultimately matter whether the College of Arts and Sciences was one college or three? Not really. Great universities have been organized with both models. Would the university have been weakened if normal search procedures had been followed in replacing the administration? Clearly not.

However, Erwin also served the interests of the University of Texas. He worked to expand its size, influence, and resources. He protected it against efforts of legislators who wanted to distribute to other Texas universities the Permanent University Fund (the large endowment derived from the university's oil revenue). He was ambitious for the university to recruit distinguished faculty and to become a university of national importance. Whether the University of Texas would have moved further faster without Erwin's interventions is an open question. The fact remains that UT had begun to emerge from regional to national prominence before Erwin began to dominate the scene, and it continued during and after his years of control.

People familiar with the history of the University of Texas will recognize much of the story Ashworth tells, because some of it has been recounted in some form before by the critical report of

Ronnie Dugger in *Our Invaded Universities* or in Joe Frantz's "opinionated" history, *Forty Acre Follies*. But Ken Ashworth provides both the eyewitness account of a participant and the analytical perspective of forty years of subsequent work in Texas higher education. Ashworth worked with, occasionally around, and sometimes against Frank Erwin, other regents, and university leaders on behalf of the university. The book is wonderfully written and entertaining; it reminds us how all leaders of universities engage both the ridiculous and the sublime. But it is also a serious book. His final chapters, whose reading would serve any prospective university administrator, consider the existential dilemmas of anyone working within an institutional structure: the conflicted nature of loyalty one owes to one's bosses, on the one hand, and to the institution one serves, on the other.

We are all educated about the nature of leadership by observing the style and methods of others. Having witnessed the heavy hand of Frank Erwin's leadership, Ashworth has drawn the opposite and, I believe correct, conclusion. "The futures of universities," he writes, "should be determined more by what originates with their faculties than what comes down from some central office or governing board." Amen to that.

Robert M. Berdahl

President of the Association of American Universities
Former President, the University of Texas at Austin
Chancellor Emeritus, University of California, Berkeley

Acknowledgments

Without imputing to any others endorsement of my accounts of events or for responsibility for my accuracy in describing them, I wish to acknowledge and thank the following individuals for their willingness to talk with me about their memories of some of the individuals and episodes of the years I cover in this book: Nancy McMeans Richey and Andy Yemma, former editors of the *Daily Texan*; John McKetta, Eldon Sutton, Ira Iscoe, and Robert Mayfield, UT Austin faculty members and administrators; Art Dilly, Frank Graydon, Sheila Simmons, and Henrietta Jacobsen, all of whom served with the UT System staff during the years covered by this book; and Lloyd Lochridge and Will Davis. The poem about the Waller Creek trees came from Hugh Sparks's memory of the events of the fall of 1969.

And I must acknowledge the memories shared with me by Norman Hackerman, Don Weismann, and L. Joe Berry, close and departed friends from the UT faculty, about their relations with John Silber.

At the Dolph Briscoe Center for American History at UT Austin I was assisted immensely in the editing and final copy of the book by Erin Purdy and Holly Taylor. And Ralph Elder deserves special praise for his work in the archives to turn up the many photographs from which those in this book could be chosen. And my special appreciation goes to Don Carleton, the Center's executive director, for his early interest in the book and for his suggestions and continuing encouragement.

Michele Kay Schultz was especially supportive and helpful in assisting me to organize the material for the book and in advising me on improving the manuscript for publication. She provided critical editorial advice and guidance just when I needed it most. And to her husband, Robert Schultz, I am grateful for his candid comment on an early draft that readers would surely be more interested in the history of the University of Texas during those troublesome years than in a litany of my travails and internal struggles. As a result, the reader suffers through much less introspection about "what I learned from life."

For her early reading of the manuscript and her suggestions and guidance I thank Joanna Hitchcock.

I wish to thank James Huffines, who as chairman of the UT Board of Regents directed the staff to open the files of the UT System and the board to permit me to refresh my memory on a number of the events of those years.

For their support of the Dolph Briscoe Center for American History in making possible the publication of the book I am most grateful to Ray Bowen, former president of Texas A&M University, and John Hagler, an Aggie and enthusiast for publishing this book about the damage done to a university by political intrusion. And for additional support I am indebted to Harry Reasoner, former chairman of the Texas Higher Education Coordinating Board, Jess Hay and James Huffines, former UT Board of Regents chairmen, and Larry Faulkner, former UT president and president of the Houston Endowment. Another knowing expert on the harm of political interference in universities and former president of UT Austin is Robert Berdahl, who supported my efforts and generously provided the foreword.

The Lyndon Baines Johnson School of Public Affairs at UT and the George Bush School of Government and Public Service at Texas A&M University supported my teaching at those schools for the past thirteen years and my research and writing for this book.

And most noteworthy, to Emily, my wife, I am especially grateful for her support, patience, and tolerance during the gestation of this memoir.

Preface

The years 1969 to 1973 were critical for the University of Texas at Austin, for Frank Erwin, for Harry Ransom, and for me. In telling my story of those years I am rounding out a bit of the histories of the other three.

These years were critical for UT Austin because the school could have been derailed from its climb to national prominence and was not, although at times that seemed possible.

They were critical years for Frank Erwin, as chairman of the UT Board of Regents, because, to use a phrase by Laurence Veysey, his "idiosyncratic taste for display" peaked and declined. These were significant times because Erwin was utterly unyielding in keeping students from taking over the UT Austin campus. These were years in which Erwin relished taking revenge on his enemies. And during this period he suffered a major setback when his political protégé was defeated, cutting off his means to a third six-year term on the Board of Regents and limiting his ability to acquire still greater influence and power.

These years were critical for Harry Ransom because midway through them, the regents, led by Frank Erwin, took from him his power to continue directing the future of his university, after he had spent more than a decade to set the school on its course toward greatness and national recognition.

During a few of those most formative years as UT moved toward greatness, I had the privilege of working on the inside in the UT System Administration near the policymakers who were directing and attempting to control events in those troubled times. Drawing on my personal experiences from those years, I have tried to describe the roles Frank Erwin and Harry Ransom and others played as the University of Texas struggled to come of age and achieve academic prominence.

These years of interference by the Board of Regents in the internal affairs at UT were critical for me for choices I had to make. On occasion I had to decide to what and to whom I would be loyal. And in having to choose, disloyalty became unavoidable. On one hand, it was so easy, as a member of the university administration, to remain silent and follow orders and be warmly accepted, and, on the other hand, so hard to speak up and disagree and put myself on the outside. How to function in that milieu was my challenge.

Marie Arana, commenting on her memoirs, says she believes there is a place in the mind where "thoughts can wander from the rigorously factual to the flamboyantly imagined." In this recounting I cannot swear that after forty years every detail is absolutely rigorously factual, but I will firmly deny that anything here is flamboyantly imagined.

My use of quotation marks in the conversations and dialogues is no way intended to represent that these were the actual words spoken. I have used quotation marks stylistically in order to capture the mood, content, and direction of conversations and decisions. The outcomes and consequences of the dialogues are real.

Some of what I say here is controversial. But I would observe, as did Truman Capote when some of his rich friends were dismayed at his recounting from their pleasure cruises their most intimate and puerile conversations, "Did they think I was not taking notes?"

To anyone aggrieved by events I recall, I can say only that I have done my best to be true to my story, and consequently, I have not tempered my chronicle to avoid offense. If I were not trying at my age to describe as closely as I can what actually happened, why bother to record it?

With a familiar episode here and there, some may feel, as with *Rashomon*, that this is a witness report on an already thrice-told tale.

CHAPTER 1

The Good Chance

In 1969 the University of Texas was in turmoil. Not as roiled as some other campuses across the country, but strife was far above the usual level of excitement and normal ferment at the Austin campus. Students were vigorously protesting the war in Vietnam, demanding greater equality for minorities, and resisting traditional paternalism from the faculty and administration. Faculty members were opposing plans by the regents to divide the College of Arts and Sciences and were deeply concerned about continuing legislative efforts to establish minimum teaching loads and demands for more time in the classroom and less research. Regents were displeased with student demonstrations and faculty rhetoric about the war and political intrusion, and the board was totally frustrated and disappointed with administrators for not keeping students and faculty under control and in their proper place. Campus administrators, already out of favor with the regents, found little support from students and received much faculty criticism for not standing up to regents, legislators, and other politicians.

To make matter worse for all parties, the offices of the UT System Administration, another layer of managers and executives overseeing a growing number of universities in addition to UT Austin, were located at the very center of the campus in the Tower Building, alongside the UT Austin administration. This physically framed the question whether the Austin president and his staff were in any way independent or separate from the System Administration. Offices for the regents, along with their meeting rooms in the Tower, put the Board of Regents where they witnessed too much and found it too easy to interfere and impose their judgments on the UT Austin president and his staff.

The System Administration of the University of Texas oversees extensive activities across the state. The UT System consists of all the component universities, the medical and dental schools, the public health school, and other financial, investment, and construction arms that come under the governance of the University of Texas Board of Regents. The System Administration includes the chancellor, vice chancellors, and subordinate heads of units and their support staffs. The System Administration is independent of any component institution and the arm of the Board of Regents that implements its policies throughout its conglomeration of universities and medical schools.

UT Austin, the Medical Branch in Galveston, and UT El Paso, formerly the School of Mines, were the original components of the UT System, which over the years grew to more than a dozen institutions. Such growth brought with it financial influence and awesome political clout when it could be organized.

As tensions continued to build on campuses across the country and dissent spread from one school to another, student protesters began to perform for each other, create networks, and raise the bar for outrageous manners, egregious behavior, and even violence.

Rumors ran rampant. The president of the university was going to be fired. Splitting the College of Arts and Sciences was a poorly disguised plan to displace the dean. The chancellor of the UT System Administration was in trouble with the regents. The National Guard and local police were being trained to put down demonstrations. The Nixon administration and the military had spies on college campuses. The regents and the administration were cooperating with the government and the military in suppressing civil rights and opposition to the war.

Immediately on completing my Ph.D. in May 1969, I was plucked from a routine state administrative position and dropped into the midst of this swirling maelstrom of campus upheaval. I was there when the president, under extreme pressure from the regents, chose to move to another university. I was there when cutting the trees along Waller Creek on the campus triggered student outrage and protests. I was there when the dean of Arts and Sciences was fired. I was there when the students marched on the state capitol after the Kent State shootings. I was there when the student and faculty's favorite candidate for president was refused the position by the regents. I was there when the presidency was denied to the acting president over the desire of the regents. I was there as presidents on other campuses were fired or pushed out and replaced. I was there when the much loved and heralded chancellor was forced out and replaced. And I was, at times, the handmaiden to the chief orchestrator and ramrod driving controversy and policy and action, the chairman of the Board of Regents, Frank C. Erwin Jr.

In the forty years I spent in public service, the years 1969 to 1973 were the most intense in pressure and personal stress that I experienced in my entire career. But as a consequence, they were also the most instructive to me in my professional development. Although I had been in some pressure-cooker situations and in confrontational circumstances for months on end in other jobs, in contrast to what I encountered in the University of Texas System Administration, I had been serving in the backwaters of public service.

Some of the issues I would face came to create major internal conflicts for me. How I would eventually resolve those struggles would have serious consequences for the University of Texas.

But how did I, a newly minted Ph.D., end up in a position at the UT System Administration from which I would soon be elevated to vice chancellor for academic affairs?

After graduating from the University of Texas in Austin with a B.A. in economics in 1958, I spent a year at Syracuse University to earn a master's degree in public administration. From 1959 to 1966 I worked in Washington, D.C., with several federal agencies. Two of those seven years I spent working in urban redevelopment for the city of San Francisco. Then, already fairly well embarked on my career as a civil servant, I decided I was not going to spend the rest of my life dedicated to public housing, code enforcement, and slum clearance. So I took a pay cut to move my family back to Washington to work in education and pursue a doctoral degree in hopes of landing a college presidency someday. Upon returning to Texas in 1966 from the U.S. Office of Education, I worked for the state until, in 1969, I completed my doctorate at UT in the history and philosophy of education.

In 1966 while I served as assistant commissioner with the Coordinating Board for Higher Education, I became acquainted with Harry Ransom, chancellor of the UT System Administration and former president of UT Austin. Ransom did so much to shape UT Austin for coming greatness and international recognition that I discuss his role in more detail in Chapter 2.

Chancellor Ransom often attended meetings of the state Coordinating Board to explain or justify an item from one of the UT System universities. It did not require any special sensitivity on my part to notice that Ransom was not included in the camaraderie among the other university presidents. This was obvious to most everyone. I could not decide whether this was because the other presidents held him in awe because of his national reputation or because he kept himself aloof from them. He simply did not participate in the casual conversations and cajolery of the other presidents as they caught up on events with each other.

When I did begin to speak with Ransom, I found him at first much easier to approach than I had thought, but it was clear to me he was not at ease with small talk. There were long silences in conversation with him; every moment did not have to be filled with talk.

I made it a point over those years I worked at the Coordinating Board to spend a few minutes at our meetings chatting with him, even if at times it was a little difficult to keep the conversation going. Sometimes we just stood together in silence until one of us would try to start another topic. From time to time during those intermittent conversations at Coordinating Board meetings, Ransom would ask about progress on my doctoral degree.

I did not know at the time that Ransom's laissez-faire style of administration had run up against a new nastiness in higher education that was entirely foreign to this gentle and soft-spoken man. To this point in his career there had not been anything affecting or touching on UT that was beyond his grasp and competence. But recently he had had a student pound on his desk with his sandal, police officers had to be posted in the hallway to prevent students from taking over and occupying his office, and occasionally even faculty members were acting uncivilized. All his years of unparalleled contributions to the university seemed little appreciated as he came under personal attack as a symbol of the so-called establishment.

Only later would I learn that the Board of Regents had begun to have doubts that Ransom was strong enough to stand up to increasingly obstreperous student and faculty demands. He had tried to prevent a rally on campus led by three of the most aggressive protesting organizations, the Students for a Democratic Society, the Student Nonviolent Coordinating Committee, and the Black Panthers. The rally was headed by Stokely Carmichael, a nationally known and notorious militant. These groups epitomized the new pressures on higher education arising across the county. When Ransom's efforts to prevent the rally failed, he was attacked by the students for interfering and by the regents for how he had handled the situation. The civilized world Ransom had spent his life promoting and securing was coming apart at the very spot on earth where he had focused his energies. Who would have thought it possible? Civilized discourse was failing in the temple of reason.

Over the months leading up to completing my doctorate, I had begun to look for a position at a university. To take on a college presidency some years down the road, I needed to start getting campus experience. I applied for positions at several out-of-state institutions, and when I asked Harry Ransom for help, he agreed to be a reference for me.

Then one day I received a call from Otis Singletary, Ransom's vice chancellor for academic affairs, inviting me to lunch. While I was an undergraduate at UT a decade earlier, Singletary had just begun his own administrative career as assistant to the president. He had been a guest lecturer on the Civil War in an American history course I had taken. Now, after having served in the Lyndon Johnson administration in Washington, he had returned to Austin as vice chancellor under Ransom. While I was working at the Coordinating Board, Singletary and I had crossed paths, and I reminded him that when I was an undergraduate he had autographed for me his book *Negro Militia and Reconstruction*.

These may seem like calculated efforts to extend my network and further my career, but both my contacts with Ransom and Singletary were truly innocent of such intent. Small talk was difficult for me too, and I desperately grasped at whatever topic might ease a conversation. Singletary's approach was exceedingly assertive and overpowering; he was the kind of person I found especially difficult. Mentioning his book was about the only thing I could think of that we might have in common.

Over lunch Singletary revealed that Ransom had told him it would be a mistake to let me go to an out-of-state university. Singletary said he was there to convince me I should accept a position as his assistant at the UT System Administration.

It did not take a lot of convincing for me to decide to accept his offer. Here was an unbelievable opportunity, and it meant I would not have to uproot my family again, having just moved us from Washington, D.C., three years earlier.

After Singletary had persuaded me to take the job, he said, "Now I want us to stand up and shake hands on it. I want an unbreakable Texas agreement." And although I felt foolish doing it in a room full of people, I went through the ritual with him.

When we sat down he said, "Ken, you need to know, now that you have taken this job, that I am leaving in three months to become president at the University of Kentucky."

In disbelief I asked him why, then, had he gotten me to agree to take a job with such a tenuous future? He said it would be a good position for me and that Ransom wanted me on his team. He added, "I'll help you in the time I have left here. I'll make you a '90-day wonder.' My successor will not be able to function without you."

Consequently, within a few weeks I was immersed in the turbulence, rivalries, and politics of the University of Texas at Austin and the University of Texas System Administration as assistant to the vice chancellor for academic affairs. It would be a mad dash to try to keep up—and to keep my head.

CHAPTER 2

A University on the Prairie
Makes Its Move

It is not possible to do justice to the many leaders among presidents, deans, faculty, and regents who over the years conceived of greatness for the University of Texas. From its very beginnings on the prairie in 1881, leaders envisioned a bright future for the new school. High aspirations drove leaders early on as graduates increasingly filled scientific, business, engineering, and other professional positions across the state. However, gains in academic rankings were slow in coming against the progress being made at the same time by the university's principal competitors.

Standards were not all that rigorous, and the school was still small and insignificant on the plains of Texas. T. V. Smith, philosopher, poet, political scientist, professor, early radio talk-show host, and member of Congress from Illinois, was a University of Texas graduate. In his autobiography, he titled his chapter about coming to UT in 1913, "The Higher Learning on Texas Prairies." About arriving in Austin without a high school diploma Smith said, "In what seemed to me a generous moment the Admissions Office permitted me to register as a sophomore."

At the turn of the twentieth century, UT was seen on the national horizon as no more than a regional institution. Provincial, parochial, or regional, whether described on the prairie or on the range, UT did not receive much recognition from the rest of higher education or others ranking institutions of higher learning. Even after the university had finally "arrived," as it were, and was being recognized as one of the better schools in the nation, the *Saturday Review* referred to it as "Cambridge on the Range."

Completed in 1937, the University Tower with thirty-one floors remained, even at the end of the Second World War, the tallest building in Austin. Seen from any perspective, from an airplane, train, or automobile from anywhere in or near Austin, the school was still in the midst of the prairie.

Graduates began making their mark in the professions, in science, and in graduate schools elsewhere. And although the school was also attracting some nationally recognized scholars, hopes for a larger role and greater recognition for UT remained unrealized for decades. Then, in the 1950s, the first aggressive moves toward a larger future began to take shape.

With the end of the war and surging enrollment, thanks to veterans arriving under the auspices of the G.I. Bill, new opportunities arose for the school. At the same time, the value of the oil-rich lands that underpinned the university's endowment grew as the demand for oil and gas continued beyond the war and into the peacetime growth of the U.S. economy.

Texas students and parents shared with the rest of the nation a growing recognition of the importance of a college education as a way to achieve personal advancement. Industry and business demanded a better educated workforce as the United States became a manufacturing colossus. Business leaders increasingly looked to higher education for new scientific discoveries and technologies and for business and engineering graduates who could function internationally.

At midcentury, UT was still a small institution with a total enrollment of 7,000. There was little development along the two-lane and, in places, three-lane road connecting Dallas and San Antonio through Austin. Although Austin was the state capital, it only had a population of 133,000.

The first leader of those years to recognize the new opportunities for the university was President Logan Wilson. Looking very much the prototype of a university president, silver-haired, suave, and sophisticated, Wilson arrived in 1953, shortly after UT had been blacklisted by the American Association of University Professors (AAUP). This censure was imposed after the Board of Regents fired its president in 1944 for resisting the board's encroachments on academic freedom and insistence on firing certain economics professors. President Wilson persuaded the AAUP to lift its censure of the university. He then turned his attention to securing a stronger financial base for the school and began extensive faculty recruitment and construction programs. Wilson saw the university's potential, and he led the school in significant moves toward national recognition.

Among those veterans returning from the war was Captain Harry Ransom, reclaiming the position he had left in the English Department. It did not take Ransom long to make his mark in Austin. Within a few years President Wilson promoted him to Dean of the College of Arts and Sciences and then to the top academic position on campus, provost and vice president. Ransom immediately began to improve the university through aggressive recruiting. He solicited the names of the best faculty in different fields across the nation and then brought them to the campus as lecturers to size them up. Those he wanted, he signed on while they visited, or he followed them back to their institutions to recruit them.

Ransom was a popular choice for provost. In his new job, with authority over academics across the entire campus, he pushed for excellence. He quickly seized a new opportunity when the legislature removed restrictions on how the university could use its endowment from the oil lands in West Texas. He began to spend endowment income on faculty needs other than construction. He aggressively used these monies for libraries, equipment, research, and to help researchers procure matching funds to attract government and business grants and contracts.

Since Wilson's and Ransom's drive for excellence, UT Austin has continued on the upward trajectory they established. UT has doubled its buildings to more than 11 million square feet, degrees conferred each year have increased from 700 to 1,300, and doctorates awarded grew from just over 500 to a 1,000 a year. The number of doctoral offerings doubled from 40 to 82. The most phenomenal growth, however, has been in funding. The annual operating budget for the Austin campus has grown from $100 million to more than $2 billion.

What specifically did Harry Ransom achieve? And how did he go about it?

Very early in his career Ransom was asked to advise the university on buying rare books, and his attention to this opportunity shaped his vision for UT for his entire tenure. He envisioned establishing a library of international repute, one patterned on the oldest and grandest of European libraries. As part of his grand plan he set out to acquire not just rare books but the manuscripts of contemporary writers. This became his focus rather than trying to compete with Harvard or Yale for the rarest books. He would buy the early drafts and edited copies of literary works to provide researchers with a paper record of the creative process. Although some rivals accused him of buying "trash," it soon became evident that UT was becoming a favored destination when biographers and critics and scholars researched major authors and dramatists. The Austin campus attracted scholars because the library held authors' entire literary collections, often their whole libraries. The home for these new holdings was the Humanities Research Center, the brainchild of Harry Ransom.

In 2010, paying homage to the center renamed for its founder, John Howard Wilson said, "The Ransom Center conserves the works of . . . writers and artists so that they are available to scholars as long as our civilization lasts."

Another of Ransom's initiatives that attracted national attention was the *Texas Quarterly,* a journal he envisioned to reach audiences across all of the arts and sciences. The new publication was a runaway success from its first issue and brought praise and recognition from across the country.

Ransom was truly an institution builder. Much of what he achieved both survived and did well because of the organizations he founded, such as the Arts and Sciences Foundation, Friends of the Library, and the Chancellor's Council. He initiated ways to bestow recognition and honor on those who supported his causes and who aspired to become acquainted with other donors and patrons of influence.

Among his most important permanent improvements to the campus was the Academic Center, established on the West Mall as an "open stacks" library of 400,000 books for undergraduates. Until that time undergraduates had not been permitted access to the stacks. Ransom's idea, first implemented at UT, was soon replicated on campuses across the nation.

After he was promoted to president and then chancellor, Ransom had to work hard at times to maintain support from the regents for his aggressive acquisitions for the new Humanities

Research Center. As they began to see how university rankings were affected by his improvements to the library, the regents became more willing to open the purse of the university endowment to him. Whether he ever actually was authorized a "line of credit" to buy books, as alleged by his envious competitors, for all practical purposes he created his own line of credit by owing some booksellers hundreds of thousands of dollars over months and years. His buyers would allow him to fall in arrears, but they remained willing to treat him as an "account receivable" because he always paid, even if belatedly.

On occasion he would have an acquisition locked in before the regents had actually authorized the money. But when he would explain to the board the merits of the particular buying opportunity he had on the line, they almost always would come through with the funding, albeit sometimes reluctantly. He would set the hook not only with a seller but then would do the same with the Board of Regents.

Ransom became known as "the fastest dean in the West" for his aggressive faculty recruitment and the deals he made in acquiring materials for his library. His practice of acquiring whole libraries or collections rather than individual rare books brought donations of a number of private collections. In fact, Ransom bought and accepted books and manuscripts so fast that boxes and crates sometimes remained unopened for months after their arrival. When the benefits of some of Ransom's acquisitions were not immediately apparent, Frank Erwin sometimes chafed at how much Ransom was spending for "a bunch of used books." Erwin's weak joke was a thin disguise for his concerns about how much the regents were devoting to Ransom's acquisitions. Erwin did not want any reduction in expenditures for buildings, which could readily be seen and admired by all.

It can be argued that most of what Harry Ransom did for the university he did off campus: buying, recruiting, fund-raising, speaking, and charming donors and supporters. With his hiring he competed hard for stars, but once they arrived, he left them on their own to do their scholarly work because he was off to his next acquisition or recruitment.

Ransom had a concept of where he wanted to take the university, but he had a very light touch on his campus. In fact, he was not a typical hands-on administrator at all; he was more of a visionary about where the university needed to go and about what it needed to do to get there than he was a chief executive officer who sat behind a desk and issued orders by memoranda and gave directions to subordinates. He manifestly disliked mundane administrative tasks. He could bargain, bid, and bluff with the best when operating off campus, but on campus he was quiet and subdued and often inattentive to campus routine.

Some went so far as to call Ransom a "dreamer." He clearly was not a manager. He enlisted support from the regents for what excited him most, pursuing his particular vision of greatness for the university. He then went off campus to do the recruiting, buying, and persuading to build the base for his vision. What he did in the field began to show up on the campus as crates got delivered and new academics arrived for work. The university's visibility and reputation continued to rise. He was its principal spokesperson, fundraiser, cheerleader, drummer, explicator, pleader, and visionary.

But Ransom knew executive and managerial decisions had to be made during his absences and periods of disinterest and neglect. While he was out doing what he did best, he turned the responsibility for running the university over to Norman Hackerman. Ransom retained the dual titles of chancellor of the UT System Administration and president of UT Austin from 1963 to 1967. During those years, Norm, as he was known on the campus, served as vice president.

Having come to UT as an assistant professor of chemistry after obtaining his doctorate from John Hopkins University and after having spent World War II working on the Manhattan Project to produce the atomic bomb, Hackerman began his administrative career as department chairman. When the regents divided the administrations of the UT System and UT Austin in 1967, it was fitting that he should be promoted to president to continue and expand the duties he had been carrying for four years. Ransom remained as chancellor of the System.

Hackerman was undoubtedly the strongest administrator on campus. He could be acerbic and blunt. But he was decisive. He was known for beginning to shout at supplicants as they came through the door to his office, stating his position before they could even find a seat. In his office one day I heard him yell on the phone, "Goddamn it, John, shut up and listen to me. The answer is no," and he hung up.

When a professor at Rice overheard a similar telephone exchange, he remarked to Hackerman that you couldn't please all the people all the time. Hackerman shot back, "I have never felt the need to please any of the people any of the time."

Norm remained cool in the face of controversy, and the faculty liked and supported him. He had the reputation of standing up to the regents and legislators, a rare trait and one admired by the faculty and students. They saw him as forceful and independent and always in touch with the academic side of the university. Even while president, he taught an early morning freshman chemistry class every semester and maintained a research laboratory.

Then, in contrast to the usual gradual pace of transition in higher education, events forced quick changes that were very much at odds with Ransom's style and leadership. Protests and demonstrations erupted on campuses across the nation.

UT students became part of the antiauthoritarian milieu as protesters and demonstrators undertook to extend free speech on campus, to challenge sexual mores, to promote civil rights, to shuck in loco parentis, and, in particular, to oppose the war in Vietnam. Campus disruptions across the country included picketing administrative offices, sit-ins to occupy presidents' offices, and shutting down universities as a protest against public policies. Student and faculty and off-campus organizations resorted to pressure and even violence to use universities as instruments to rectify policies on civil rights and the Vietnam War. University neutrality was not acceptable. Acts of violence increased as administrative offices, ROTC buildings, and some research laboratories were trashed and firebombed on campuses.

The prominently published picture of a student at Cornell University sitting in the window of the president's office with a shotgun across his lap epitomized what was happening on many campuses across the country. It was not surprising that academic leaders like Harry Ransom discovered they were not prepared to deal with unreasoning, uncompromising, and uncivilized behavior and demands. Ransom preferred the light touch in directing the university. Students were quick to exploit this weakness.

Frank Erwin, who had served on the nine-member Board of Regents since 1963 and became chair three years later, was beginning his second six-year appointment. In reward for Erwin's staunch support, John Connally had planned upon his election to place

Erwin on the Board of Regents in 1965. But one of his 1963 appointees, W. St. John Garwood, was denied confirmation when a conservative cabal in the state senate came together and in a sneak attack labeled him an extremist liberal, condemning him as a "one worlder" who supported the United Nations. As a result Erwin was immediately appointed in Garwood's place. This early appointment made it possible for him to serve a second six years as Connally reappointed him at the very end of his third term as governor, just days before Preston Smith took office.

Erwin became an immediate power on the board through his close association with W. W. Heath, who Connally had just reappointed to his second term on the board. Heath and Erwin conferred almost daily on university business. Heath, as chair, recognized Erwin's talents and similar political views and concerns about student disorder. Heath made it easy for Erwin to come to power by appointing him chair of important committees and giving him favored assignments. After Heath resigned to become ambassador to Sweden, Erwin succeeded him as chairman.

In this time of student protests, Erwin immediately took a stand. As campuses across the nation were taken over by students, Erwin was adamant this was not going to happen at his alma mater. In pressing for stronger positions by administrators he considered indecisive and irresolute, he increasingly took a hand in directing campus events. To him student demonstrations and rallies had not been met with sufficient vigor. He absolutely refused to permit administrators to give in to students' "nonnegotiable demands" or to tolerate any form of campus disruption. Erwin would stand behind any president on any UT campus who would confront disruptive students or prop up any president who appeared to falter in standing up to student demands. He would even replace that president, or, if necessary, personally stand in place of that president. He resolutely refused to permit any school in the UT System to close in response to student demands.

Erwin particularly resented the damage he sensed that students and recalcitrant faculty were inflicting on UT. He was quick to blame students and troublesome faculty for holding UT back in making its mark among the great universities of the nation.

The university had come a long way from its quiet beginnings on the Texas prairie.

CHAPTER 3

Building the University's Political Clout

Through the early decades of the twentieth century, the initial growth of UT Austin was inextricably tied to population increases across the state. But the future of the Austin campus was even more intertwined with the increased dependency of the state on scientific discovery and technological innovations. Out of such conditions Frank Erwin was able to extend the influence of the UT System and the Board of Regents into every major city in the state.

Texas's internationally famous native son, Walter Prescott Webb, described the extreme difficulties of settling frontier Texas and of establishing its economic base. In his 1931 book *The Great Plains*, he described how the state's economy had been founded on several modest technologies. The original moldboard plow in progressively improved models had enabled the farmers to plow deeply and to turn the hard sod and break the unyielding roots of native grasses. The new plows increased the area of farmers' cultivation and in turn supported more people and promoted urbanization.

The windmill had enabled settlers to raise water from wells to irrigate their crops and support their cattle. Barbed wire had made it possible for ranchers to keep the higher meat-yielding cattle imported from abroad separated from the native longhorns, which provided little meat and less milk, and were mean and ornery and prevailed in the wild, inbreeding to yield rangy and tough meat.

And then there was the six-shooter that provided the new settlers with the firepower to win horseback gun battles with the Comanche and Apaches, who were the best horsemen in the world. Until the revolver came along, the Comanche had so completely dominated the land of West Texas and other parts of the Midwest that mapmakers had simply labeled the unexplored area the Great American Desert. Then the Texas Rangers obtained the new Colt revolvers, and the Indians were subdued and driven off their lands or killed.

General economic progress ensued in succeeding generations through rapid settlement, land speculation, consolidation of ranches, enlarged farms, and the installation of railroad lines. Webb described how little by the little the conditions of the people improved, attracting more migration into the state.

By the middle of the twentieth century, cattle raising on open range had given way to cotton production, and the oil and gas industries had come to predominate and become the major new contributors to the Texas economy. However, each of these enterprises had required new technological developments and scientific discoveries, whether it was disease and screwworm control among cattle, mitigating the effects of the boll weevil, or new drill bits and advances in geological mapping.

With the agricultural capacity of the state and the dependence on oil for ships and the other vast machinery of World War II, Texas developed a booming economy. Metropolitan areas began to grow, and Dallas, Houston, San Antonio, and even Austin and El Paso began to appear among the larger and faster growing cities of the nation. Banking, insurance, and other service industries were on the rise.

Then, after the war, the veterans, drawing benefits under the G.I. Bill, showed up in large numbers on the Austin campus. What came as a surprise to many faculty members was that under enormous growth pressures and with inadequate housing and labs and classrooms, the quality of students and their performance rose significantly. The veterans, older and more mature, brought a new seriousness to their studies and set higher standards that the regular students had to rise to meet as well.

The result of all this was geometric increases in college and university requests for financial support from the state legislature. As the colleges grew in enrollments, their leaders asked not just for buildings and more money for salaries, but they demanded support for new programs in engineering and sciences and business administration. There were new demands for graduate degrees in the humanities and liberal arts as well. College and university budgets that had been in the hundreds of thousands of dollars jumped to tens of millions. Legislators could not determine which requests were legitimate and which were opportunistic uses of the present growth to fulfill the ambitions of presidents, regents, and chambers of commerce. Legislators soon gave up trying to coordinate the growth and to set priorities through legislative committees. In 1959 the legislature created a Commission on Higher Education and gave the new agency authority to try to make sense out of the multitude of new requests pouring in from institutions of higher learning.

In 1963 John Connally, the newly elected governor, and his team had already seen how ineffective the Commission on Higher Education had been in the face of the continuing demands of higher education leaders. The agency had authority to collect data and write monographs and to preach about quality, but the commission could do little effective planning or devise or enforce rules that were needed.

And the runaway growth was totally unplanned. Private colleges and universities were being converted to public institutions by the legislature, thereby becoming dependent on continuing state funding. Two-year junior colleges were converting to full four-year status to become new state colleges, and as a result also becoming dependent on state support. New master's degree programs opened in many colleges, and universities began to offer doctoral degrees on the grounds that they needed to produce faculties for the continuing onslaught of coming enrollments. State teacher's colleges became state colleges and then became universities through frequent name changes pressed on the legislature.

For example, in the years just before Connally became governor, a junior college in Wichita Falls became Midwestern University; a private university in Houston, which had begun as a private junior college, became the University of Houston; and a private junior college in Edinburg became Pan American University. The public junior college in San Angelo became Angelo State College. At the time of Governor Connally's election, there was a proposal pending to convert the junior college in Odessa into a state college or university. Other cities and regions of the state were lining up to get on the bandwagon to boost local economies and fulfill the ambitions of local college presidents. As the president of West Texas State University in Canyon said, "If the state would just get out of my way, I could make WTSU into another MIT."

On Governor Connally's transition team in 1963 was Frank Erwin, who had helped convince Connally to leave his position in Washington as secretary of the navy to run for governor. Erwin had then worked diligently for his election and gained a position of influence in Connally's new administration.

One of the new governor's first assignments went to Larry Temple, a young lawyer in Austin who would later become special counsel to President Lyndon Johnson. Temple had the job of writing a bill to strengthen the coordination of higher education in state government. As Temple wrote the bill, Erwin made suggestions on what the bill should do. The higher education situation had gotten so badly out of hand that even the college and university presidents and their boards signed on and got behind the effort to replace the old Commission on Higher Education with a stronger agency.

The new Coordinating Board for higher education created by the legislature was given the assignment to prevent and eliminate unnecessary duplication among institutions of higher education to improve quality and to reduce costs to the state. The agency was granted authority over expenditures on buildings and was given the authority to deny or approve new campuses or branches of universities.

As the new board members and staff went to work, they quickly identified the dire circumstances about to be confronted by the state. By 1965 Governor Connally and his advisers recognized that the enrollment crisis of the returning veterans in the late 1940s and 1950s had only been a prelude to what was coming. The state was now about to be inundated with an even larger second wave of demand for higher education. Next in line were the children of these veterans, the baby boomers. This new wave of students could be counted right then in the public school classrooms across the state. Those young people were undeniably there, and they and their parents were going to be even more demanding of opportunities for higher education than the previous generation.

By 1968 I was working at the Coordinating Board as an assistant commissioner while I pursued my doctorate. The Commissioner of Higher Education and the members of the Coordinating Board knew the state had to act to address this coming increase in college enrollments. We recommended to the governor and the legislature the establishment of at least six new state universities and large increases in higher education funding.

Under the early domination of state government by rural legislators, colleges had been placed in remote locations away from the bright lights and distractions of large cities. For example, colleges and universities existed in cities such as Canyon, Commerce, Denton, Alpine, Huntsville, and Kingsville. Therefore, it was no surprise that the Coordinating Board found that locations for the new campuses should be Dallas, Houston, San Antonio, and Corpus Christi. New schools in Midland-Odessa and Laredo were recommended in response to political pressure.

By 1969, when the Texas legislature began to address the Coordinating Board's recommendations to authorize the creation of the new universities, Erwin was at the peak of his power in his position as chairman of the UT Board of Regents. Very conveniently the Board of Regents had separated and strengthened its System Administration apart from UT Austin. And that System Administration and its governing board under Frank Erwin's leadership now had experience in overseeing multiple campuses. Even though Erwin's first concern was always the welfare and advancement of the UT campus in Austin, he would not neglect opportunities that could strengthen the political base in the legislature to ensure the betterment of that flagship campus. An expanded UT System with campuses in the major urban areas would increase the ranks of those Erwin could mobilize in support of his beloved alma mater. He could see ahead to the deals and swaps and trades and favors that made up the toolbox of his political bartering.

But Erwin was not the only opportunist on the scene. Community leaders in Dallas had closely tracked the changes occurring in the Texas economy. Dallas businessmen had been deeply involved in the successive economic drivers of the state: cattle, cotton, oil, and gas. Dallas entrepreneurs had subsequently used this involvement to make their city a center for banking, financial, and insurance corporations.

By 1969 the primitive technologies of the early settlers of Texas described by Walter Prescott Webb had long been surpassed by the scientific and technological advancements of the modern age.

As technology became more important to the nation, scientific and engineering industries emerged in the Dallas-Fort Worth areas in the form of aircraft manufacturing and transportation and in the electronic fields, exemplified by the development and manufacture of the transistor as a replacement for vacuum tubes in radios, televisions, and countless electronic devices.

One of the three founders of Texas Instruments was Dallas mayor Erik Jonsson. Another was Cecil Green. The third, Eugene McDermott, was serving on the Coordinating Board for higher education, the very state agency now recommending a new campus in the Dallas area. The city had long lamented the deficiency of state-supported higher education there, and this was especially felt by the founders of new industries and businesses such as Texas Instruments. These three men were now placed in a unique position to follow through on an educational thrust they had begun several years earlier.

In their positions as leaders of Texas Instruments they had begun to experience acutely the shortage of engineers and scientists they needed to expand their corporation and to stay on the cutting edge of technology that was leading them to wealth and corporate success. Finally they saw no solution but to create their own research and training institute. They set up the Southwest Center for Advanced Studies (SCAS) north of Dallas in a building in the wheat fields near their transistor plant. The purpose of their new center was to attract scientific and engineering experts and researchers and to provide graduates and apprentices for their industry. By the mid-1960s, the center had become a very expensive institution to maintain without substantial results. The plan had called for two thousand scientists and Ph.D.s, but by now they had only a few dozen doctoral students enrolled, and only a half dozen had completed their doctoral work. The triumvirate that had established SCAS were finding their new enterprise of only limited success, and their institution was becoming a major financial drain, especially after Lloyd Berkner, the founding president and eminent atmospheric scientist and the school's driving force, had died.

The Texas Instruments founders had tried to give their failed enterprise to Texas A&M University and to North Texas State University and to Southern Methodist University, but there were no takers. They had tried to arrange for long-distance and joint degrees with UT Austin, but these arrangements had not worked out. The next effort was to try to pass SCAS on to the state, but the legislative effort in 1967, with Erwin trying to help the Dallas leaders, failed.

The predictable result of the Coordinating Board recommending a new campus in the Dallas area was that these various circumstances and needs came together in a natural confluence. In the 1969 legislative session, the new university the Coordinating Board had recommended for the Dallas area got assigned under Erwin's careful stewardship to the University of Texas System Administration.

Similarly, the new university to be created in San Antonio was placed under the UT Board of Regents. John Peace from San Antonio, a close political ally of John Connally, had been appointed a UT regent as a result of delivering the Mexican votes for San Antonio, sealing the election for Connally in his hard-fought race against an incumbent governor and a field of four other well-known candidates. Peace worked with Erwin in influencing the assignment by the legislature of that city's new campus to the UT System.

In making these deals to strengthen the UT System as a way to promote his alma mater, Erwin also accrued favors owed to him. He expanded his network of political movers and shakers whom he would be able to call on to help in his larger strategic politics as well, such as his efforts to promote the future of the youthful lieutenant governor Ben Barnes.

Once the new universities had been authorized, there remained the problem of finding the money to pay for them. In authorizing the new universities in 1969, the very parsimonious legislature had carefully arranged it would never have to buy land for the new campuses. The legislation required that the city in which a new university was to be located must provide a tract of land of not less than 200 acres, free of cost to the state.

This did not provide an obstacle. Developers quickly competed in offering land for the new campuses in anticipation of big gains off their remaining properties. Some developers offered land in excess of the 200 acres to influence site selection in their favor.

The selection of specific sites for the new campuses presented Erwin with still another opportunity for deal making and trading of favors for his political use.

CHAPTER 4

A Standard Frank Erwin Operating Procedure

Within a few days of taking my new job with Otis Singletary in the UT System Administration, I received my first exposure to the "Erwin treatment." Singletary took me along to a meeting with Erwin.

Singletary said, "Now watch how Frank tries to push me around and how I'm not going to let him do it."

Over drinks at the Forty Acres Club, Erwin began a prolonged interrogation about which of the several sites being proposed for a new UT campus in the Midland-Odessa area Singletary preferred. They were both enjoying their drinking and jousting with each other. Each dragged out his portion of the exchange. I was there as audience and apprentice.

Just approaching fifty, Erwin had started at the university in 1937 and had stopped out to serve in the U.S. Navy in World War II. By 1948 he had completed his law degree at UT and entered private practice.

Erwin was a large man, standing well over six feet and carrying enough extra weight to be called robust at least, and portly at most. His jowly face, beneath a head of wavy, graying hair with only a slightly receding hairline, gave the impression he was heavier than he was in fact. He always dressed formally, in a suit and tie, making an exception only when he wore an orange sport coat for UT athletic events. He wore shirts with French cuffs.

His was a noteworthy face—plastic, extremely pliable, and malleable. When he registered disgust or skepticism or irritation or impatience, words were superfluous. His repertoire ranged from dark scowl to engaging smile, with the former predominating. Yet he could freeze his face and be as enigmatic as a poker player.

All parts of his physiognomy were employed, his heavy brows and his eyes, his cleft chin, his jowly cheeks and mouth. And they were all aided and abetted by his half-moon glasses. When he questioned or doubted what you were saying, he would incline his head toward you and look over the flat top of the lenses and raise his eyebrows. As though to ask, "Is that true?" or to show surprise he would sometimes suddenly toss his head back and look at you through his glasses as if to try to focus on you. When he was dividing his attention between reading and listening to you, he would let his glasses slide down his nose to be able to shift his eyes back and forth between the page and you without moving his head. Then he might forget they were down on his nose and pursue a vigorous conversation, ignoring them. In casual conversation, he would cross his legs with one foot on the other knee, remove his glasses, and, holding one earpiece and with his arm resting on his crossed leg, swing his glasses back and forth endlessly. When he became impatient or angry, he might twirl his glasses in a circle around his hand.

When he was enjoying himself he did not seem rehearsed or calculating. He could be spontaneous, jovial, and friendly. People who thought he was totally detestable had never seen him in his likable mode, and when exposed to this side, they might come to think more benignly of him.

The puzzlement to me over the years was what motivated Erwin to work so hard and assiduously for the University of Texas. And knowing how despised and hated he was on the campus, what kept him going.

There was speculation, often voiced, that when his wife June died of cancer, he was devastated and his intense work with the university diverted his mind from his loss. I have no views on these speculations. Everyone who knew them as a couple said June was the love of his life and her death was his greatest tragedy. He was well along in his deep involvement with the university when I joined the System Administration.

Now, as Erwin questioned Singletary, probing for information on the sites for the future Permian Basin campus, he alternated between leaning forward with his elbows on the table or slouching down in his chair. In his slouched position he would place his fingertips together over his paunch and rock his hands back and forth from the wrist while glaring at Singletary over his half-moon glasses.

After the 1969 legislature had authorized a number of new university campuses, Erwin and local supporters had gotten the new campus in the Midland-Odessa area assigned to UT. In recognition of the region, famous for the prolific Permian Basin oil and gas fields, the new campus was to be named for the area, the University of Texas of the Permian Basin, UTPB.

The UT System was now in the process of implementing the legislative condition that the land for the new schools be provided at no cost to the state. Developers in the Midland-Odessa areas were competing to donate land to the Board of Regents for the new campus. They were eager to provide a campus site, knowing that a new school on their land would be a magnet, an economic generator, to attract residents and businesses to enhance the value of their surrounding property.

Singletary had just made a visit to Midland and Odessa to inspect the several sites being offered in those cities, and now Erwin wanted his judgment about the various offers. He wanted to know which site Singletary was planning to support in order to influence his recommendation if he needed to before it reached the Board of Regents.

After he and Erwin had parleyed awhile, Singletary finally said, "Frank, I drove around every site out there and I counted the sage brushes and the oil jacks and the tumbleweeds, and I can't see any difference between 'em. Any one is as good as the next. They'll all make a campus. They all look the same. You tell me which one you like, and that'll be the one that will get my unqualified and unwavering endorsement as unquestionably the best site."

A couple of weeks later Singletary sent me to Odessa to make my own evaluation of the sites. I thought my report would be to him. But when I returned to Austin the next evening, there at the airport waiting for me was Frank Erwin. With him was Michael Levy, the future founder and publisher of *Texas Monthly* magazine, then a twenty-three-year-old UT law student. Levy was with his girlfriend and another young man. They were Erwin's drinking companions for the evening.

It was not unusual for Erwin to take along for cruising around Austin several students from his Kappa Sigma fraternity or friends from one of the bars where he was drinking. Sometimes he wanted to drive past some building under construction at the campus or at the Balcones Research Center or just to drive around.

Out front of the airport terminal we gathered around Erwin's car. That evening he was not driving his orange-and-white Cadillac but a large dark sedan. Levy opened the trunk to put in my bag, and there were a couple of dozen drinks in capped plastic containers. As I moved toward the side of the car to get in, I overheard Levy whisper to Erwin, "We've got lots of bourbon left, but we're already running low on scotch."

As I started to get in behind the driver's seat Erwin called out, "What would you like, Doctor, scotch or bourbon?"

I knew what my answer had to be. I replied, "I'd prefer bourbon, if you've got it."

"We got it; come and help yourself," he said, and I could palpably feel their more ready acceptance of me to join their party.

Levy and his girl got in back with me, with the girl in the center, and the other student sat in front with Erwin.

As I sat behind him, Erwin adjusted the rearview mirror so he could see me. Then for close to three hours Erwin slowly cruised around Austin, across the old Montopolis Bridge toward Bergstrom Air Force Base, then working our way slowly on back roads west to South Congress. From there we came north through the Capitol grounds and then out Lamar toward Route 183. We stopped from time to time for a restroom break and to get new drinks out of the trunk. And during that time I endured a continuing grilling from Erwin on what I had found in Odessa and what I would recommend pertaining to the selection of a site for the new campus.

In his report to Erwin earlier, Singletary had just about summed up everything that could be said about the sites being offered. It became a struggle under Erwin's cross-examination to try to make distinctions or elaborate on Singletary's earlier description. How much can you say about the attributes of undeveloped West Texas desert?

I strung out my reasoning under three headings. First, we should probably pick a site in Odessa rather than Midland. Erwin wanted to know why. I said because that was where the lower-income and working students lived predominantly. Those were the prospective students in the area; they would be less able to afford to leave home to go to college elsewhere. Students from more affluent families in Midland would be much more likely to leave the area to attend college. If we were to build the new campus in Midland, the students would still come primarily from Odessa, so why make the largest number of students travel all the way to a Midland campus?

Then he said that if we didn't pick a site in Midland, Tom Sealy, a former member of the UT Board of Regents from Midland and currently vice chairman of the Coordinating Board, would be very unhappy with us.

I acknowledged that was certainly true. I did not tell him Sealy had already called me, telling me how he had worked to get the new college approved by the legislature. Sealy had told me that as a favor to him and as a former employee of his at the Coordinating Board, I needed to help him locate the school in Midland.

"What else?" Erwin wanted to know.

Second, we should not consider choosing the site being offered by the city of Odessa near the community college. Even if a campus on that site would permit a closer integration of the new UT campus and the community college and facilitate joint enrollments of students and permit sharing of faculties and libraries, the site had problems. The land for a campus there was in a federally assisted urban renewal project. I explained that it would take years to clear titles, assemble the land, relocate the present occupants, and raze the structures to make a site available to start a new campus.

I dwelled on this because I had worked in Washington, D.C., and San Francisco in slum clearance and urban redevelopment. I knew from experience the protracted delays that we were likely to encounter. I was able to spin this out for some time, speaking as an expert on the subject.

Tiring of that, Erwin asked, "What's wrong with the land out by the airport?"

He had anticipated my third point. I said the land between the two cities at the airport was nothing but a compromise offer and not a good location for the new campus. Erwin said that lots of people thought that was a good compromise. I couldn't tell whether he really supported that view. I pointed out that the airport was halfway between the two cities, a distance of about 10 miles in each direction. I said this site would make the new campus equally inconvenient to everybody in both cities.

I summed up by saying that other than these three points, I felt that any site around Odessa would be acceptable.

The others in the car hardly said a word all evening, and the girl never said anything other than whispering to Levy.

Then Erwin made me go through the whole recital again. When it became clear he had milked me dry, he turned onto Airport Boulevard and delivered me back to the airport. When he dropped me off at my car, it was after one in the morning.

As I staggered in, groggy and sleep deprived, the next morning, Singletary motioned for me to come into his office.

He said, "Just heard you spent the evening with Frank. He came by early. He didn't tell me what you talked about. All he said was, 'That new guy you hired? Well, he's not a complete idiot.'"

The experience that night of being cross-examined by Erwin was one I would endure or witness a number of times in the years ahead. He was a sponge for information, soaking up everything he could squeeze out of a victim. He did not stop pressing for more information or what I thought or what I thought someone else might think until he had finally decided he was not going to get anything more out of me. The long pauses after I had answered a question and before he would put a new question to me made me feel I had to have something more to say just to fill the silence. After I had told him everything and he kept pressing for more, I was even tempted to tell him more than I actually knew. Or I might elaborate on a point I had already made to build it up more than the matter deserved. His long pauses may have been intended to make me feel uncomfortable. He certainly made it hard to continue to remain silent.

He would say, "And? What else?"

After several rounds of that I would finally reply, "That's all."

"Come on," he'd say. "There's got to be more."

"No, I've told you all there is."

"I don't believe you."

A long pause would follow.

Then sometimes he would say, "Okay, then take me through it again."

And he would want to hear it all over again.

His method of interrogation was effective because he made a victim feel he wanted to please him. It did not take me long to recognize the dangers of telling more than I knew just to fill empty time. I tried that only once and quickly found myself in territory I could not defend under his continuing questioning.

On other occasions I found myself covering the same ground over and over. I had to learn that as long as I kept responding to his questions, he would not let me go. It would get to the point I just wanted the grilling to end. I decided finally that if he wasn't uncomfortable with silence, I wouldn't be either. So I learned to let the long silences lie there between us, regardless of how uncomfortable I might become. In time it became easier to just sit in silence even as he would be scowling at me over his glasses. My silence was the signal that he had finally obtained all he was going to get out of me. Only then would he leave me alone.

The other thing I came to learn over time was that what had happened to me that evening coming back from Odessa was not unusual. He frequently met on the campus and around town with faculty, students, and administrators from various parts of the university. Those of us on the staff sometimes wondered how Erwin so often knew what his opponents were planning to do before any of us administrators had heard the first thing about it.

Erwin would spend much of each day walking around the campus and meeting with faculty and students, especially during breaks between classes. Or he would simply pick up the phone and call a faculty member to ask for information or an opinion. For example, two faculty members he had nothing in common with were Forrest Hill and Tom Philpott. Hill, a liberal-leaning economics professor, was useful to him as an expert on faculty retirement options and how they were funded. Improving faculty benefits was an issue Erwin fought for in the legislature to help with recruitment and retention. He found Hill a reliable source of information. Philpott, a historian, provided a contrary point of view on most everything Erwin believed in. Erwin apparently enjoyed jousting verbally with him.

Erwin could be extremely personable and congenial when he wanted to be. Because of his notoriety on the campus and his recognized power and influence in the legislature, it was flattering for a person to have Erwin want to spend time with him. And many discovered to their surprise that he could do this in a nonconfrontational and totally unthreatening way. Faculty and students found he could be completely disarming and surprisingly fun to be with. When he wanted to, he had a way of being charming and interested in finding common ground. One of his techniques was to nod his head and even say he agreed with criticism leveled at the administration or board policies. And when he would follow up on a faculty or student complaint, he became credible and laid the ground for subsequent encounters. These qualities, along with the favors he might bestow on his prey, gave him a formidable advantage in finding out what was happening on campus.

Vartan Gregorian, a history professor, once said that Erwin would have made a good double agent; he was able to deal on both sides of an issue. I could not tell whether Gregorian said this out of admiration or denigration.

Erwin was notorious for his evening drinking soirees at the Forty Acres Club, the Quorum Club, and other watering holes around town. At his table almost any night there would be a constant flow of people from across the campus and from the state capitol and the city as a whole. Some of these would be invited by him. Others would arrange during the day to meet him for a drink to talk over something they needed to resolve with him. But many of those who sat with him for a drink or two were summoned to his table by a bonhomie wave of his arm to join him for some good-natured kidding and discussion.

His kidding could be rough and pointed. His ostensibly genial joshing often contained an edge of intimidation. Sometimes it was hard to tell whether he was working over a difference of opinion between the two of you or just having some good-natured fun.

On occasion he might force you to deny some view he would accuse you of holding. By seeming to be kidding, he partially disarmed his victim. It was very uncomfortable.

One reason so many people passed by Erwin's table each evening in one club or another and moved on was in part because few could keep up with his drinking, and it was hard to nurse one or two drinks for hours on end with no break for dinner. When he would order another drink for himself, he would often ask for a new round for everybody at the table. Typically his drinking went on until the early hours of the morning, having started sometimes at the end of the previous working day. Then he would be up early the next morning and back on the campus for another go. His evening repast often consisted of the popcorn and bar nuts served with his drinks.

After I had been working for the System Administration for a couple of years, Erwin returned from a trip to Galveston or Houston for a health checkup. I asked how his exam had gone.

He answered, "They told me I have the heart of a thirty-year-old and the liver of an eighty-year-old."

What some of us could not understand was why Erwin ended so many evenings driving himself home when obviously he had had far too much to drink. Why had one of his drinking companions not driven him home? I am sure it was in part because he would refuse such help. He was not a man you easily told he had had too much to drink. And perhaps his late-drinking buddies were not in much better shape than he. More than one of his drinking companions had their own DWI arrests to contest. But it did seem he was often left alone when he most needed help from friends.

The result was that he was stopped from time to time for erratic driving and on at least two occasions was charged with drunken driving. John Fainter, a lawyer and longtime confidant to Democratic governors, recounted a story of Erwin being stopped one evening by a policeman. The police all knew who was driving the orange-and-white Cadillac. That evening the policeman stopped him and said, "Mr. Erwin, I would like for you to get out of the car and walk for me."

Erwin promptly replied, "But, officer, everybody knows anybody can drive further than they can walk."

CHAPTER 5

A Plagiarized Dissertation

That summer of 1969, Otis Singletary handed me a large file and said, "I'll be in Kentucky by the next board meeting. You need to decide what to do with this."

The folder contained an extensive analysis of the dissertation completed fifteen years earlier by James McCrocklin for his Ph.D. in government from UT. At that moment, McCrocklin was president at Lyndon Johnson's alma mater in San Marcos, Southwest Texas State University.

Everyone who followed Texas higher education politics knew McCrocklin was Lyndon Johnson's protégé. While Johnson was Senate majority leader, he had arranged for McCrocklin to obtain a position at the Pentagon after McCrocklin had completed the course work for his doctorate.

Then, as Johnson's golden boy, McCrocklin had, upon receiving his Ph.D., become president of LBJ's alma mater in San Marcos. Southwest Texas State University was at that time conveniently governed by a Board of Regents chaired by LBJ's longtime adviser and business manager, J. C. Kellam.

Now in 1969, as I began perusing McCrocklin's file, he was serving out a second appointment from President Johnson. He had taken a leave of absence as president of the San Marcos school to become undersecretary of the Department of Health, Education, and Welfare. There were those who thought he had sought the appointment in hopes of duplicating Connally's career of moving from Washington into Texas politics.

While with the Coordinating Board, I had gotten to know McCrocklin. He was a vain, loud-mouthed, profane political operator. My personal dealings with him related to his requests for construction grants, land acquisition, and building plans at his university. He was abusively aggressive in pushing for approvals required by our board, letting us underlings know that he had talked with our board members about his request and he already had their approval. Nor did he fail to mention that he was close to President Lyndon Johnson and was friends with the governor and key legislators.

McCrocklin tended to talk big and as a result sometimes told stories that would have been better kept to himself. He told me, confidentially of course, that just a few months before the fateful visit in November 1963, when Vice President Johnson brought President Kennedy to Texas to help patch up the breach between the conservative and liberal branches of the Texas Democratic Party, he had gotten a late-night telephone call. It was from a distraught Vice President Lyndon Johnson. According to McCrocklin, Johnson had come to the conclusion that Kennedy was planning to drop him as vice president from the 1964 reelection ticket. McCrocklin told me that Johnson had called him that night in tears to ask McCrocklin if he would be willing to step aside if Kennedy did drop him from the ticket. Johnson could then come back to Texas and take up the presidency of his alma mater in San Marcos.

While serving at the Pentagon in the first position arranged by Senator Johnson, McCrocklin had settled on a topic for his dissertation for his UT doctorate, the American occupation of Haiti from 1915 to 1934, an operation largely carried out by the U.S. Marines. At the Pentagon he had discovered as a basis for his doctoral research two obscure reports on that military operation.

McCrocklin worked with these reports to prepare a "compilation" subsequently published by the Naval Institute as *Garde d'Haiti 1915–1934*. This distillation of the earlier reports became the basis for his dissertation. Marine colonel R. D. Heinl, at the Naval Institute, was disturbed by what McCrocklin was doing. He said, "All felt that this is a hell of a way to earn a Ph.D., but what was the point in doing anything?"

In the meantime, McCrocklin's wife had completed her master's thesis at Texas A&I University, on the same topic. Her husband, still working on his dissertation, served on her thesis committee.

Now, in 1969, there lay before me faculty documentation from the school where McCrocklin was president, comparing his dissertation to his wife's thesis. The Southwest Texas State University faculty analysis showed that only 30 percent of all the sentences in her thesis did not appear in his dissertation and that more than 50 percent of her thesis sentences appeared in his dissertation word for word.

Even more damaging, Colonel Heinl, now retired and a writer for the *Detroit News*, had published a story alleging that McCrocklin had plagiarized government studies and reports for his dissertation. This story had been picked up by the *Texas Observer*. After setting out all the horrific allegations, the *Observer* article said that McCrocklin had been mentioned as a possible president for the University of Texas when his mentor, Lyndon Johnson, would come back to teach at UT.

Despite these revelations, McCrocklin's Board of Regents issued a statement of confidence in him. Faculty members from San Marcos, unable to obtain on their own campus a fair investigation of McCrocklin's alleged plagiarism, came to Austin to be certain the UT faculty was aware of their charges against their president.

Gordon Whaley, dean of the UT Graduate School, obtained copies of the obscure Pentagon documents alleged to have been copied. He had his staff undertake a comparison of McCrocklin's dissertation with these materials.

That analysis was what Singletary had handed to me. What I was looking at was incredible. A page-by-page, word-by-word comparison had been made, and each page of his dissertation was rated as to its congruity with the text of the government documents. Those ratings read, 98 percent congruity, 99 percent congruity, 98 percent congruity, 95 percent congruity, on and on, page after page. The evidence of plagiarism was irrefutable.

In reporting on a meeting of the UT faculty committee appointed to investigate the case, William Livingston described McCrocklin as "impervious, imperious, and unashamed."

As this case unfolded, the question in the minds of UT faculty members was where would LBJ's close friend Frank Erwin stand on James McCrocklin's degree from UT?

I prepared the staff recommendation to the board that the Ph.D. conferred on James McCrocklin be retracted. In fact, the university had already been told by the attorney general that the board could not withdraw or take away a degree it had awarded. But the attorney general had helpfully suggested that the law did not prohibit the Board of Regents from in effect canceling the degree by publishing notice that the university would no longer recognize the degree it had granted.

The members of McCrocklin's dissertation committee had been lied to and misled, and they were eager to see the university take action against him. University committees, the graduate dean, and all other top UT officers were unanimous in recommending the removal of McCrocklin's degree. In the face of the evidence, no top-quality university could refuse to withdraw the degree, but what the regents chose to do with the matter would in the end be determined by Erwin as chairman and chief manager of board actions.

Erwin knew I was the staff person working up the material for the board meeting, and he stopped me one day in the hall to ask what would be the effect if the university did nothing and let the matter drop. I was surprised that he would ask me this; he could get more informed advice on this from Dean Whaley, someone he greatly respected and conferred with regularly.

I felt sure Erwin was aware of the damage that would be done to UT's reputation. I told him word was already spreading around the country, and he challenged me on that, saying that only one reporter in Ohio and the *Texas Observer* had shown any interest in the story, and it was already becoming old news. I could not read what he might be thinking. Was he testing my command of the issues or rehearsing arguments he would have to answer? Or was he really considering dropping the issue? I went on to say that the evidence the graduate dean had pulled together could not remain unknown for long, and it was extremely damaging to our university. What the faculty at San Marcos had put together had already been shared across several campuses.

McCrocklin was not present when the board considered his case, but he was represented by an attorney who asked for more time to study the action proposed by the regents. Erwin granted a postponement without further discussion. This did not seem to bode well for those acutely concerned with the issue. We searched in vain for clues to how the regents viewed our recommendation. Not everyone was sanguine about the outcome.

It was at that August 1969 meeting of the board that I got my new boss, or rather bosses. Engineering Dean John McKetta was elevated to executive vice chancellor for academic affairs and William Livingston from the Government Department became vice chancellor for academic programs. I was designated assistant to Bill Livingston, but McKetta told me he wanted me to be involved in everything in his office and to report to him as well.

McKetta was the most lovable man on the UT campus. He never had a bad word for anyone. Always smiling, he held a positive view of every situation regardless how unpleasant or difficult. When Chancellor Ransom approached him about taking Singletary's position as vice chancellor, McKetta said he was not comfortable about how the humanities and liberal arts might look upon an engineer in the position. He asked that Ransom create a complementary position to his to deal with those areas, and he suggested Bill Livingston for the position.

Livingston, during his academic career, probably held more important administrative posts than any other person in the history of UT. Titles included department chairman, dean, at least two vice presidents, and numerous chairmanships of programs and committees, as well as acting president for a time. One of his most prominent responsibilities was head of the committee for establishing the Lyndon B. Johnson School of Public Affairs.

McKetta's first encounter with Erwin had occurred early when both were young and starting their careers in Austin. There had been an explosion at Nussbaum's Barbeque, and McKetta, as a new engineering faculty member at UT, was hired to serve as an expert witness in a lawsuit brought by employees for injuries. When McKetta met with Jay Brown, Nussbaum's defending attorney, Brown told him he was assigning a new lawyer at the firm to McKetta to do anything he needed on the case and run errands for him. The new attorney at the firm was Frank Erwin.

When McKetta accepted the executive vice chancellor position, Erwin came to his office and said, "Well, Johnny, now you work for me."

McKetta replied, "No, Frank, I work for Harry Ransom."

Erwin said, "We'll see about that."

The first indication that I might have misread Erwin's intentions about the McCrocklin case from our short conversation in a hallway came at the end of that meeting in August. I told him that McCrocklin's lawyer had said that if the regents attempted to lift McCrocklin's degree, Erwin would be sued as chairman of the board.

Erwin grunted, "Well, they won't get a virgin."

It wasn't until almost three months later that we knew for certain how this would play out. The board took up the recommendation again, and practically without discussion and without argument from McCrocklin's lawyer, they declared his Ph.D. degree null and void and of no effect. The board further instructed university officials to strike James H. McCrocklin's name from the list of Ph.D. recipients for 1954 and to reduce by one the number of Ph.D.s awarded that year.

About a year later, I asked Erwin if President Johnson had said anything about the board's action on the McCrocklin affair. Erwin did not answer and changed the subject. Then he came back to my question.

He said, "Everybody knows Johnson hated those Kennedy ivy-league sons a bitches even if he did have to keep them on his staff and in the cabinet. He was self-conscious about his degree from Southwest Texas State when their degrees were from Harvard and Yale and Princeton.

"One night he told me he'd put all his faith in McCrocklin as a bright young man who could show them what a Texan with a Texas Ph.D. could do."

Erwin stopped abruptly and stood up. He ended, "Enough said."

McCrocklin resigned as president of Southwest Texas State University and established a very successful and lucrative real estate business in Dripping Springs.

CHAPTER 6

Denying Instruction to an Army Officer

There never seemed to be an end of new crises. Events and challenges and policies in the making accumulated and rolled on top of and past each other. In our academic world there was nothing quietly cloistered or encrusted in ivy.

During registration in the 1969 fall semester, an associate professor, Warren Dean, a tenured faculty member in the history department, refused to accept an army major into his course on Latin America. Professor Dean, although a young air force veteran, declared himself a pacifist opposed to war and would not instruct the major in his course. When pressed for his reasons, he argued that he would be ruined with the people he was working with in South America if he let this man in his class. They would never trust him again if an army officer took his course and learned how he might undermine their governments and social institutions. He said he would very likely no longer be welcome in South America to continue his research.

There was immediate reaction from students. Contrary to expectations in that time of opposition to all things military, nearly every student who spoke up or wrote letters or articles for the student paper criticized Professor Dean for his position. They did not believe a faculty member should be able to refuse a student from enrolling in his class.

What few on campus sensed was that the UT Regents might seize on Professor Dean's action as an affront to the obligations of the university to serve the nation and the military in a time of war. The remedy would be obvious to the board: fire the disloyal professor. This would clarify policy and send a message to the rest of the faculty.

There were, in fact, few restraints on the power of a Board of Regents in overseeing campuses they governed. Whereas European universities were historically governed primarily by their faculties, America established its universities on the corporate model, with governance resting in the hands of boards of trustees. The result, particularly among public institutions, was that by law the supreme authority rested with institutional governing boards. Most boards found from experience that the organization they had undertaken to rule worked most efficiently and made more progress when trustees did not disregard the views of their faculties but instead were willing most of the time to be guided by them. Although actual approval of faculty appointments and organizational structure and the awarding of tenure and salaries had to be approved by the board, regents at a first-class institution could not continually override faculty recommendations on such matters without losing professors and researchers to other schools.

Most regents sought to be on university boards because they wanted the prestige and to bask in the glory of being associated with the achievements and reputation of an institution of higher learning or to serve on the board of their alma mater to flaunt their success and become the envy of all their former classmates. Yet, on the whole, regents were politically conservative and came to expect that their professors should hold similar views. The previous century and a half of American higher education was replete with cases in which regents chose to force their views of the so-called real world on a university. If that meant confrontation and faculty displeasure, some regents chose that rough path and disregarded the consequences.

As soon as Professor Dean's action became public, I could see what might happen. With the level of intrusion by regents into university affairs on the increase, interference in such minor issues had by then become all too commonplace. I could imagine the board insisting that Dean be fired for his refusal to accept the army major in his class. The fact that Dean was a veteran might save him, but I doubted it. And with the students lining up to criticize the professor's position, I could see the regents using student sentiments to justify firing him.

The university had suffered through periods in its past when pressures were exerted from outside on the administration and regents to discipline or dismiss certain individuals from the faculty. In 1915, the very year the American Association of University Professors (AAUP) had been created to protect academic freedom among faculty members across the nation, the governor of Texas, James "Pa" Ferguson, had exerted extraordinary pressure on the University of Texas. He wanted the regents to fire certain faculty members and their president. Failing in that, Governor Ferguson threatened to veto the state appropriation to the university if the regents and the administration did not dismiss the professors objectionable to him. He replaced regents until he got a slate of regents who fired the faculty members he objected to. Then, in addition, he carried out his threat to veto the school's appropriations. This resulted in such an outcry that Ferguson was impeached by the Texas house of representatives and convicted by the senate and removed from office. New regents were appointed and the fired faculty rehired.

Not all threats to faculty members have been resolved so promptly or so clearly in support of the autonomy of UT. Many of the problems in the past were in house, between the Board of Regents and members of the administration who refused to give in to board encroachments on academic freedom or administrative prerogatives. One of the most notable of those incidents occurred in the 1940s, again a propitious time because in 1940 the AAUP had just updated and restated its 1915 principles protecting academic freedom and tenure.

Governor W. Lee O'Daniel, upon reelection to his second term, achieved his goal of appointing a majority of the nine members of the UT Board of Regents. At the first meeting after the new members took office, President Homer P. Rainey was handed a card by a new regent listing the names of four full professors in economics. The regent said, "We want you to fire these men." All were tenured, and not one of them had been at the university for less than fifteen years. When Rainey asked why, the regent replied, "We don't like what they are teaching."

President Rainey refused to fire these men or others the regents wanted him to dismiss. Regents objected to what they labeled dirty books in English and progressive ideas, namely Dos Passos's *1919* and *The 42nd Parallel* and New Deal economics. Rainey managed to stall action by the regents for months, but they did ultimately fire three of the economics professors. The firings took place in a meeting during which the regents discussed the matter by telephone with Governor O'Daniel.

The AAUP immediately investigated the firings under their stated principles protecting academic freedom. In the meantime, President Rainey obtained support for his opposition to the governor and the regents from the attorney general. But his resistance to the board continued to rankle, and in 1944, Rainey in a faculty meeting charged the board with gross interference with university matters and itemized their encroachments on faculty rights. The regents then immediately fired him.

Despite the outcry of many against the efforts of the Board of Regents to rid the university of "radical professors," the harassment of faculty continued. One prominent literary figure a number of regents despised was the folklorist J. Frank Dobie. His popularity and reputation rested in part on his ongoing ridicule of conservative Texas politics. At one point Dobie wrote, "When I get ready to explain homemade fascism in America, I can take my example from the state capitol in Texas." Despite Dobie's international fame, the board refused his request for an extension to his leave of absence in England and, in effect, fired him.

Now, in 1969, in the middle of a war, with an associate professor refusing admission of an army major into his course, we could not ignore what the regents might be capable of in the situation. Political intrusion into university affairs had a long legacy.

I thought we should be prepared to offer some kind of alternative course of action to the regents if they did begin to consider a step that would damage the university and put us at odds with the AAUP standards.

AAUP had over the years become increasingly effective in reprimanding institutions of higher learning when they departed from the procedures and principles of the association adopted to protect tenured faculty members. Early in the century, universities had frequently and without proper cause simply fired teachers who became objectionable to regents or to presidents or even to fellow faculty members. The firing of the great American economist Thorstein Veblen by the University of Chicago was one of the most egregious examples.

AAUP maintained a blacklist of institutions that had been found to have violated the principles and procedures adopted by the organization. To many smaller and less recognized institutions not aspiring to national recognition, to be included on the list was relatively meaningless. In fact, for the more obstreperous and uncaring boards, being on the list was sometimes taken as a mark of pride, a clear recognition of the conservative character of the institution.

But UT in 1969 had its eye on becoming recognized as a major American university. The school was actively working to attract and hold the kind of research and publishing faculty who would make a name for the school. Being placed on the AAUP list would be anathema to recruitment and the university's further advancement toward recognition as a quality institution. Across the nation, faculty members of worth and merit consulted the AAUP list of censured institutions. If UT was blacklisted by AAUP, the most sought after faculty from elsewhere would have nothing more to do with UT recruitment efforts.

But with an opinionated and impulsive Board of Regents, no one could be certain that in a moment of pique over a particular faculty member they might not act with total disregard for consequences with the AAUP. It was for this reason that I thought we needed to have a backup option on which the board might vent their spleen. I knew there would be some regents willing to consider a reasonable alternative to firing Professor Dean. They might be satisfied merely to slap his wrist and send a message to the faculty—if an alternative to firing him were presented to them.

My proposal was not much, but I thought we should be ready to throw the regents a bone. I was aware that the American model of protecting academic freedom and the awarding of tenure as a way to protect faculty members against arbitrary dismissal was based on the principle of *Lehrfreiheit* from German and European universities. This word describes the freedom of learning and freedom in teaching guaranteed to faculty members. And the UT Board of Regents' Rules and Regulations spelled out the controls the regents had in the past imposed on themselves to protect academic freedom and tenure, controls that tracked closely the stated AAUP principles of 1940.

What the regents' rules did not have was the complementary German or European concept of *Lernfreiheit*, the idea of the freedom of learning guaranteed to students. *Lernfreiheit* was defined as "the absence of administrative coercion in the learning situation." I thought this might be a useful concept to apply. So I drafted an amendment to the Regents' Rules and Regulations that spoke to this point. A simple amendment would make clear that students should be guaranteed the right to choose whatever courses they wished to study and that the university and its faculty should not be able to presume how a student might apply what he learned or arbitrarily deny a student access to certain learning.

This was merely stating the obvious, but the rule change might save Professor Dean's job and the reputation of the university. And because days were passing, if we could somehow stall long enough on getting the amendment adopted, the army major perhaps would have found another course to enroll in and his denial in taking this particular course would have become moot. Dr. Dean would not have to back down and admit him to his class after all.

I took my proposed amendment to Deputy Chancellor Charles "Mickey" LeMaistre and President Hackerman, and they both pooh-poohed the idea that the regents might get out of their corral on this issue. They both told me to forget it. My rule change would not be needed.

As deputy chancellor, "Mickey" LeMaistre was beginning to handle more of the campus affairs coming to the System Administration from all of the campuses under the governance of the Board of Regents. An epidemiologist, having joined the System offices from the Southwest Medical Center in Dallas, he also dealt with health affairs issues.

LeMaistre was a couple of inches over six feet and an extremely handsome and striking man. He was well known for his ability to explain complicated issues and to promote and sell plans and ideas. Aside from financial matters, which rested in the hands of Don Walker, the vice chancellor for planning and finance, most administrative items were handled by LeMaistre. Bit by bit, Harry Ransom's authority was becoming attenuated.

The Saturday following the report on Professor Dean's refusal to admit the major to his class, the regents held a reception for invited guests and dignitaries in the art museum across from the stadium. Just before the Texas-Navy football game that afternoon, the regents called an emergency meeting in a back room of the museum. Those were the days before advanced notice of a meeting had to be given to the public about the time and place and topics to be considered. The regents could close their meetings to the public, and there was no requirement to announce what had been decided.

Midway through the football reception, LeMaistre and Hackerman found me among the crowd and asked me if I still had a copy of the proposed rule change I had shown them; the regents were about to meet to fire Professor Dean.

I made a mad dash across campus to get my draft. By the time I returned, the board had acted. They adopted a rule change to guarantee *Lernfreiheit* to UT students.

President Hackerman's version, much simpler than mine, said, in the form adopted by the regents, "The teacher must recognize that the right to academic freedom includes students. No faculty member may refuse to accept a student in a course because of conflict in beliefs and opinions with the views of the faculty member."

Would the regents have fired the professor without having available an optional course of action? I like to think they would not have. But who knows? In those times it wasn't just students suffering from impulsive distemper.

And in the meantime the army major had found another course of interest to him.

Only a week later some of the regents were again up in arms over the nationwide student moratorium on university campuses. Students were insisting that UT dismiss classes in protest over the war in Vietnam. Several regents remarked openly that faculty members who did not hold their classes should be fired. That would have required firing over half the UT faculty during that particular moratorium.

Close on the heels of these events came the episode that led the students and some faculty to label Frank Erwin as the true villain, ruling over the university with an oppressive hand, a role he seemed increasingly to relish and flaunt.

CHAPTER *7*

The Trees of Waller Creek

As the 1969 fall semester began, Erwin got off to mixed reviews. He supported Project Info, a program funded by the university to inform economically deprived young people about higher education and financial aid opportunities.

The *Daily Texan* gave Erwin positive marks for endorsing this program. And even though he objected strongly to another student idea, the Program for Economic Opportunity (PEO), the paper editorialized in support of his position on that as well. PEO was an effort to recruit African American and Mexican American students and admit them even if they could not meet the entrance requirements of the university. Erwin criticized this program as admitting these selected ethnic minorities when "thousands of applicants of Irish, Scotch, Yugoslav, Japanese, Chinese, Italian, French, and other descendants" were turned away for failing to meet the same lower standards.

But the *Texan* continued to criticize Erwin for his ongoing interference in university matters. The students needed a target, and he made himself conveniently available with his frequent press releases and rejoinders to criticism. For example, he was highly visible in his opposition to *The Rag*, a radical off-campus paper being hawked on the campus. To hoots of derision from the students, Erwin argued that the paper was interfering with the university's educational mission and the ability of students to learn.

Next, Erwin was out front in wanting to restrict accessibility to the student union to students only. Almost daily, some news event kept Erwin in the campus news. No one at UT was getting the press he did.

That fall the contract for Larry Caroline, an outspoken young assistant professor in philosophy, was not renewed. Caroline, a tall, unkempt professor who in the growth of hair could compete with the most outrageously hirsute student, had been highly visible in his attacks not only on the university but much of the rest of American society. He accused UT of being elitist, authoritarian, and capitalistic. Among his many causes, he held the view that the university should not require grades for students and should have no salaried staff or faculty. Even if students did not agree with much of what Caroline promoted, they thought he was fun, and he was popular for his outrageous sallies against the establishment. Although Erwin did not play any public role when the university did not renew Caroline's contract, students assumed he had to have been behind it because Erwin had become the university's principal spokesman on almost every controversial policy. Explaining that Caroline had failed to complete his dissertation had no traction with the students as a reason for not rehiring him.

One night at Gregory Gym, protestors hooted and yelled outside a university dinner held to honor Governor John Connally. Former president Lyndon Johnson and Lady Bird were present. Erwin called the demonstrators "a bunch of dirty nothings."

"I'm a Dirty Nothing" buttons appeared on campus within days. Erwin was quick to acquire one and wear it prominently on his lapel.

This was the calm before the storm compared to what Erwin was about to do. He was on the verge of his most flagrant intrusion into campus events. His confrontation with students over the cutting of trees to expand his football team's stadium would bring him national notoriety. His heavy-handed involvement in this situation also altered how many of the UT faculty saw his role at the university. Questions began in earnest about whether he was hurting the institution more than he was helping it in its reach for excellence and academic recognition.

That fall the Board of Regents authorized enlarging the west side of the football stadium by fifteen thousand seats. The plans for expansion were ingenious, both in the architectural design and in its financing. The university would construct, immediately abutting the stadium, a new multistory instructional building containing physical education facilities, dance studios, gymnastic and exercise rooms, and kinesiology labs. Thus as a new classroom building, it could be paid for with funds for instructional facilities even though the building would become totally incorporated into the structure of an income-producing intercollegiate athletics stadium. The ingenuity of the design was its sloping roof that would support the upper deck and seats being added to the stadium.

Erecting the new building with fifteen thousand seats on its roof meant the street on that side of the stadium had to be moved west. This, in turn, required a number of large trees along Waller Creek to be uprooted or cut down. When it became evident to the students what was about to happen, the narrow line of green space along the creek became a cause célèbre. Several architectural students quickly devised an alternative plan that would save the trees.

The 1969 episode of students attempting to protect the trees along Waller Creek began on October 20. By the next day, Tuesday, the picketing students had grown to around fifty. The cutting and bulldozing of the trees was to begin the following day. A number of students spent the night on the site for fear the workmen would take down the trees under the cover of darkness. The workmen arrived early Wednesday morning with bulldozers. A number of students then climbed into the trees to protect them from being removed. The workmen could not proceed.

Frank Erwin was also on the scene and called in the police. Erwin was quoted in the *Daily Texan* as shouting, "Arrest all the people you have to. Once the trees are down, there won't be anything to protest."

Police had to pull the students from the trees, and a hook-and-ladder fire truck was required to extract some of the students who had climbed ever higher to evade the police. In total, twenty-seven students were arrested and removed from the construction site. The university was fortunate that no student was hurt in this dangerous confrontation high in the trees.

Although serious about the confrontation, students made the most of the situation. One student taken from a limb, Bruce Elliott, was the subject of a poem addressing the times by his friend, Ben Branch.

> He climbed a tree into the air;
> Was plucked to earth, though hardly fair.
> The leaves and nightsticks then did fall,
> His prints are now in city hall.
> Victim of a system crass,
> Tis true. But please explain to me:
> I always knew he loved the grass,
> But just how does one smoke a tree?

Once the protesters were arrested, Erwin directed the workmen to get about their task. The cutting and bulldozing began. The next day the *Daily Texan* ran a picture of Erwin applauding as the trees came down.

In angry frustration the students dragged piles of tree limbs from the site on Waller Creek to the main building in protest and stacked them around the doorways at the base of the Tower. Students rallied at noon, demanding that President Hackerman come out and talk with them. There was much complaining and venting of feelings, but the removal of the trees was a fait accompli. Funds were collected by students for those arrested.

Student body president Joe Krier met with President Hackerman, who agreed to try to arrange a meeting of students with Erwin. When Krier announced their agreement, the crowd dispersed.

That afternoon the Sierra Club obtained a restraining order to stop work along Waller Creek for a week. The *Daily Texan* editorialized that this episode was an example of how "many of the university's decisions are made—by one man." They saw President Hackerman as left "holding the bag" by Erwin and demanded that decisions be returned to administrators, faculty, and students.

The next day the students walked out of the meeting Hackerman had arranged with Erwin when he refused to drop charges against the arrested students. Both the Young Democrats and the Young Republicans called for Erwin's resignation.

By Monday Erwin had gotten the Sierra Club injunction overturned, and site work for the stadium resumed. The remaining trees were removed along with dozens of saplings that students had planted over the weekend.

The next day a resolution submitted by six professors to the general faculty calling for Erwin's resignation passed 242 to 197. This vote came even after Chancellor Ransom and President Hackerman spoke against the motion, trying vainly to explain the many good things Erwin was doing for the university.

Erwin responded to this vote by stating that the Students for a Democratic Society (SDS), a national student protest organization, had also called for his resignation in the past. By lumping the faculty vote together with this radical student group, Erwin further offended faculty members already angry with him.

Now Erwin was in his fighting element. He called into question the validity of the faculty vote, pointing out that less than 20 percent of the faculty had been present for the tally. To underscore his intransigence, he refused to make any apology for what he had done.

Asked about the possibility of impeachment Erwin said, "I can think of no forum in which I had rather have this matter heard than the Texas House of Representatives." He went on to add, "The people of Texas are sick and tired of paying taxes to support that kind of conduct on the part of both faculty and students."

When a student referendum was held and the vote was heavily against him, Erwin compared the votes against the total student body and had the university release a statement reading, "In view of the bitter and personal vendetta which the student newspaper has been carrying on against me daily for the past several months, I am surprised that they were able to persuade only 17 percent of the students to cast a negative vote."

Aggressively unrepentant, he further called on the faculty and students "to accept the realities and get about the business for which they are supposed to be at the university."

This episode brought Erwin a national reputation as one of the few strongmen across the country standing up to students. In the eyes of the UT students it spotlighted his role as point man for every oppressive university policy they objected to.

Meanwhile, tensions were not permitted to abate. The board, led by Erwin, amended their Rules and Regulations to require that any disruptive student on any UT System campus be immediately suspended until a hearing could be held. Students saw suspension as punishment before trial. The rule prohibited any president from negotiating with "persons engaged in disruptive activity on campus." The presidents were directed to eliminate all disruptive activities on their campuses.

The students interpreted this as a rebuke to President Hackerman, who had restrained fifty police officers from arresting more students during their protests about cutting down the Waller Creek trees.

The Chuck Wagon, an eatery in the Student Union where some of the organizers of protests met, was then closed to nonstudents. Enforcement of the prohibition against nonstudents in the Chuck Wagon resulted in violent resistance to arrest and the use of mace on protesters by Austin police officers. More arrests were made. This in turn triggered a rally of thousands of students.

As students organized an additional moratorium against the war, the conflicts continued to fester. Within one month there were seven fires in the Student Union, most in wastebaskets, all attributed to arson.

Erwin continued to be the focal point with the students for all that was wrong at the university.

It was hard for me to believe all this had happened in only the first six months of my new job.

CHAPTER 8

Professional Dilemmas

P art of my work was satisfying and even fun at times. It provided latitude for creativity and initiative. But those aspects of the job were offset by incipient doubts about how we were pursuing some of our goals in the System Administration and how those goals got defined and were affecting UT Austin.

On the positive side of my job, I found the opportunity to help the state build the new campuses the legislature had authorized but absolutely did not want to pay for. By 1970 new campuses were in the process of getting established. Land had been offered by developers or acquired by the cities where they were to be built. The Texas A&M University System of schools had acquired Laredo. A campus in Corpus Christi had been assigned as a branch of Texas A&I University in Kingsville. The University of Houston was set up for a new campus in Clear Lake City near NASA headquarters. Texas Tech University was about to get a new medical school in Lubbock thanks to Governor Preston Smith, a native of the city. And the UT System had come away with new medical schools in San Antonio and Houston and academic campuses in Dallas, San Antonio, and Odessa.

While sites were being provided for the new campuses, this still left the universities with the unanswered question of how they were going to convince the legislature to appropriate the hundreds of millions in tax funds required to construct the new campuses. Serendipity had placed me ideally to see a solution to this problem.

From 1966 to 1969, while I had been assistant commissioner for facilities planning at the Coordinating Board, I helped the colleges and universities with their various sources of funds to construct needed buildings. In fact I had been hired into that job at the Coordinating Board from the U.S. Office of Education, the predecessor to the later Department of Education at the federal level. My work in Washington and Austin had been to administer the federal facilities grants program that had been created by President Lyndon Johnson in 1965. The federal programs provided grants and loans to colleges and universities for academic facilities and offices. But the federal dollars had to be matched with state or local funds.

There were a few little pockets of money the colleges and universities could draw on to provide those matching funds. In earlier years when inadequacy of state support for institutions of higher education became acute, a legislator named Skiles had found a way around the stinginess of the legislature to provide a small fund for construction.

Here is how his program worked. Under the Skiles Act, each semester a state college or university could set aside $5 of the tuition paid by each student to retire bonds issued for the construction of facilities. That seemed innocuous enough and was easy to compute and administer. Even when tuition was only $25 a semester, that did not seem like very much money, and it made it possible for the legislature to avoid new taxes for college construction. But as I helped the schools use these new funds to match federal dollars, we developed some doubts. There appeared to be a rub constitutionally.

The state financed the operations of its universities by calculating in each appropriations bill what it would cost in the upcoming two years to run each institution. Then from that total cost, the state subtracted the estimated total tuition, and the state would appropriate the remaining balance to cover operating costs.

In an underhanded way the Skiles Act did this: if a portion of the tuition income at each school had already been set aside to pay to retire construction bonds, there was that much *less* tuition available to subtract from the institution's total costs. Although it appeared that the legislature did not have to appropriate new money to the universities, that absent tuition income pledged to retire bonds, in truth, had to be replaced by new state revenues.

In effect, taxes were being used to cover the issuance of bonds. And the Texas constitution required all bonds to be presented to the voters for authorization.

Voilà! Here by sleight of hand was a way to appropriate more money for funding higher education without appearing to have to do so. It was an ingenious "back-door" financing scheme. The constitutional problem was that bonds had been issued by the state of Texas through its institutions of higher education, which were backed by the full faith and credit of the state and paid for by the taxpayers. But the voters had never been asked to authorize those bonds or to extend state credit and bond guarantees. That certainly looked like it was unconstitutional.

But being dedicated as we were at the Coordinating Board to our task of trying to increase classroom and laboratory space, faculty offices, and libraries on our university campuses around the state, we were certainly not going to publicize the fact that much of the money the universities were using to match the federal funds flowing to Texas might be provided unconstitutionally.

I had not given a thought to these arcane financing procedures in a couple of years until I began to hear about the next big problem facing the UT System: where was it going to get the money necessary to construct the new campuses that Erwin and the Board of Regents had gotten control of? Clearly the niggardly state legislature was not going to pass new taxes for those buildings.

Bernell Waldrep was a much maligned and underappreciated university attorney with the UT System Administration. One day I went to his office and explained to him how the Skiles Act worked. Then I extrapolated that idea to the problem we faced on our new UT campuses. I opined that if the legislature really did want to finance those new campuses but did not want to be identified by the voters as guilty of imposing new taxes for that purpose, the legislators might be willing to let the UT System find its own way of paying for the necessary new buildings. They could allow the UT Board of Regents to pledge a part of the anticipated tuition from the new campuses to pay for the buildings the students would later be occupying.

The beauty of the scheme was that no university would suffer any loss in income from the state because the legislature would replace the tuition siphoned off to retire the construction bonds just as was done on a very modest scale under the Skiles Act. And the legislators would not have to explain how all those new bonds got funded without asking the people to vote to authorize the new state indebtedness.

Waldrep was maligned and underappreciated precisely for the kind of close scrutiny of proposals that he now gave to my idea. His job was to try to keep regents and administrators out of legal trouble. His analysis started and ended with, "Is it legal?" If it was not legal, he never got to the next question, "Is it right?" He had a major problem if someone asked him the more indulgent question, "How can we find a way to do it?"

Waldrep was not a "can do" lawyer who endeavored to help administrators or regents who wanted to find a way to do something marginally legal. If he ever tortured an opinion, it had to be under orders.

On my proposal he ruled exactly as I suspected he would. He said what I was proposing was, by his interpretation, unconstitutional.

Even though he did not like the proposal, Waldrep agreed to join me to discuss this idea with Don Walker, the vice chancellor in charge of finance.

E. Don Walker or just Don, as he was known, had come to the UT System from the Galveston Medical Branch. He was a big man, standing probably five inches above six feet. Don was a master at garnering the favor of members of the board. He could be both ruthless and insidious in how he dealt with colleagues. The poison he spread quietly and cumulatively about those he disliked or who would not do his bidding undermined the respect and acceptance of regents for some of their administrators. And he turned staff members against some of their coworkers to gain favor with him.

I had watched how obsequious Walker was with members of the Board of Regents, making himself available to them above anything else and pandering to their every need. It was a shock one day for me to see him refuse to take a call from a former regent he had formerly fawned over after the regent had been replaced by a new member just the week before. He turned and said, "Thank God we don't have to put up with that son of a bitch anymore."

But Walker could deliver when it came to financial manipulations and hiding and then finding money. As a result he became extremely useful to Erwin, to the point that many came to see him as an Erwin tool and operative.

That day Walker listened as I laid out the plan for funding construction on the new campuses and Bernell Waldrep tore it apart as being unconstitutional. Walker did not seem particularly interested. Waldrep and I left his office, and I thought that was the end of that idea. Waldrep was relieved. From my position on the periphery, I felt a little disappointed.

In less than three weeks Erwin had lined up the leaders of both houses and Governor Preston Smith behind a new financing vehicle. He had gotten the University of Houston and Texas A&I University, which had been authorized to build new campuses, to support his new plan. Even Texas Tech University supported it because Erwin now provided a way to finance their new medical school. The new campuses across the state would be financed at no new cost to the state through the use of "tuition revenue bonds."

Do I look back on coming up with this idea with any feeling of guilt? Not a bit. If this is what it takes to entice the Texas Legislature into doing what it should do anyway and to trick the public into paying for improving its own society, then my suggestion was in perfect keeping with the needs of the times. Similarly, Don Walker taking credit for the idea with Erwin was in perfect keeping with his usual practices. And Erwin was the ideal protagonist with just the right network and influence to sell this approach as a bootstrap operation by the universities, without in any way reducing their appropriations. Erwin's plan avoided placing any new financial burden on the taxpayers—that is, any burden they would ever be aware of.

This was the kind of creativity and initiative that made the job rewarding and fulfilling. But there were some serious downsides to working in the System Administration.

Upon receiving my doctorate in 1969, I had not expected to work at the University of Texas. When I did accept Singletary's offer to become his assistant, I had no idea what I was getting into. I certainly did not expect the job to have such a profound impact on me, opening me to question concepts that I had thought clear and resolved. I found myself forced to grapple with how loyalty and betrayal interrelated. It turned out they were not givens with simple definitions. Each required choices that affected the other. When loyalties were in conflict, a choice resulted in betrayal of one or the other. What was betrayal but a choice between loyalties? Loyalty was not necessarily a lofty virtue any more than betrayal was by definition a lowly sin. The test was what merited loyalty and what deserved betrayal.

The years from 1969 until 1973 I spent with the UT System Administration were most important to me in forming the kind of person I would become, personally and as a public executive. Making that observation now is entirely a matter of hindsight. During the events of the six months I have described to this point and into the next year, I knew only that I was having a really difficult time. I felt acutely the conflict between how I was responding to the expectations of my bosses and the reservations I had about how I had to function in my job. Had I had to articulate what was bothering me about my work I would not have been able to do so with precision. I knew certain values I held were being compromised. I assessed the kinds of things I was finding myself doing, and I began to wonder where was the limit of how far I could be pushed to do things my bosses wanted me to do. In the meantime I would just have to struggle on to discover where I was going to come out of these personal conflicts.

Where does a person's sense of moral discomfort come from? And *moral* may be too precious or affected a word for what I actually felt uncomfortable about in my work with the UT System Administration. Moral often implies a sense of righteousness that I never felt. I was burdened rather with nagging misgivings. At the heart of my discomfiture was my sense that we could perhaps create a greater sense of fairness in how we did things, a conceit that we could get the same result by sharing more information and perhaps by allowing more consultation in decisions with those affected.

My internal conflicts were playing out against a backdrop of the Watergate episode, and I realized that men smarter than I, men with far more experience than I, had succumbed to the pressures of their bosses to compromise their standards and to violate their oaths to uphold the Constitution and the laws of the land. As with them, I lived in the midst of groupthink, and as much as I despised what they had done, I could empathize with them and the pressures they were under. I could fully relate to those working in the White House who had strayed because they were willing to accept without question the directives from the president and his principal spear carriers. I found myself thinking that were I in their places, I too might have done what they did. That truly scared me because

I was forced to look closely at myself and realize I had not set limits to what orders I would not carry out.

I could not help but see the parallels to my own work, even though the particular assignments and tasks I had to carry out were relatively inconsequential compared to the egregious violations of ethics and the law that had taken place in Washington. At least I was not having to decide whether to do something because I was told it was essential to protect national security.

This kind of thinking and self-flagellation led me to measure more carefully what were the basic values of the university I served. Were those values and interests being injured or eroded?

Agreed, these were times of unreasonable demands and outrageous behavior by some students and campus hangers-on, but I felt we were, in some of our actions, making things worse for everyone, including ourselves, by imposing decisions without at least having given our opposition a chance to be heard. After all, not by any means were all our students and faculty unreasonable in their wants and expectations about how a university should be run. Probably the entire faculty would abhor the thought of a student pounding his sandal on Harry Ransom's desk. And most students would share that sentiment. Who could say? Perhaps through more openness with the larger population of students and faculty, we might even separate the radical malcontents from the more reasonable people on campus.

I certainly did not feel that some of the positions being demanded of the administration as "nonnegotiable" should be accepted. There were demands to close the campus upon call by students. Admissions requirements should be abolished. There were demands for the university to formally oppose the war in Vietnam, to denounce the Nixon administration, to remove all representation of the military from the campus, to reject and close down all research that might relate to the military. There were demands for separate departments for black history and Chicano history with courses to be taught by professors hired by the students, with the university paying the bills, of course. There were objections to degree plans: why not just let students choose whatever courses they feel like taking and grant them a degree for their efforts? There was a call for a major in gardening as offered by the University of California at Santa Cruz.

But certainly not everyone was beyond negotiation and compromise. I could not understand the harm that would be done by talking with opponents and sharing information with them on what we were about to do and why we were going to do it. I did not believe that meeting with opponents constituted an abdication of authority.

It was no wonder that faculty governance was deteriorating into gripe sessions; the faculty was not being consulted on matters that directly affected them. A strategy of the UT System under Frank Erwin's direction was to figure out when was the best time to announce policy proposals and changes to generate the least reaction from faculty and students. Gathering the submission deadlines for the different media became important to be certain to schedule calls to reporters after their stories had to have been put to bed. And we wondered why we got bad press?

I came to feel that our methods were not always the best approach to addressing our problems. Similarly, I became conflicted between what we were doing and how we were doing it when measured against what was best for the organization and the basic academic tenets of the university. It became increasingly evident to me that some of our actions were eroding the gains the university was making as it reached for preeminence among institutions of the first class. Our practices and approaches to campus issues were becoming known on other campuses across the country to the detriment of our reputation.

With such doubts I began to question much I felt I had already resolved about how I should be pursuing my career. After ten years in various public jobs, I had begun to believe I was making progress toward discovering the formula for success and advancement in my professional field. Now much I thought I had learned was thrown into disarray. My expertise in the science of management did not provide answers to real-life tough dilemmas. My desire to try to please my bosses was not a sufficient guide to define where my duty lay. As an ethical proverb, speaking truth to authority was not as easy to live by as it sounded. Maintaining the high regard of your bosses for future advancement became problematic when you might effectively end your career by giving your frank opinion to those who had no doubts whatsoever about what needed to be done.

Two basic precepts, loyalty to the organization and maintaining my principles, were sometimes in direct conflict. Abiding by organizational hierarchy and maintaining loyalty to my boss lost all meaning when I had many bosses and none of them had any regard for hierarchical relationships. Making ambition for advancement my touchstone for deciding how I should conduct myself would quickly leave me with no principles or moral base at all.

Such professional and personal issues made me doubt anew that I had found the answers about how to pursue my professional career. Within months of taking my new job it became clear that I was not yet fully formed professionally or personally as I undertook growing responsibilities and duties in the UT System Administration.

It was out of the discomfort of these conflicts that I would have to find my answers to how I was going to do my work. I had reached the level of management where what I thought and how I decided to do my job could make a difference in an organization. For the first time I had to decide: was I going to try to have my own actions make a difference in the organization or would I be content to be a mere instrument of others, carrying out directions, even if they violated my integrity or resulted in harm to the organization?

CHAPTER 9

Ambitions, Achievements, Celebrities

Early in 1970, Deputy Chancellor LeMaistre asked me to join him and Dean Silber one morning for breakfast in the dean's office. They began by discussing the directions from the Board of Regents to divide Silber's college. The dean made clear his continuing opposition, saying there was far too little communications among academic disciplines even under the university's present structure and it would only be made worse by splitting the departments into narrower divisions. Silber tried out a new pejorative label; he referred to the proposal as "disunifying" the disciplines.

Then the discussion turned to the presidency of the university. Silber said forthrightly that he was not trying to take the presidency away from Norman Hackerman. But to my utter astonishment, he announced unabashedly that he did want the position after Hackerman left it.

In my experience it was simply bad politics to announce one's aspirations so openly. Why set yourself up for those who opposed you? Everyone might know what you aspire to, but it was wise to maintain at least a pretense of deniability. It was better to be courted for a position than to outright declare for it the way Silber did. And having said this to LeMaistre with a witness, he apparently had no reluctance about advertising his ambitions.

Upon meeting John Silber, several things struck you immediately: his intellectual brilliance, his handsome and trim appearance, his persuasive eloquence, his combativeness, and his stunted right arm. Of these you forgot first the physical ones. He was a man of the mind, and when you were in active confrontation with him you had to concentrate on coping with his rhetoric and arguments.

When you arrived in Silber's office, it was not unusual to find him doing one-arm push-ups while leaning over his desk as he began to talk to you. He was careful about his weight and appearance, always dressing smartly and formally. He was undeniably good looking. His suits and shirts were tailored to accommodate his right arm, which, from birth, had reached to about where his elbow would have been and tapered to an end almost like a finger. His tailored shirts and coats permitted him to extend his arm out of his shortened right sleeve. Some people thought he flaunted his arm, but anyone paying attention could see it was useful to him. He had learned to rely on it since childhood. He used it effectively and unselfconsciously; if anyone had a problem with how he used his shortened arm, it was not he. Without its use he would have been crippled, and he refused that.

As to Silber's brilliance and combativeness and his verbal skills in exercising them, Otis Singletary once said to me, "John was born with a sharp mind and he took it to Yale, where he honed it to a fine edge. And he's been cutting people up in little pieces with it ever since."

Irwin "Chet" Lieb, a classmate with Silber at Yale and chairman of the philosophy department at UT, was in less than total awe of Silber's debating skills. He said Silber didn't play fair. He was not above ad hominem argument; if an opponent scored against him on facts or substance, Silber would instinctively resort to attacking his intelligence, honesty, and integrity.

At our breakfast that morning, Silber turned to explaining his plans for a new residential college and a building he envisioned to house the new college. He had selected a site on campus and went to an easel holding a rough rendering of the structure as he laid out his justification for building it. He waxed on about why this was a necessary addition to the growing campus and a way to promote interdisciplinary exposure among students, especially in his college.

I left Silber's office wondering what his purpose had been. I presumed the breakfast had been requested by him because he hosted us in his offices. Perhaps he had met with us to use LeMaistre as a messenger to let Erwin know he wanted to be the next president of UT Austin. Other than that I could not fathom what he had gotten out of the meeting.

There was one thing that Erwin guarded jealously. He would not tolerate any interference with his relations with the legislature. Handling the legislature on behalf of the university was his exclusive domain. This was one of the issues that had most annoyed him about a speech John Silber had given in Dallas in early 1970. Returning from Dallas, Erwin could barely control his anger and concern about the talk he had heard Silber give to a group of wealthy and influential leaders.

When I read Silber's speech, I was impressed. It was well crafted and carefully balanced to address the concerns of this particular audience, which contained regents and former regents of the university as well as Dallas leaders and their spouses. In fact, Silber showed a great deal of political savvy in how he handled himself. For example, he knew everyone in the audience was concerned about the demonstrations and protests on college campuses across the country and the takeover of numerous campuses by students.

In setting out his opinions, Silber addressed the issue of student disorder by criticizing the presidents of major universities across the country for not being prepared to handle violence and protests on their campuses. He said they all knew protests were coming from the earlier turbulence at Berkeley and Wisconsin. Silber said their managerial ineptitude had hurt all public universities. In contrast, he said, at the University of Texas it is "not beneath our dignity to enter into confrontation politics." He said that we know from experience how "to avoid highly destructive campus unrest." He gave reassurances that he knew how to anticipate threats of violence and how to deal with them.

I was sure he addressed this to Erwin, both to flatter him for his toughness and to make the point that, if appointed president, he knew full well how to continue Erwin's policies in dealing with troublesome students.

Then Silber explained that we did not, however, want "to stop ideological debate or dampen the intellectual excitement that is the work of great institutions of higher learning."

He then went back to the other argument and explained that when an assault on the university is proposed, the administration would obtain a court order. By obtaining a court order, the university would change the debate from whether, for example, ROTC should be removed from the campus to whether protestors are going to obey the law.

If this seemed severe to anyone or appeared to be a limitation on free speech, Silber pointed out that this dialogue about whether to obey the law was a way to educate students, make it a learning experience. He did not advocate overwhelming force. A single police officer with arrest warrants, in his judgment, would be sufficient to explain the options available to students. They needed to know that society must enforce respect for the law and those who resist the law will be arrested and punished. To enthusiastic applause Silber said students need to understand "that the right of revolution has only one corollary—that the revolutionaries had better win—and that there is no corollary right to amnesty." If students wish to oppose a law or policy, and violating the law is the only way to express their opposition, they could do so but they needed to recognize the price they might have to pay. In publicizing their opposition to the law, they must be ready to accept arrest and punishment.

Next he addressed another concern of his audience, the apparent loss of religious belief by students. He called this a problem of the generation gap. He said the younger generation is "largely secular in its attitude and is remarkably ignorant of our religious traditions." He added, "The theological inexperience of students has brought about a retrogression in religious insight." These were views that resonated well with his audience.

And he could use humor. On the subject of parents' concerns about what the university was doing to their children, he had a suggestion. He said that all new freshmen should be required on their first night on the campus to write to their parents and list every obscene and scatological word they knew so parents would understand they knew these words before beginning instruction at UT.

At the end of his talk, Silber received an enthusiastic and prolonged standing ovation. President Hackerman, who had preceded Silber as speaker, had not received the same audience response.

I sensed what was behind Erwin's extreme displeasure about the talk. He had to have recognized the potential political threat that Silber could present to his own plans to promote the career of his protégé, Ben Barnes, from the lieutenant governor's job to governor, then senator. Already the press had begun speculating about Barnes being a natural to become vice president or president in years to come after serving as Texas governor or U.S. senator. Erwin must have seen from the audience reaction to Silber that here was a possible rival to his own candidate for higher office.

But there was more to it than that. Twice in his talk Silber had asked those in the audience for help. He said that the only way for UT "to fulfill its constitutional mandate to become a university of the first class is for the citizenry to disassociate in the minds of the legislature what has happened elsewhere from what has happened at (the University of) Texas."

At the end of his peroration, Silber said, "I know this group gathered here tonight can be instrumental in seeing to it that the legislature of the state of Texas continues to honor the university at budget time by appropriating what is necessary to accommodate the needs of an institution of the first class."

To Erwin, this was beyond the pale. Silber had crossed into his personal political arena. Relations with the legislature were Erwin's prerogative and his alone. He knew there would be house and senate members soon taking umbrage that a dean at his university had been pushing the public to pressure them to provide more funding for higher education.

While this was going on, Harry Ransom's tireless efforts over more than a decade to bring international recognition to the University of Texas came to abundant fruition in 1970. *Great Libraries*, by Anthony Hobson, one of the world's most eminent bibliophiles, listed the UT library among thirty-two selected as the very best in the world. Ransom's library was one of five from the United States, in the company of those at Harvard and Yale, the Pierpont Morgan Library in New York City, and the Huntington Library in San Marino, California. Even more impressive was Hobson's statement on why he included the UT library in his book.

He said the UT library's "expansion and rise to prominence have been as rapid and remarkable as the British Museum's expansion under Panizzi in the nineteenth century, or the Vatican Library's in the seventeenth." And in a ringing endorsement of Ransom's unusual and sometimes criticized pursuit of authors' manuscripts and edited drafts, Hobson said, "Texas will certainly be the centre of future scholarship on English and American twentieth-century literature."

Ransom's vision, dating back to the 1950s, to build at UT a great library modeled on the grandest of those in Europe was fully realized—and during only a small portion of one man's lifetime. His vindication and achievement were lauded all over campus and across the nation.

Throughout each year there was a continuing round of receptions, recognition dinners, awards ceremonies, and other social gatherings, many of them to court wealthy donors. Rarely a weekend passed without some sort of celebration of a university achievement or the unveiling of a new plan for growth and innovation.

On occasion there would be someone of special interest at a social event. In Dallas one evening I was placed at a table with James Michener and his wife. We got off to a bad start as we located our table at the same moment. After I introduced myself to him, he said, "When you came across the room just now, I thought I had met you before. You remind me of John Dean on President Nixon's staff."

I must have looked thoroughly horrified because he burst out laughing. He moved a place card so I could sit next to him.

Michener and his wife were being courted by Harry Ransom to place their collection of twentieth-century art at UT Austin. Despite the many other universities and museums trying to obtain their art collection, the Micheners chose to make their donation to UT. They said they made their final decision based on Harry Ransom's pledge to provide space for displaying their paintings. Here, again, Ransom's Humanities Research Center (HRC) played a major role in bringing a coveted donation to the school. And, indeed, pieces from the Michener collection were displayed immediately, many of them hanging in offices around the campus as well as in the HRC.

In the meantime, the Board of Regents continued for the most part to be mystified by the wants and demands of students and the faculty who supported student dissent. One day as the regents sat in closed executive session in the room off the main meeting chamber in the UT Tower, several of them were again complaining about how dirty, unkempt, and unruly the students had become. To make the point, one regent described a tall young man he had just seen on the west mall: barefoot, no shirt, wearing only cut-off shorts, a top hat, and a cummerbund. It was hard to keep a straight face when not a single regent laughed or even smiled.

Another regent commented, "Looks to me like everything they eat turns to hair."

And we sat in a room where there hung on four walls the portraits of former members of the Boards of Regents back to the nineteenth century, the great majority of whom had gone through adult life heavily bearded and mustachioed.

CHAPTER 10

To Fire or Not to Fire
President Hackerman

"Well, Professor, I just had a most interesting conversation with John Silber."

I had learned in the six months I had worked with the university that in conversations with Frank Erwin I had to say little. When he wanted an audience, it was sufficient to sit and listen.

Erwin continued, "I ran him down by phone in Michigan. I told him about the troubles we're having with Hackerman. I told him we may have to fire him at our meeting in Houston this week. I told him Hackerman is still refusing to do what we told him to do about dividing the College of Arts and Sciences."

We were sitting in my cubbyhole of an office on the second floor of the UT Tower. It was January 22, 1970. Erwin was in the side chair beside my desk.

With support from Chancellor Ransom, Silber had been hired into the Philosophy Department, where he rose to become department chairman. Later, when Hackerman became president and had to appoint an arts and sciences dean, he had sent the list of recommended candidates back to the search committee and insisted that Silber's name be added to enable him to appoint Silber as dean.

To Erwin saying he had told Silber that Hackerman was refusing to divide the College of Arts and Sciences I responded, "That should be good news for Silber."

The dean had been fighting for months against dividing his college.

Ignoring me, Erwin shook his head and went on, "You know what Silber told me? Get this. He said I didn't have to take on that burden. I didn't have to fire Hackerman. He would destroy him for me."

What could have motivated Silber to make such a statement to Erwin? Silber was renowned for his cleverness, and he often worked in convoluted ways and could put reverse spin on proposals. It was part of his style of keeping others guessing. Was he just kidding? Was he trying to open Erwin's eyes to what a drastic step the board would be taking to fire Hackerman? Was he using a good dose of cold water with Erwin on such a move by the board to save Hackerman? Was he putting Erwin on? Was he grandstanding as he liked to do and ingratiating himself to Erwin by making such an offer? Was he showing Erwin he could talk and be just as tough as Erwin? Was this conversation the result of two power brokers matching each other in talking big? Was he positioning himself to become president?

I did not know Silber's intentions any more than I knew why Erwin was telling me this story. Was it even true? I was to come to learn that Erwin was not above mythologizing about his role in affairs at the university.

Erwin let Silber's offer to destroy Hackerman register with me and then added, "Yeah, that sort of surprised me too. So I asked him how he proposed to do that, and he said the College of Arts and Sciences teaches over two thirds of the student credit hours in the whole university and he's got half the students. He's got half the university budget in his college. He produces over half the graduates every year. But get this, while he's been dean he's appointed twenty-three of the twenty-seven department chairmen in his college, and he said they will do what he tells them to do."

When Erwin stopped there and sat, put his fingertips in a tent over his chest, and did not go on, I finally commented. I said it was hard to believe Silber would actually say that.

Erwin nodded and said, "He may oppose us breaking up his college, but if he could be president. . . ."

I was acutely aware of the back story on why Erwin was so angry with President Hackerman. Earlier in the day I had heard him talking openly about firing Hackerman. High among Erwin's injunctions to UT Austin was the demand that the College of Arts and Sciences be divided into smaller colleges.

The board, principally Erwin, had been pressing Hackerman for months, and then they had flat out ordered him to bring them a proposal on how to divide Silber's oversized college. Hackerman had dallied and delayed and dragged his feet about finalizing such a plan. He said that such reorganization should not be done without extensive faculty consultation.

Despite having told Erwin his personal reservations about acting too quickly on splitting the college, President Hackerman had for months done nothing to dissuade the board from continuing to believe he was actually working on a proposal to divide the college. Then when he was finally forced to bring forward a plan before the next board meeting, he submitted a two-page letter instead just a few days before the upcoming board meeting.

In his letter, Hackerman said he found no base of support at present for reorganizing arts and sciences. He pointed to evidence of some movement in that direction with the formation of a Division of Biological Sciences within Silber's college. He stated again his opinion that there should be extended discussion among the faculty about any reorganization. He estimated that "if changes occur, they might be two to five or more years off." Hackerman did say he felt there appeared to be long-term benefits to a division of the college. In his closing paragraph, however, he said that any division of the college should wait for "spontaneous nucleation" to take place among the faculties, drawing on a term from his field of chemistry.

Unsurprisingly, this was totally unacceptable to the Board of Regents, and to Erwin especially.

The irony of the situation was that Hackerman's position completely supported Dean Silber's resistance to dividing his college. The president's position added weight to Silber's continuing arguments that his college should not be hastily segmented.

When Erwin read President Hackerman's letter, in effect disregarding the board's repeated directions to him, Erwin made it clear to everyone within hearing that this was grounds for dismissal. He was clearly not content to wait "two to five years or more" to have his way on dividing the College of Arts and Sciences. He used "spontaneous nucleation" as a term of derision. Erwin was accustomed to having administrators promptly follow his orders. To him,

Hackerman, given the most generous interpretation, was uncooperative and, at worst, downright insubordinate.

Now, sitting in my office, Erwin did not say why he had decided to tell John Silber he might have to fire Hackerman. Nor was I about to ask him. I was astonished at what he had just sat there and told me.

Erwin did not say any more but shrugged and got to up to leave. Then he sat down again and said, "You know, I owe John a lot. I got myself in a pickle one afternoon when I was supposed to meet with a bunch of students. Then I learned they'd set me up to debate some faculty bomb thrower."

Erwin continued, "So I called Hackerman to see if he could help me out, but he was off on the East Coast. And I called Ransom, and he was off on the West Coast. Then I called Silber and told him the mess I was in and he said, 'Hell, I'll go with you.' And he did, and it turns out the faculty member was that long-haired tramp Larry Caroline. Silber beat the socks off him and had the students laughing with him while he did it. He admitted to me later he'd hired Caroline. He knew how to deal with him."

Then Erwin got up to go again. "We'll see," he said.

As he left my office that day I remember my feeling of great relief. It did not appear at that moment, as it clearly had seemed earlier in the day, that he planned to try to get the board to fire the president.

And from his seeming wonderment as he described his conversation with Silber, I guessed at a couple of things. First, he had not agreed to let Silber destroy Hackerman. Otherwise he would never have told me what he had. And second, from his recounting of Silber's description to him of his accrued power in his college, it seemed to me Erwin might be reassessing the control Silber had gained over what was happening at the university that Erwin thought he was running.

A couple of days later the Board of Regents held its scheduled meeting in Houston. President Hackerman's letter advising the board to wait for "spontaneous nucleation" was distributed to the regents as an executive privilege item with no public acknowledgment or discussion. Its very existence went unnoted publicly. However, in the open session the president was again admonished that to improve teaching and make the student experience at the university more personal, he must bring to the board a plan for reorganizing the College of Arts and Sciences. There was no suggestion in the public sessions that the president was in any way out of favor with the board.

During the proceedings of that meeting in the ornate and heavily chandeliered Castilian Room of the Shamrock Hotel in Houston, I noticed at one point a hotel employee come in and speak with someone sitting by the door. He was directed toward Erwin at the head of the board table, where he presided as chairman. The messenger handed a note to Erwin, who looked at it and nonchalantly put it in his coat pocket.

A little later in the meeting as the regents were discussing one of the many mundane subjects on the agenda, Erwin got up and started around the room, stopping briefly here and there to speak to someone. As he walked past me he took the message out of his pocket and casually handed it to me without a word.

After Erwin had moved on to speak to others, I unfolded the note and read, "In case you need me, I'm in room 806. John."

Why was Frank Erwin, with all his power and influence, sharing with me, someone most people had never heard of, personal confidences from his phone call to John Silber and Silber's note to him at the Shamrock Hotel? Why would he tell me, a mere subordinate in the UT System Administration for a mere six months, about his conversation with Silber while Hackerman's presidency was hanging in the balance?

Frankly, I think he needed an appreciative audience. He found me a good listener. I believe he felt he was making history for the university and he needed someone with whom to share his machinations and victories. I was only one of a number of such witnesses to events he was directing and managing.

CHAPTER 11

UT Students React to the Kent State Tragedy

Moving into the 1970s, opposition to the war in Vietnam increased on campuses across the country, and UT Austin was no exception. There were calls for moratoria at the school, that is, the canceling of classes by faculty or the refusal to attend classes by students, as a demonstration of solidarity with other students and campuses opposing the war. Antiwar speakers on the UT campus at rallies included liberal professors David Edwards and Irwin Spears, among others; Ronnie Dugger, editor of the *Texas Observer*, a liberal news journal; Abbie Hoffman, one of the "Chicago Seven"; and Robert Sheer, an anti-Vietnam War journalist and editor of the new left *Ramparts* magazine.

Abbie Hoffman was one of the protesters arrested at the 1968 Democratic National Convention. Over months in an unruly and at times uncontrollable courtroom, he was tried in Chicago. Upon being sentenced to five years in prison, Hoffman suggested the judge try LSD and offered to fix him up with a source. He, along with others in the trial, became instant pop heroes as "the Chicago Seven."

Campuses were fast losing their ambiance as a place of serenity, contemplation, and calm. Universities were constantly criticized and attacked by students and by hangers-on around the periphery of campuses. With student protests growing across the country, there was a perennial threat of campus violence.

At UT an open forum outside the student union was set aside for the daily harangues on any subject that students and community speakers wanted to address. Establishing this location had been a compromise by the administration to set aside a place for freedom of expression while prohibiting such speechmaking wherever and whenever a group might decide to congregate and expostulate elsewhere on the campus. Such impromptu speeches arising noisily at any time anywhere on campus had disturbed classes and interfered with other university activities.

Saying the university should be shut down because it was filled with bigoted bureaucrats brainwashing its students did not mean it was about to happen, but this was continually argued. Saying the faculty was completely out of touch with the country did not mean it was so, but this was a constant theme. Stating the university was a tool of the army and the government did not make it so, but this was repeated in nearly every attack. Accusing the administrators and staff of being dupes and pawns of the military-industrial complex promoting the war did not make it so but was repeatedly alleged to be true. Calling for taking over the administrative offices and staging sit-ins in the president's office did not mean it was on the verge of happening, but it was nonetheless threatening.

What took place in the open forum on campus as well as elsewhere may have been only speech, but with the intense anger expressed and the vehemence of delivery and crowd responses, it often felt close to action. This went on day after day, week after week from one semester to the next. The emotionalism of the speakers left listeners wondering when some speaker might actually find the words to fire the tinder of actual violence. Every speaker hoped that he or she might be the one to do just that.

All of this was democracy at work, but it did not seem an entirely civilized way of going about achieving change on a university campus. The result was a disturbing and unnerving tension that brought into question every day the security of the campus as a sanctuary for thought and learning or a safe haven from physical injury.

The most tragic day of those years on American university campuses occurred on May 4, 1970, when the National Guard at Kent State University fired into a crowd of students. Whatever squabbling and arguing went on and however contentious and bitter differences were over the disagreements on the UT campus, reconciliation short of this kind of tragedy was always an option.

Firmness did not imply deadly force any more than a willingness to talk implied acquiescence.

Although Erwin stirred animosities and seemed at times to enjoy fomenting fights with the students and faculty, with this event he immediately became cold, disciplined, and deeply worried. Order need not be purchased at the cost of student lives. But that did not imply he would easily accede to disorder or let his campus fall into the hands of rioters. The turning point in the UT campus protests over the Kent State killings would come from a totally unexpected source.

On April 29, 1970, President Nixon announced he was sending troops into Cambodia to pursue the Vietcong into their sanctuaries and bases there. This triggered especially vigorous new protests. Not only students and faculty denounced Nixon's decision. President Robert Goheen of Princeton, for example, said he was dismayed and had a feeling of betrayal at Nixon's actions.

At Ohio State University the campus had calmed down after two days of confrontations between students and National Guardsmen deployed with fixed bayonets.

Then on Tuesday, May 5, 1970, America awoke to ask what was happening to this country. How could we have come to the point that national guardsmen were not only carrying weapons loaded with live ammunition on the Kent State University campus but had actually fired a fusillade that killed four students and wounded nine others? Much of the nation was in a state of alarm and foreboding not felt since two years earlier when Martin Luther King Jr. and then Robert Kennedy had been assassinated.

With students killed at Kent State, campuses across the country erupted in outrage and indignation to condemn a government and a military system that could permit such an atrocity to occur in America. The Austin campus was among the scores of schools with spontaneous protests and organized demonstrations. The day after the killings, three thousand students marched to the Texas capitol, and police used tear gas to disperse them.

This moved the students from sorrow to belligerence, and by the next day, Wednesday, students were in an even uglier mood. A microphone was set up on the steps of the UT Tower. Students and faculty members began taking turns speaking against the war in Vietnam and about the dreadful events that had just occurred in Ohio.

The broad sweep of steps leading up to the main entrance to the building is capped on each end by two wings of the tower that extend to the south. The UT System offices were in the east wing overlooking the steps. Our second-floor offices provided an overview of the speakers below and the demonstrators and audience gathering on the plaza and the mall that sloped away to the south. The president's offices were in the west wing complementary to ours, overlooking the scene from the opposite end of the steps.

Out of concern for what might happen next and in the event they might be needed to approve or suggest possible administrative actions, several members of the Board of Regents, including Chairman Frank Erwin, had assembled in the UT Tower in our offices at the UT System Administration.

With the speakers just outside our offices and the continuing anguish and outrage expressed to the growing student audience, everyone suspended work to watch what was developing. Within hours the great plaza in front of the tower was filled to overflowing, and students began to gather as well on the grassy open mall leading down from the plaza to the Littlefield Fountain on 21st Street. Students were now covering a distance about 200 yards in length and about 50 yards wide. A few protesters began to appear with blankets. They were obviously coming to stay as they lounged on the grass and under the oak trees lining the mall on each side.

Among the crowd of seven thousand, students conversed and listened only desultorily to the speakers. But they came alive when a speaker announced that police officers and the National Guard had assembled near 21st Street, just to the rear of the gathering students and between the UT Tower and the state capitol. Some students began to get up from their blankets and pallets to look in the direction of the Littlefield Fountain. After the shootings at Kent State and the use of tear gas on students at the capitol the day before, the presence of the police and military dressed in riot gear was very intimidating. The students were slow to resume their places on the ground. They stood in groups, and their talk became more animated and serious.

For those anxious to spark student indignation and anger into another national incident in opposition to the war, the presence of the national guardsmen was a godsend. Some speakers began to harangue the students to attack the police and National Guard and drive them away from the campus.

As all this was unfolding outside, we in both wings of the tower overlooking developments watched with growing concern. Tensions were increasing both out on the mall and inside among us.

Vice Chancellor Bill Livingston's office was at the extreme end of the second floor of the east wing of the tower. His office offered a commanding view across the steps where the speakers and leaders of the demonstration stood and across the plaza and down the mall to the street where the guardsmen and police were stationed. Soon those of us watching from Livingston's office were asked to leave his office, and two men entered the room and closed the blinds. They then set up a tripod and camera and opened a couple of the slats. Through the blinds they began filming the students, particularly the speakers at the microphone on the steps.

They obviously were not university personnel. Upon inquiring who they were, I was told they were from the U.S. Army and were making a record of the demonstrators to identify the major troublemakers. One of them told a member of our staff there were leaders of similar demonstrations spreading out across the country to foment a revolution and the government needed to know who they were. There was a rumor that overnight communist organizers from Houston had come to Austin to stir up the crowd just outside our windows.

With earlier large gatherings of crowds and demonstrators on the campus, I had felt some apprehension that protests might turn ugly. There had been violence in the Student Union when the police made arrests. There had been arrests of students protesting the cutting of trees, and just the day before police had used tear gas on students on the state capitol grounds. But those earlier concerns were nothing compared to what I felt now. For the first time I felt genuine fear. I remember well the sinking feeling in the pit of my stomach.

Not only had the military killed students on a campus just days earlier, now, in civilian clothes, our military, which was supposed to protect us from foreign enemies and was not to be used domestically, was filming students demonstrating their feelings of sympathy for the Kent State deaths and expressing outrage for what was happening to our nation. This was our government using our army inside our country from inside our own offices to gather intelligence on our students. And apparently this was happening on campuses across the country.

This, indeed, made us in the universities complicit with the military and the FBI, as claimed by the Students for a Democratic Society and the Student Nonviolent Coordinating Committee.

Until now things had seemed manageable. Suddenly they had slipped beyond our control at the university. If our military could do this on our campus, then what were our protections against our own government? What were we in charge of on our campuses at this point?

And we were just standing around cravenly letting it happen.

If there were others threatened or offended by the presence of the U.S. Army photographers in our offices and what they were doing, we did not manage to find each other.

Unknown or forgotten at the moment to most everyone present was an event long previously scheduled for that afternoon on campus. I had marked it on my calendar and had planned to attend. In view of what had occurred, I had not given the event another thought. A talk was scheduled to begin at 3 P.M. in the Student Union by John Kenneth Galbraith, the renowned economist, writer, and social critic.

When Galbraith got off the plane in Austin that Wednesday, several students were waiting for him. On the drive to the campus they explained to him that rather than addressing the four hundred students and faculty in the Union as had been planned, they were taking him to the campus to speak to thousands of students assembled on the mall. They told him with eagerness what was happening.

When Galbraith was introduced, I was standing in a group including Erwin, a couple of other regents, and several administrators at the windows behind the speaker.

Someone said, "That's all we need. Some damned Harvard liberal to set this off."

Galbraith, standing seven feet tall, towered above the students around him. Slowly he began speaking. Among our group inside there was more general grumbling about outsiders on the campus and how we didn't need them.

Erwin said, "Wait a minute. Wait. Listen to what he's saying. He's helping us."

Galbraith started off saying how he shared the students' grief and loss at the shootings and deaths of their colleagues at Kent State. He told them they had every right to be indignant and it was their constitutional right to gather and express their sympathy for those killed and what those students had been protesting at Kent State.

He said, "We are no longer a minority. We are a majority on this issue. Cambodia and Kent State have turned public opinion strongly on your side. Don't blow that."

He commended them for the disciplined and controlled way they were going about expressing their views. He told them they should be proud they were part of a nationwide movement that was bringing the American people to their senses about the war in Vietnam.

He said, "Antiwar sentiment, which began with a tiny and eccentric minority, has grown into the major feeling by a great and sensible majority." He went on, "The past few days—Cambodia and Kent State—have changed opinions. Never has there been such a thrust of public opinion on our side. Now, for God's sake don't blow it engaging in mock heroics with those police watching down the street."

He continued by saying that life catches up with those who use violence in the name of law and order. He said students throwing rocks and bricks was not excusable.

Then he pulled the teeth of all those trying to get the students to attack the National Guard and police officers on the street at the bottom of the mall.

He said, "And don't have animosity toward the national guardsmen. Why do you want to pick on them? They're just a bunch of draft dodgers like the rest of you."

With the roar of laughter it was clear the crowd was hanging on his every word.

He ended by saying, "You have power in your capability for peaceful persuasion. I urge action within the system—time is on your side."

There is a story that has become part of the legend of the time and I doubt its veracity. But it was reported that after Galbraith put that volatile situation in perspective, some students passed a hat for cold drinks for the guardsmen. The story continues that the National Guard commander would not let his men accept the drinks for fear they were laced with LSD. It sounds too neat and romantic to be factual, but the story made the rounds.

On another evening of grief, October 31, 1984, Galbraith told me what had happened on the way in from the airport to the UT campus in 1970 and how he had felt that afternoon on the UT campus. I was moderating a debate between Galbraith and William Buckley, and Galbraith had just finished talking with President Jimmy Carter. The president had asked him to fly to India the next day to represent the United States at the funeral of Galbraith's very dear friend, Indira Gandhi, who had been assassinated that day.

On that October evening in 1984, Galbraith told me in all of his public career, including some very touchy circumstances while ambassador to India, he had never faced a situation more pregnant for tragedy than appearing before those students that day in Austin. He said all he knew when he stepped up to the microphone was that the students had been harangued at length to bring about another confrontation that could end in deaths. He was afraid the least wrong word from him could set off an additional tragedy. He said on the way to the campus from the airport the students in the car had talked to him incessantly the entire time, and he had to decide what he was going to say only as he stepped up to the microphone.

The protests that afternoon became demonstrably peaceful from that point on. A further calming contribution was made by a blessed faculty member who for almost an hour in the heat of that long May afternoon read over the microphone an abstruse paper he had written on the Vietnam War. Speeches continued well into the evening as more blankets and pallets showed up and the unmistakable aroma of cannabis wafted across the calm crowd. By midnight the gathering had shrunk to about three thousand sun-baked protestors, some of whom were planning a peaceful march and demands for a university moratorium for the next day.

As I walked among the students lounging quietly on the grass that evening, I encountered Erwin making his own rounds. We nodded to each other but did not speak.

President Hackerman refused to close down the university the next day but said that the faculty would hold teach-ins to discuss the war. That morning there were very few classes being met, but I met mine. Although I held a full-time administrative position, I was trying to gain experience in the classroom. That morning I held my class in Parlin Hall, our room facing out onto the mall where we had so recently witnessed bad options end peacefully.

Midway through the class a sleepy-eyed couple came in and asked me to dismiss the class as an expression of unity with the student moratorium against the war in Vietnam. I told them we were discussing what had been happening and asked them to come in and join us. They demurred, said it was probably all right for us to continue if we were discussing the war, and left.

The students' request for a parade permit for the next day was denied by the City Council, but that decision was overruled by the District Court. That Friday twenty thousand people held a peaceful march through the streets of Austin from the campus downtown past the capitol and back to the East Mall.

CHAPTER 12

Some Unexpected Moves

When President Hackerman formally told the regents at the May 29, 1970, board meeting that he had accepted the presidency of Rice University, the regents placed him on leave from July 1 until he would take his position at Rice. The board then appointed Hackerman's vice president for students affairs, Bryce Jordan, as president ad interim, until a successor to the presidency could be officially appointed. All of this took place very quickly. So quickly, in fact, that the announcement of Hackerman's resignation and Jordan's appointment had to be delayed until the Rice Board of Regents could meet and announce Hackerman's appointment as their new president.

Norman Hackerman had not sought the presidency at Rice University. The institution was in a distressed state, and their Board of Trustees worked hard to recruit him. They had watched Hackerman as he ran the University of Texas and decided he was the man to give their institution new leadership and direction.

At that same May 29 meeting of the Board of Regents, held on the UT El Paso campus, the board made a number of other momentous decisions. For me personally, that meeting was the end of my brief career with the UT System Administration in Austin and my working with the Board of Regents. Happily, it was to be my last attendance at a meeting of the regents.

As far as I was concerned, this relationship was ending none too soon. My position as staff assistant to Executive Vice Chancellor

John McKetta and Vice Chancellor for Academic Programs William Livingston had become untenable.

Structurally, the UT System Administration fit the standard hierarchical organization chart. The chancellor was at the top with vice chancellors under him for such areas as finance, health affairs, academic affairs, student affairs, and operations. Other mundane operating offices also were responsible to the chancellor. All of the presidents of the many campuses reported directly to the executive vice chancellor for academic affairs. The campus vice presidents for business and police forces reported to Don Walker, the vice chancellor for finance.

Whether Erwin influenced or directed the appointment of any of the people heading the offices from chancellor on down, I do not know. I had heard that Don Walker, who later became deputy chancellor and ultimately chancellor, had been brought to the System Administration from the Galveston Medical Branch by Erwin. It was also generally understood that Richard Gibson, head of the law office, had been appointed at Erwin's direction. But I do not know for certain that even these two were appointed at Erwin's direction.

The fact is that Erwin did not need to appoint individuals to specific positions; he roamed the halls of all the offices of the System Administration, freely expressing his views on what needed to be done and giving direction to everyone. When he wanted information or to discuss how an issue was being resolved or to communicate his preferences on how something was progressing, he went directly to the person handling the matter. He was an early practitioner of the administrative technique later known as "management by walking around." Often he was just trolling for information: what projects were bottlenecked, who was saying what, how was a particular problem being handled, what was going on?

In operating in this way, Erwin completely destroyed the "unity of command" in the organization. Authority rested with him if he chose to interfere. You never knew for certain who your boss really was. If Erwin's directions countermanded those of one of your other bosses, that boss understood when you went with Erwin's decision. Responsibility for decisions and actions, as a result, was hard to pin down.

A couple of episodes will make clear why I wanted to escape from the UT System Administration after only a year. In addition to Erwin working around my two bosses to ask me to tell him what they were up to, I was also being called into the chancellor's office to read over letters and recommendations that either or both my new bosses had sent forward for action by the chancellor or the Board of Regents. Finally, I asked Art Dilly, the chancellor's chief of staff, why I was being called in to review these kinds of materials and comment on them to the chancellor and the vice chancellor for financial affairs. Dilly explained that these letters did not have the initials "nn" at the bottom of Nancy Neuenschwander, my secretary. He told me that materials lacking Nancy's initials had clearly not originated with me. In the chancellor's office they wanted to get my opinion on what McKetta and Livingston were recommending on their own. This turned the organization upside down.

For me, grounded in the expectation of loyalty to my immediate boss, this situation put me in a most uncomfortable position, to say the least. In time McKetta or Livingston would discover how I was expected to function outside what should have been a clear-cut hierarchical structure. After they had inherited me from Otis Singletary, for them to find me disloyal and commenting to their superiors on their executive documents behind their backs was a situation I knew I had to escape. This was not just awkward; it was intolerable.

Then one day I received a call from the vice chairman of the Board of Regents, John Peace of San Antonio. He asked me what kind of university we envisioned for his new campus in San Antonio. I told him we were largely leaving that to the new president to decide once he was on board. Peace, in his usual slow and methodical way, said that was the answer he had gotten from McKetta and Livingston. He let me know he was not happy with that plan.

Then he started to interrogate me about what thought we were giving to the particular kind of students most likely to attend his new university. He said that in time most of the students to enroll in San Antonio would be Mexican Americans. He then drawled on and asked me what we knew about the special needs of such students and what experience other universities might have had that enrolled large numbers of Mexican Americans. I told him we had not yet compiled that kind of information. After a long pause he asked if there were any universities in the country that had enrollments of over 50 percent Mexican Americans. I told him we had two in Texas, UT El Paso and Pan American University in McAllen. And there was one in Arizona.

After another long pause he said, "Wouldn't it be useful if we could find out what their experience has been to help us with our planning for my new school?"

Then he waited awhile and asked, "What are you doing next week?"

I told him I was scheduled to be on a panel at a national conference out of state.

He said, "Oh," and we soon ended our conversation.

I may have been slow, but I could not miss what he was interested in me doing next week even if he had not directed or ordered me to do it. And, besides, he was right; it was a good idea. I canceled my trip to the conference and visited the three schools I had mentioned to him.

When I returned, I prepared a lengthy memorandum to my two bosses about what I had discovered and why I believed this information could help us in our planning sessions with the new president and his staff in San Antonio. I ended by saying I was aware that Regent Peace was interested in these kinds of issues for the new school in his city and that I was sending him a copy of my memorandum for his information.

In this case I had at least not violated my obligations of loyalty to my bosses.

My response to John Peace's request did not satisfy his wants. Unfortunately, I had identified myself as someone he could talk with on other topics. One reason he liked to call me was because I had figured out how to talk with him, that is, not to interrupt his long pauses or fill them with verbiage or to become impatient or try to end the conversation before he had completed his thoughts.

But I had also stimulated his desire for more information on various subjects. Or at least it must have seemed to him that I had encouraged him to call me on his other ideas about UT San Antonio and about the new UT Medical School in San Antonio. For soon he was also asking me for information related to the new Institute for Texan Cultures that had recently been placed under the UT regents after it had completed its run as a state-supported part of HemisFair, the 1968 world's fair held in San Antonio.

One evening my wife and I were dressed and about to leave for the bar mitzvah of a neighbor's son when John Peace called me at home as he had begun to do. After I had been on the phone with him for more than half an hour, my wife was pointing at her watch and making motions that we needed to go. I motioned for her to go ahead with our kids and without me.

One of the topics Peace wanted to discuss that evening, again, at length, was what we were doing to find a president for his new university. I explained that my bosses had begun a national search to identify outstanding candidates for the position.

He said, "Yeah, that's what they have told me several times."

I assured him I had seen dozens of letters to my bosses' colleagues at universities across the nation inviting nominations of outstanding candidates. But mostly in this conversation with Peace, as usual, I just listened—and waited out his long pauses. He was clearly unhappy with this situation.

When my wife returned from the bar mitzvah, I was still on the phone with the vice chairman.

As I worked in my office one afternoon a few weeks later, Graves Landrum, vice chancellor for operations and the longest serving member of the top echelon of the System Administration, came in and closed the door. He was angry and concerned. He said, "Ken, your boss is not listening, and I am here to tell you he is headed for deep trouble."

Landrum then explained he had just completed a long meeting in San Antonio with John Peace and Bill Livingston. He said that Peace repeatedly brought up the question of when he was going to get his president for his university. Bill explained that he was conducting a nationwide search for just the right person for the job. Graves explained how Peace and Livingston went back and forth on this several times and Livingston never got the message that Peace was insistently sending: he wanted a president and he wanted him now.

Landrum told me that on the drive back to Austin he asked Livingston if he understood what the vice chairman of the board was saying to him. He told me that Livingston said it wasn't important. Livingston said that Peace will be happy when he sees the high-quality president we get for him in San Antonio. He told Landrum that he was committed to the process he had underway and he wasn't going to abort it to give Peace a quick appointment.

Obviously exasperated, Landrum said he had repeatedly told Livingston that he had better do something quickly or he thought Peace might go to the board and take matters into his own hands. He said Livingston would not listen to what he was trying to tell him.

Landrum asked me if I would talk to Livingston to see if I could get him to move faster. I told him I had already had a few conversations with him on this and had not been able to get his attention.

I did not tell Landrum that Peace had given me much the same message Landrum had just brought me. But I had not kept the sense of Peace's less-than-subtle messages to me to myself. I, too, felt we needed to move quickly, and I had said so to both McKetta and Livingston.

I always listened to what Graves Landrum told me, especially when he was reading the desires of members of the Board of Regents. He had worked with the regents for decades and was keenly tuned to understanding what they had on their minds. I knew he was reading John Peace unerringly.

It was not easy for me to make suggestions to Bill Livingston or to try to provide advice or guidance as a staff assistant to him. After all, I had once been his student, and he had given me the only C in my entire undergraduate career. So now who was I to say or even presume to say that my judgment on matters might be superior to his? It was difficult for me to give him advice when he seemed, I'm sure unintentionally, to demean the suggestions that I did make.

It was a matter of the pecking order in our offices. For example, once I had misused the word *temerity*, and Bill explained to me in his usual instructive spirit that timorous and timidity had no relationship to temerity. They meant, in fact, very much the opposite. It had been valuable counsel, and I resolved to be more certain thereafter of the precise meaning of any new word before I began to use it. Nonetheless, he had, once again, underscored the ranking of our relationship in the office. So it was that if I became not exactly diffident in giving him my views, I did not do so with brash temerity.

So it became almost inevitable that a few days later I would receive a call at home in the evening from John Peace. After a few preliminaries about where we stood on appointing his president in San Antonio, he asked me what I knew about Dr. Arleigh Templeton.

I was frankly horrified and did not pull any punches. I told him as bluntly as I could without being disrespectful what I knew about Templeton. I told Peace he was president at Sam Houston State University in Huntsville and had worked as part of the staff that had prepared a report on the status of higher education in Texas for Governor Connally recommending the creation of the Coordinating Board for higher education. I told him I knew from Bruce Thomas, the vice president at Trinity University in San Antonio and an acquaintance of Peace, that Templeton had claimed authorship of the report that Thomas had written for the governor's study committee. I told him Templeton was a wheeler-dealer, that he was above all a politician, that he had a reputation for being able to raise money, that he did not have the respect of the academic community because of the way he operated and pushed faculty around and ran a strong top-down administration at his university. I told him as well that Templeton was a close personal friend of the powerful chairman of the House Appropriations Committee, Bill Heatley, as well as A. M. Aiken, the dean of the senate and chair of the Senate Finance Committee.

I did not tell him I did not trust or respect Arleigh Templeton.

There was an inordinately long pause on the line after I finished. Finally, Peace drawled, "Sounds to me like he might be the right man to be our *first* president at UT San Antonio."

It was a shorter conversation than usual.

About a week later I overheard the commotion in the outer office as both my bosses were summoned to the chancellor's office immediately.

They returned in a few minutes with the distressing news that the Board of Regents had held a meeting by telephone and appointed Arleigh Templeton president of UT San Antonio. John McKetta merely shook his head and did not say much, but Bill Livingston was in a state of disbelief. He did not suppress his personal views. How could they do this? And Arleigh Templeton, of all people. Our credibility was destroyed. How would he explain this decision to all those people who were helping us identify nationally recognized candidates for the job? How were we going to work with this impossible person? What message was this going to send across the country about our pursuit of quality?

At about this time, I came to the conclusion that the position I found myself in had simply become too uncomfortable for me to continue in it. Situations came up that constantly caused me to feel disloyal to my bosses, but I could not find ways to avoid responding to those who were coming to me around my bosses and using me as their presumed ally, sometimes against my own bosses. Visits from

Erwin with his probing questions were not something I could control; I could not very well refuse to listen to him or respond to his inquiries. I could not turn down his invitation for a drink at the Forty Acres Club after work without offending him.

The same applied to phone calls from John Peace. Nor could I refuse to talk with Dan Williams, a regent from Dallas and a former member of the Coordinating Board. Williams felt he had a right to call me whenever he wanted information because I had once been one of his staff employees when he served as a member of the Coordinating Board. And regent Joe Kilgore, a former congressman and attorney in Austin, would call occasionally to let off steam about Erwin, saying, "I agree with most of what he wants to do; I just don't like the way he does it. I have to vote for the positions he takes, but I'm not happy about it." And vice chairman Jack Josey from Houston would call to ask for my help in trying to ameliorate some position Erwin was taking that he wanted to soften or undermine. In effect, Josey was asking me to work with him against the board chairman.

At one of the meetings of the Board of Regents, which all the presidents of the component institutions of the System regularly attended, I approached the president of UT Arlington, Frank Harrison, while the regents were in executive session. I told him I was in an impossible situation and I wondered if he had an opening on his campus where I might be of use to him. Harrison was immediately enthusiastic. He said, "You bet I do. I'll create a position of vice president for administration. And we'll work around that."

I agreed to his arrangements and we sold our house in Austin. I told the chancellor and his staff and my bosses that I was leaving, and my wife and I submitted a contract for a house in Arlington. From my earliest announcement that I was moving, a number of people in the UT System Administration could not believe I would leave my position there to go to a campus. Counteroffers were made to raise my salary, thinking I was merely going through all this to exert leverage for more pay. But I was determined to get out of that place. When they learned I had sold our house and bought one in Arlington, they began to believe me.

This is where matters stood when I attended my last Board of Regents meeting on May 29, 1970, in El Paso. I did not pause to ask to what extent I had perhaps created or, in part at least, nurtured my uncomfortable situation. I did not ask to what degree I had contributed to creating the bifurcated expectations placed on me. I just knew I wanted out.

Those were still the days when a governing board could agree to appoint a president through a telephone poll and when a board could go into executive session, that is, a closed secret meeting, and make whatever decisions they chose. That day in El Paso, the board went into executive session early in the day and stayed in closed session into the afternoon. Various administrators would be called into their closed meeting and would later come out, to be succeeded by others entering and leaving. There was much reticence and a few long faces among those coming out of the meeting with the regents.

One significant event did take place in the public part of the meeting. The board received material from Vice Chancellor LeMaistre on the continuing issue of what to do about reorganizing the College of Arts and Sciences. He promised to bring to the board a plan for action on the college in time for it to be implemented for the coming 1970–71 school year, that is, by that coming fall semester. This was most interesting in that Dean Silber was still vigorously opposed to dividing his college, President Hackerman had just left, and September was a mere three months away. But because I was leaving that was all going to be somebody else's problem.

Frankly, I was not paying that much attention to what might be going on in those private meetings with the regents because my mind was already very much on the new position I had taken at UT Arlington.

My first sense that something significant had been taking place in the closed meetings came when I was walking out of the building a few steps behind two regents, Joe Kilgore and Frank Ikard, president of the Petroleum Institute in Washington and a former congressman from Wichita Falls.

Joe Kilgore, a prominent lawyer in Austin, had served many years in the state legislature, representing the Valley area in South Texas. He had been an earlier worker in both of Lyndon Johnson's runs for the Senate, and he had served in Congress from South Texas. When Ralph Yarborough came up for reelection to the U.S. Senate in 1964, Kilgore decided he would run against him in the Democratic primary, and his first move was to announce he was not going to seek reelection to his congressional seat from

South Texas. Then to everyone's surprise, President Johnson endorsed Yarborough for reelection. After Johnson called Kilgore and told him he would work to see he was defeated, Kilgore decided to accept a position with a law firm in Austin. Having kept his hand in politics, Kilgore had worked hard to elect John Connally governor, and he was subsequently appointed to the UT Board of Regents.

As they went down the steps in front of me, Frank Ikard said to Kilgore, "I still can't understand why we picked Mickey for Ransom's job."

He was referring to the deputy chancellor, Charles LeMaistre.

Kilgore responded, "Well, me either. For God's sake, if you'd suggested anybody else I would have seconded your motion."

"But who is there?" Ikard asked.

While LeMaistre had served as deputy chancellor and handled items on health-related institutions, I had worked only peripherally with him and I did not know his working style. In presentations before the board he seemed to me competent and extremely articulate. He was good on his feet and quick to read nuances in board reactions to matters he presented. He was pleasant and forthcoming and told fascinating stories about the detective work of epidemiologists to run down the sources of mass infections or poisonings.

When the board returned to open session, they formally ratified the decision made earlier by telephone to appoint Templeton president of UT San Antonio.

At the dinner that evening LeMaistre took me aside and told me he wanted me to fly back to Austin with him on the UT airplane.

On the entire length of the flight back to Austin with Bill Livingston, Art Dilly, and LeMaistre, there was no discussion of the board meeting or any other university business. I decided I must have been invited along as the fourth hand to play hearts, for that was all we did the entire trip back to Austin.

When we landed I grabbed my bag and started for the terminal. LeMaistre took my arm and held me back and let the other two go ahead of us. Then he told me that Harry Ransom was out as chancellor. The board had made Ransom chancellor emeritus effective at the beginning of the next year. At that time LeMaistre would become chancellor. In the meantime he was appointed chancellor designate with full powers to act as chancellor.

Then came the final shock. He told me the regents had removed John McKetta and Bill Livingston as vice chancellors and appointed me vice chancellor for academic affairs.

I was stunned. My first stammered reaction was logistical, "But Mickey, I just bought a house in Arlington."

"Don't worry about it. Sell it. We'll cover your costs."

I was dumbfounded, as I was sure many others would be. I had held my doctorate for one year and for that year had worked for the UT System. I had taught one course at the university. What qualifications did I have for the position other than having been assistant drum major in my high school band?

That weekend I reflected on the past year. For some time I had watched Ransom's authority as chancellor eroded and encroached upon as Erwin came to have less and less confidence in his ability to handle student and faculty confrontations on the UT campuses. Bit by bit items that Ransom should have handled were reassigned to LeMaistre and to Don Walker. Now LeMaistre was chancellor designate and Walker was deputy chancellor for administration with Ransom relegated to chancellor emeritus.

As I thought about taking on my new responsibilities, I pondered what had happened to Harry Ransom. I felt the Board of Regents had been merciless in how they treated him, even as they represented his removal to the public as acceding to his request to step down. I wondered at the choices Ransom had faced at the time of his removal. Had he any intimation this was coming? He clearly could not prevail once the board aligned to remove him. But had he been ready to accept how they treated him? Why did he merely acquiesce in relinquishing his authority and position? He at least had the option to return to the English Department.

My conclusion was that he stayed in his diminished role to at least serve on the periphery to protect what he had put in place over the previous two decades. Yet there was no denying it. The regents, in effect, bought him off. They continued him at his salary and commissioned him to write the history of UT. They had assuaged their guilt at removing him and at the same time felt they had rewarded him for the many contributions he had made to the university. They made it attractive for him not to resist their removing him and, instead, to go along with the board's representation of doing all this pursuant to his desires.

Ransom was a very private and taciturn man. I knew there was no way I would ever be able to discuss these questions with him. To do so would have implied I felt he had sold out to retain what they offered to him. As well as I felt I knew him, I could not even ask him if he had anticipated what happened or how he felt about what the future held. As badly as I knew he had been hurt, I doubted there was anyone he could discuss his feelings with other than his wife Hazel.

The following Monday morning when I arrived at the office, I was called into Don Walker's office, the newly titled deputy chancellor for administration, courtesy of the recent meeting of the Board of Regents.

Walker said, "Here are the keys to the car that goes with your new job. And the credit card for your gas."

Rank had its privileges.

Erwin was sitting at the conference table and motioned for me to come over and sit down. He asked me about my plans as vice chancellor.

I said I was thinking about how I needed to staff my office. He said he thought I had better plan on getting by with my existing staff. He pointed out that the board had also abolished the vice chancellor position for student affairs and put Jack Holland under me.

When I got up to leave, Erwin said, intentionally mispronouncing the word as he often did, "Perfesser, what did you do to make John Peace like you?"

I said I couldn't think of anything specifically.

Erwin added, "Well, you did something. He made you vice chancellor. We were wondering who to put in the position after we told Livingston that he and McKetta were out. Peace said you could do the job; he would vouch for it. He said you'd been carrying those other two guys for months. Nobody objected. So, you're it."

That week the *Daily Texan* reported on parts of the El Paso meeting held the previous Friday. Aside from Ransom's retirement, which hit the campus hard, the principal news was that President Hackerman would go on leave on July 1 and that Bryce Jordan was appointed president ad interim.

But the students were far more concerned about a change in the regents' official rules Erwin had raised than in any of the resignations or new appointments. Erwin had proposed that the board amend its rules governing the campuses to prohibit the use of university buildings by nonstudents and nonemployees. The chairman was particularly incensed by what he called "classes in socialism" which he said were merely lectures on communism concocted by troublemakers from off campus.

The student paper reported on Hackerman's plan for organizing the College of Arts and Sciences that had been submitted to the regents for information. According to the plan that Hackerman had brought forward, the college departments should be grouped into three divisions: Humanities, Sciences, and Social Sciences with a fourth unit of General Studies and Special Programs. Each division would be headed by a dean of faculty. But, most significantly, under Hackerman's plan the three divisions would remain under a single dean of the College of Arts and Sciences, almost exactly the proposal John Silber had been promoting.

The regents established an eighteen-member search committee on the selection of a new president made up of faculty, students, and community leaders, with Charles Alan Wright of the Law School as chairman.

The resignations and other appointments and changes in titles, including mine as vice chancellor, were not publicized at that time.

Thus it came to pass that at the moment I was least planning on my next career move or advancement, it came to me, absolutely unsought.

CHAPTER 13

On the Precipice

Erwin was indeed the lightning rod for criticism from students, faculty, and others, and it was evident that he took that role in part because he was willing to deflect part of the blame from members of the administration having to deal with campus disorder. Moreover, it was undeniable that Erwin enjoyed being the center of controversy and attention.

Early summer 1970, almost as though anticipating the further notoriety Erwin would acquire by events just ahead, Ann Arnold, an Austin journalist, wrote an article appearing in newspapers across the country. She brought together in one place much of what had been reported about Erwin piecemeal. Some of what she included was heresy to faculty and a torch to student sentiments.

She quoted Erwin saying, "If we don't find a new kind of college administrator—university presidents, deans, chairmen of departments, people at all levels of higher education—that has more courage, more backbone than he's demonstrated in the past two or three years, then we may really lose colleges and universities as we understand them."

He told her he had no confidence in professors becoming administrators. He proposed that perhaps boards should begin to use professional executives to be presidents to replace the "weak-wilted" approach of most academic administrators. He said he saw present university leaders losing the public's confidence. He was proud that UT was the largest university not shut down by protestors while hundreds of others had been closed by student demonstrators. He attributed that to one thing, a tough stance by the UT Board of Regents, and, by implication, its stalwart chairman.

Characterizing the nature of campus protestors, Arnold quoted Erwin as saying, "Then the next day these sweet little innocent people burn the ROTC building down and the way they describe it is, 'These kids were frustrated and angry and they threw railroad flares in the ROTC building and the building caught fire!' You'd think it was the goddamn building's fault."

He referred proudly to the fact that six of the nine regents at UT had come to the campus when there was a threat of violence and spent all day and stayed overnight to back up the administrators in the event it became necessary to call out the National Guard.

He added, "What kind of irritates me is that these students and faculty members think that nobody has any high moral or ethical values but them."

When Arnold brought up the episode about him personally directing the bulldozers and the police in removing students and cutting down the trees along Waller Creek, Erwin explained that when you get tens of thousands of students in a confined area where large gatherings can occur quickly and there are inadequate campus police to deal with the situation, somebody has to act quickly. Then he remarked, "You say, but the chairman of the board of regents shouldn't be doing this? I agree."

And Erwin continued to take on all challengers. When the Coordinating Board for Higher Education proposed to set enrollment limits for UT Austin and other state universities, Erwin testified against the proposal, saying the university would handle its own business.

Manuel DeBusk, the chairman of the Coordinating Board, then asked for an attorney general's opinion whether his board had authority over the University of Texas to set enrollment caps. He raised hackles when he said, "Boards of Regents can be bought for nothing," blaming them for wanting more student growth to help local real estate developers. DeBusk said he was sure he would make enemies during his six-year term. He was well on his way when he picked a fight with Erwin.

Erwin fired back self-righteously, "While the Board of Regents of the UT System is working overtime to repulse the Marxist elements in our universities and to keep classes open and operating for tens of thousands of fine Texas boys and girls who want only a quality education, the chairman of the Coordinating Board appears to be trying to invent a power struggle between him and the Board of Regents."

Growing enrollments at UT had already become an issue on campus, with the faculty standing firmly for some kind of limitation. Erwin appeared content to let enrollments continue to grow. In direct opposition, Dean Silber led his college to a near unanimous vote to limit growth to 35,000. There was speculation that Silber should have left this issue alone and that by apparently siding with DeBusk against Erwin he had only gained the ire of the chairman.

The attorney general ruled that the Coordinating Board did not have enrollment control authority over the state's universities. There were immediate presumptions that Erwin had interceded in the attorney general's office to be certain the ruling was written to maintain UT's autonomy. This was probably true; he had done so in the past.

But DeBusk could not leave well enough alone. He then had the Coordinating Board adopt a resolution on campus disorder. He explained the resolution was necessary to encourage university presidents to expel troublesome students and bring criminal charges against them.

Even if Erwin might agree with him, this kind of encroachment on the prerogatives of the Board of Regents was inflammatory. Erwin swore to the System staff he would get his revenge on DeBusk for attempting to interfere with UT. And, indeed, he would.

John Silber was the other person on Erwin's list who had encroached into his arena of legislative politics. If he had not had intimations earlier of Silber's growing influence and political visibility, the talk in early 1970 in Dallas certainly attuned him to the threat Silber posed to Erwin's aspirations for his protégé Ben Barnes.

He watched closely as he saw Silber building an independent base. Silber had organized his college faculty to insist the university was growing too big and enrollments needed to be curtailed. He openly opposed any plan to divide his college. He was traveling around the state far more than any other dean. He had breathed new life into the Arts and Sciences Foundation, a group of supporters and donors of his college originally put in place by Harry Ransom. Most notably, he began to hold "Meet the Dean" dinners around the state. These were promoted as money-raising events for his college foundation, but they provided a ready forum for Silber to build name identification and to promulgate his political views. Continuing campus demonstrations across the nation provided a perfect foil for Silber to market his views on how to handle trouble-makers, a top political issue on the minds of all Americans and of deep concern to conservative Texas voters.

Meanwhile, as summer arrived, the tug and pull on the campus about how to reorganize the College of Arts and Sciences continued unabated. The faculty, cheered on by opponents of any division of arts and sciences, such as Vartan Gregorian from the history department and head of Plan II, Erwin Spear from botany, David DeLaura from English, and others, were drumming away at the damage to be inflicted on the entire university by dividing the academic disciplines.

Despite faculty resistance, the Board of Regents continued to press the chancellor and the president ad interim to bring them a proposal for dividing the college. The regents were unimpressed by predictions that dividing the college would result in faculty flight to other universities.

On July 1, 1970, a mere month after I had been appointed vice chancellor, a late morning meeting was called on short notice at the request of the deans of all the UT Austin colleges to hear from Chancellor Designate LeMaistre and President ad Interim Bryce Jordan on the status of the proposal to divide the arts and sciences college. President Jordan had a luncheon meeting scheduled off campus, and he made clear to the twelve deans who showed up that he could meet with them only briefly to open the session. He spoke first because he had to leave immediately, and he succinctly outlined the plans and rationale he was proposing to take to the Board of Regents. He completed his presentation and then had to leave without taking questions.

Upon Jordan's departure, Dean Silber stated again his reasons for opposing the division of his college, and other deans began to question Chancellor LeMaistre about some of what Jordan had just laid before them. The question arose why LeMaistre had directed Jordan to bring the plan forward. Then a couple of deans asked how adamant the Board of Regents really was about dividing the college. They wanted to know how tight the timeline was for moving forward on the plan.

LeMaistre then stunned me when he replied that the schedule for moving forward was in President Jordan's hands entirely and the president had not been given a timeline or any specific directions by him or by the regents as to how the College of Arts and Sciences should be divided.

At that point I interrupted him to refer to the resolution that the regents had adopted at the meeting in El Paso, just a month earlier. I mentioned how the board had said they wanted a plan in place by that fall. I rambled, trying not to be too direct, stalling for time and hoping LeMaistre would stop speaking long enough to reconsider what he had just said. I had heard him promise the board in El Paso on May 29 to have a reorganization plan in place by that fall.

I felt like a blithering idiot. I could not disagree publicly with my boss. I could not audibly remind him of the strong position the regents had taken or slip him a note as he spoke.

But it really didn't matter. I was quickly interrupted by Dean Silber and several deans saying they saw no reason to rush into such a serious matter. They liked what LeMaistre had just said to them. Well, of course. Dean Silber spoke again about the need for keeping the twenty-seven departments in arts and sciences together, at least until the faculty could decide for themselves whether some reorganization was needed and how it should be done.

At that point the meeting broke up as several deans began to stand and say they had lunch appointments.

As I walked back across the hall toward my office totally crestfallen at what I had just witnessed, Deputy Chancellor Don Walker happened to encounter me on his way to lunch and asked jovially how things had gone in the meeting.

I replied, "Terrible. Mickey just cut Bryce off at the knees."

He wanted to know what I meant, and I recounted for him what had just taken place.

He said, "Go to your office and don't leave. Frank will want to talk to you."

Within minutes Erwin was on the line and probing to know exactly what had taken place. I told him. He made me repeat it. He said, "I don't believe you. That could not have happened. Mickey wouldn't do that." Then he snapped, "Who were some of the deans there?"

I listed several, including Graduate Dean Gordon Whaley, the social work dean, Jack Otis, and the newly appointed dean of the LBJ School, John Gronouski.

Earlier in his career Gronouski had run unsuccessfully against Senator Joseph McCarthy in Wisconsin. He had gone on to be appointed postmaster general by President Kennedy and ambassador to Poland by President Johnson. Whaley was one of Erwin's closest confidants. Otis would be an objective observer.

Erwin said, "Stay in your office and don't leave."

I wasn't hungry anyway.

Within half an hour Erwin called back and said in a subdued manner, "I can't believe it. Whaley and Gronouski told me the same damn story you did. I didn't believe you. Gronouski said he might be new to academia but he knew a cop out when he saw it. Whaley said Mickey did a complete flip flop after Bryce had laid out his plan. Now get me a secretary; I'm coming over there to dictate a memo for Mickey to sign when he gets back from lunch. I'm going to clarify for everybody what he meant to tell those deans."

And, indeed, Chancellor LeMaistre did send out such a memorandum that afternoon, standing squarely behind President Jordan and his proposal to divide the College of Arts and Sciences. LeMaistre said that Jordan "has no discretion about dividing Arts and Sciences and no discretion as to the administrative character of the deanship heading each of the new colleges." In his memo LeMaistre set July 17 as the deadline for Jordan to submit his plan.

A week later formal announcements were made that Charles A. LeMaistre would become chancellor on January 1. E. Don Walker was named deputy chancellor, and my appointment as vice chancellor was announced.

When President ad Interim Jordan submitted his proposed reorganization on July 17, the *Daily Texan* printed John Silber's response and critique of Jordan's plan for dividing the College of Arts and Sciences. Silber said the plan Jordan had submitted had been tried and failed in the past. He predicted that the reorganization would foment infighting. He reminded his readers that the faculty had supported a single unified College of Arts and Sciences.

Silber had repeatedly made clear that if any subdivision of his college was undertaken he wanted four associate deans under *him*, overseeing Humanities, Science, and Social Sciences, with the fourth associate dean in charge of supervised instruction. This was very close to what President Hackerman had submitted just before going to Rice. Hackerman's proposal also left four divisions under the direction of the dean of Arts and Sciences, precisely the plan Silber favored. And Silber was absolutely correct about the faculty; a number of committees had come up with very similar configurations, again with any subdivisions of the college to be placed under the administration of a single dean.

Jordan's plan did away with the dean of Arts and Sciences and called for four *separate* units: the College of Humanities, the College of Social and Behavioral Sciences, and the College of Natural Sciences, plus a Division of General and Comparative Studies. Each of the four units was to be headed by a dean, with the four units under the supervision of a new provost of Science, Arts and Letters to ensure the unity of the different fields of study.

The *Daily Texan*, in supporting Silber's position, criticized Jordan for not having shared his proposed plan with the paper and the faculty and students before he submitted it to the chancellor.

During my twelve years of work since receiving my master's degree in public administration from Syracuse University, I had held seven different administrative jobs at the federal, state, and local levels. To that time I had never encountered a situation in which a person could expect to remain inside an organization and hold a position of authority while working against a declared policy finally decided on by the policymakers of that organization.

This was the first of two anomalous circumstances that were contrary to my experience. A person might be encouraged to speak up and disagree with proposed policy options as policy was being formulated, but after a decision was made, you went along with it, resigned quietly, or quit and took your views to the public outside the organization. I had not seen a situation where someone was permitted to remain inside the organization and use his position to openly undermine and sabotage a policy position already agreed upon.

Dean Silber had just declared to the entire campus through the student paper that he intended to continue fighting President Jordan, the System Administration, and the Board of Regents.

The second condition at odds with my experience and with my expectations about how professional administrators should behave related to the conflict between careerism and the goals of an organization. Careerism at its worst consists of advancing oneself at the cost of the organization. Everything I had seen and witnessed in Dean Silber's actions told me he was using the university to further his personal ambitions. If he was serious, there had been his proposal to Erwin to destroy Hackerman. There was his flying back from Michigan, after Erwin had told him Hackerman might have to be fired, in order to be available at the Shamrock Hotel meeting to replace Hackerman. There had been his confidence that, having hired twenty-three of twenty-seven department chairmen in his college, he could order those chairmen to vote as he wished them to. There was the unapologetic and crass ambition I had heard Silber describe over breakfast with Chancellor LeMaistre when he openly declared that he wanted to be president after Hackerman. There were Silber's "Meet the Dean" conferences around the state, ostensibly to raise money but that were thinly disguised opportunities to promote his personal political agenda.

My lack of understanding that disagreement inside the university community had few limitations and was widely tolerated constituted one of my deficiencies in holding my new position as vice chancellor. Not having come to my position through the ranks of academia, I did not yet understand that a policy set inside a university by the administration, or even by the regents, was not, in the eyes of the faculty, a legitimate policy until the faculty had had its say in its formulation. This understanding was to come to me only later, but at this point I was operating from my earlier experience. I was not mindful of the great differences between a university and government or business organizations. My lack of sensitivity to this essential nuance of university governance was about to have serious consequences.

Kenneth Ashworth, vice chancellor for academic affairs. *Photo by Frank Armstrong, UT Office of Public Affairs Records, Dolph Briscoe Center for American History, di_06962. Unless otherwise noted, all images are from the Briscoe Center.*

Otis Singletary, Harry Ransom's vice chancellor for academic affairs. *UT Office of Public Affairs Records, di_06985.*

Frank Erwin, December 6, 1971. *Photo by Ike Baruch, Prints and Photographs Collection, di_06976.*

William S. Livingston, vice chancellor for academic programs, 1969–1970. *Prints and Photographs Collection, di_06984.*

Former UT chancellors Logan Wilson (left), Harry Ransom, and James Hart at the dedication of Burdine Hall on the UT campus, December 14, 1970. *Prints and Photographs Collection, di_06983.*

John Silber (standing) and Frank Erwin (foreground) at a UT Regents meeting, November 3, 1968. *Prints and Photographs Collection, di_06969.*

Student selling the underground newspaper *The Rag*, which the Regents tried to ban from campus. *Prints and Photographs Collection, di_06990.*

Students fighting with police during the Chuck Wagon incident, when non-students were banned from the campus restaurant, November 10, 1969. *Prints and Photographs Collection, di_06989.*

UT students protesting the shootings at Kent State, 1970, looking across the mall with the tower out of the frame on the right. The speakers' microphone was at the upper right between the tree and the visible west wing of the tower. *Photo by Johnny B. Jenkins, Prints and Photographs Collection, di_06984.*

Former president Lyndon B. Johnson, right, and interim UT president Bryce Jordan, left, with Kenneth Ashworth in his favored spot, in the background. *Photo by Texas Student Publications, Inc. Copy courtesy of Kenneth Ashworth.*

Frank Erwin at Waller Creek, 1969. *Prints and Photographs Collection, di_06992.*

Norman Hackerman, president of UT, 1967–1970. *UT Student Publication Records, di_06967.*

W. Page Keeton, dean of the UT Law School, 1971. *Prints and Photographs Collection, di_06964.*

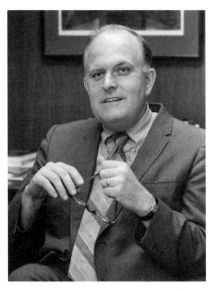

Bryce Jordan, interim president of UT Austin in 1970–1971 and first president of UT Dallas. *Photo by Frank Armstrong, UT Office of Public Affairs Records, di_06965.*

UT history professor Vartan Gregorian. *UT Office of Public Affairs Records, di_06971.*

Stephen Spurr, president of UT, 1971–1974. *Photo by Frank Armstrong, Prints and Photographs Collection, di_06966.*

Former president Lyndon B. Johnson with Frank Erwin, January 1971. *Prints and Photographs Collection, di_03306.*

John Silber addresses a UT faculty meeting, February 11, 1970. *Prints and Photographs Collection, di_03310.*

John Silber, dean of UT's College of Arts and Sciences. *Photo by Frank Armstrong, Prints and Photographs Collection, di_02389.*

Former UT Regent John Peace. *UT Office of Public Affairs Records, di_06977.*

John J. McKetta, executive vice chancellor. *UT Office of Public Affairs Records, di_06981.*

Harry Ransom, left, and Charles "Mickey" LeMaistre at a Regents meeting. *Prints and Photographs Collection, di_06978.*

UT Board of Regents, 1969–1971. *Prints and Photographs Collection, di_06973.*

Chancellor Charles "Mickey" LeMaistre, 1973. *Photo by Frank Armstrong, Prints and Photographs Collection, di_06980.*

E. Don Walker, deputy chancellor. *UT Office of Public Affairs Records, di_06979.*

Bauer House, the UT chancellor's official residence. *Photo by Frank Armstrong, UT Office of Public Affairs Records, di_06987.*

O. Henry Hall. The UT System offices moved here from the Main Building in 1971. *UT Office of Public Affairs Records, di_06986.*

UT Board of Regents at a meeting in San Antonio, July 21, 1972. *Prints and Photographs Collection, di_06972.*

CHAPTER 14

Firing John Silber

On Friday, July 17, 1970, the afternoon following the release of Jordan's plan for reorganizing the College of Arts and Sciences and the day of John Silber's rebuttal to the plan in the student paper, Erwin came into my office in the UT Tower and wearily dropped into the chair beside my desk.

Without any preliminaries, he shook the *Daily Texan* at me and asked, "Well, Doctor, where is all this going to end?"

I opened my desk drawer and pulled out a sheet of paper and handed it to him.

It was a draft letter. It was addressed to Dean Silber, listing several of his most recent acts of defiance of the policy positions and directions of his superiors in the university. The letter went on to say that in view of his continuing acts of insubordination this left no alternative but to relieve him of his position as Dean of Arts and Sciences effective immediately.

Erwin read the draft, revealing nothing of what he was thinking, and handed it back. Then he asked, "Why do you have Bryce signing it?"

I replied, "Because Silber doesn't work for you—or the Board. And he doesn't work for LeMaistre. He works for Bryce."

He nodded and told me to put the letter in my desk and not to tell anybody about it or show it to anyone.

So that was the end of that, I thought.

A week later, the afternoon of July 24, I got a call to come to the chancellor's office.

When I entered, there sat Erwin with Chancellor "Mickey" LeMaistre, President Bryce Jordan, Deputy Chancellor Don Walker, LeMaistre's chief of staff, Art Dilly, and the assistant to the chancellor, Mike Quinn.

No one was saying anything. But it was clear they were expecting Erwin to explain why he had called them together in LeMaistre's office.

When I entered, Erwin said, "Go get that letter and put today's date on it."

No one saw that as remarkable. Everyone did what Erwin told them.

When I came back with the letter, he took it from me and walked over to LeMaistre's desk and laid it in front of the president.

He said, "Sign that letter, Bryce. You just fired John Silber."

Jordan signed the letter with alacrity, and Erwin sat down and began to describe the meeting he had just had with Silber.

Erwin met Silber in Donald Weismann's office. Weismann was a university professor of the arts, a position in which he could write, paint, compose poetry, and indulge his broad compass of interests and talents.

Erwin described how he arrived in Weismann's office. He had said, "John, I'm going to make you famous today. I am going to fire you."

Erwin said Silber did not flinch or try to talk him out of it. Erwin said Silber proceeded to tell him he was relying on a bunch of lightweights who knew nothing about running a great university. There in the chancellor's office Erwin went around the room and related how Silber called LeMaistre a political hack and a congenital liar. Jordan he called a sycophant and "climber." Walker he called a self-promoting lackey and Erwin's errand boy who had no idea what a university was.

Then he turned to me and said, "And, *Doctor* Ashworth, he had a few kind words for you too. He wanted to know how I could be taking advice about my university from somebody who got his Ph.D. just last year."

From there on, after Erwin had taken such a momentous step, the discussion turned to how to handle the media and the expected outcry from the faculty and the students. He had acted on a Friday to permit the situation to cool down over the weekend. Of course it was statewide and national news that the University of Texas had once again fallen under the control of politics and an overbearing Board of Regents and its chairman.

It was almost twenty years later that I learned from Don Weismann the rest of what had happened in his office that afternoon. Weismann told me that he had just arrived home, where a university policeman was waiting for him. The officer told him Erwin wanted him to call. Erwin told him he wanted to use his office for a meeting with Silber that afternoon. Weismann had readily agreed, of course, and he told Erwin he would leave his office to them when they arrived. Erwin told him, no, he wanted him there when he talked with Silber.

Weismann said he returned to his office and Silber showed up early for the meeting. He was grinning and said, "I suppose you're wondering why Frank wants to talk with me."

Weismann said he confessed he was curious. And John replied, "Frank is coming to tell me I'm going to be the next president of UT."

His version of what else Erwin had told us about what was said at the meeting tracked Erwin's version, with the exception of how it ended.

Weismann said, "When Frank had finished and went to the door, I said, 'But, Frank, never forget. We love you.'"

He added, "Frank turned around, and he had tears in his eyes."

At the time there was no one in the UT System Administration who was at all displeased to see John Silber stripped of his power and brought down. Within UT Austin the judgment was divided. There were probably few in the university administration who sided with Silber, but he had many admirers and supporters among the humanities faculty and the students. However, a number of faculty members were not displeased to see Silber removed as dean.

Following the firing, the deans voted to support Jordan, as they put it, in a "very difficult and highly pressured situation." But they made clear their vote was not intended to endorse the firing of John Silber. Even at that, two deans voted against the statement to support the ad interim president. Rumors started immediately that they would be the next to be fired.

Of course John Silber at the time was entirely correct in his assessment in Weismann's office of those on whom Erwin had now become dependent for his advice.

Chancellor LeMaistre came from a medical school to his job and could not begin to match Harry Ransom's vision of greatness for UT Austin. President ad Interim Jordan was indeed ambitious, and rising from student services to the top job, he was untested in leading the school to greatness in academic matters. Deputy Chancellor Walker was narrowly focused on orderly procedures and immediate tactical goals, as he was instructed in those by Frank Erwin. And then there was me, fresh out of my doctoral program in the theoretical field of the history and philosophy of education.

We were the residue of leadership after our predecessors had been driven off, taken better jobs, or been demoted or fired.

Otis Singletary had left for Kentucky, one of the few who spoke directly and candidly to Erwin and who would disagree with what he planned to do with the university.

Next had been the departure to Rice University of President Hackerman, who would not follow Erwin's directions and plotted his own course for what was proper and fitting for policies and procedures at a great university.

Harry Ransom had become such a mild-mannered person by that time that although he might delay and sometimes find ways to temporize and convince regents or the chairman to reconsider a decision in the making, he did not stand in direct confrontation to the Board of Regents or their actions. By then he had been demoted by the board to chancellor emeritus at the end of the year, and in the intervening months Chancellor Designate LeMaistre had full authority to act as chancellor.

William Livingston had resigned as vice chancellor for academic programs, saying the purposes of his office had been accomplished. The new universities in Dallas, San Antonio, and Odessa had been established and a president appointed for each of them.

John McKetta had also just announced his resignation as executive vice chancellor for academic affairs on July 7, with the statement, "If you want to know the reasons, call Dr. LeMaistre and he'll tell you why I'm resigning."

In effect, McKetta was daring LeMaistre to say what had really happened: that he had been fired by the regents on May 29 in El Paso even though he had not been present.

But Chancellor LeMaistre instead issued a prepared statement praising John McKetta for his devotion and commitment to the university.

Livingston and McKetta had been poorly used. When Arleigh Templeton, at John Peace's instigation, had been peremptorily appointed by the regents as president of UT San Antonio, both McKetta and Livingston had gone to Harry Ransom, who at that time still retained the title of chancellor, and told him they wanted to resign. Ransom asked them both to stay, pointing out that their resignations so close on the heels of Hackerman's and Singletary's could be harmful to the reputation of the university. In fact, at that time Ransom asked McKetta to become a candidate for the UT presidency, but he refused. At Ransom's urging, McKetta and Livingston agreed to stay awhile longer, only soon afterward to be dismissed by the Board of Regents at the El Paso meeting—along with Ransom.

Ironically, at that same May 29 meeting, Arleigh Templeton was confirmed as the new UT San Antonio president.

And now Silber was gone as well, seemingly the last administrator at the university in Austin or inside the University System Administration who would stand up to Erwin.

Within two months Regent Jack Josey would resign as vice chairman of the board but retain his position on the board, saying enigmatically, "The chairman and indeed the board should have a vice chairman whose ideas and views on methods and procedures are more closely akin to the chairman's views."

The frequent disagreements between Josey and Erwin were well known by the members of the board. And Josey did not work to cover them up with the administrative staff either. But his giving up the vice chairmanship while staying on the board was a puzzlement to many of us. Perhaps he did this to make public that the board was not unanimously behind all Erwin did and proclaimed on behalf of the board.

Who was I to make the audacious suggestion that John Silber should be fired? What right did I have to put such an idea in Erwin's head? By right or not, I had done it. I had had an opinion, I had made a judgment, and I had made a recommendation. In any event, I believe Erwin would in time have come to the decision on his own to fire Silber.

CHAPTER 15

A Few Items Get Resolved

Once fired, John Silber accepted Erwin's action as final and irrevocable. When the faculty called a meeting to discuss his dismissal, Silber asked that it be canceled.

Approval of President Jordan's proposal to divide the College of Arts and Sciences moved resolutely forward despite continuing opposition. A petition opposing the division and signed by 350 faculty members was sent to President Jordan, the chancellor, and the Board of Regents. A petition endorsing the proposal was signed by only twenty-one faculty members. A student petition opposing the plan drew six thousand signatures.

Heated letters and statements continued from the faculty and students. Erwin could not let those lie, and he responded in language that could have served as a model for the later White House denials of the Watergate revelations. Erwin's statement read, "Through the use of innuendo attributed to unidentified 'informed sources' these character assassins have publicly attacked the University President, chancellor-elect and the chairman of the Board of Regents, and yet neither they, nor the reporters have had the honesty or integrity to identify the source of the calumnies."

English professor Norman Farmer commented, "Corporate rather than academic values are being applied to the university."

The popular cliché used across the country was often heard on campus, "What we have here is a failure to communicate."

A number of issues rose almost simultaneously requiring student and faculty involvement. In addition to the ongoing disagreements about dividing arts and sciences, decisions were needed on how to handle the runaway growth of enrollments at UT Austin, who the search committee was going to recommend for president, how the regents would deal with the radical off-campus paper *The Rag*, and how the president and regents would deal with the request to register the gay liberation club as a recognized student organization.

If speculation was true that aggressive support from the College of Arts and Sciences for limiting UT enrollment was behind Erwin's drive to divide their college, the faculty did end up with half a loaf. One projection showed UT growing to over eighty thousand students within a decade unless some action was taken. Problems with the oversized College of Arts and Sciences were symptomatic of the campus as a whole. Consequently, while the division of arts and sciences was moving ahead, Erwin did come to share faculty sentiments for setting enrollment ceilings.

On July 31, 1970, the board of regents met in Port Aransas at the Marine Science Institute to consider Jordan's proposal for dividing arts and sciences. The evening before the meeting, the regents and members of the System staff met informally over drinks before dinner to discuss briefly the hearing to be held the next day.

Shortly after we got into the informal evening session, Chancellor LeMaistre asked me to comment on what arguments I thought John Silber was likely to raise in his appearance the next day. I began to set out some of the arguments that we had all heard from Silber and started to suggest some responses.

Regent Ikard interrupted, "We're not going to answer any of his questions."

At that point I was much relieved when Harry Ransom stood up and said, "John is not going to lead a rebellion of the faculty about dividing the college. He wants to be heard. He needs to be heard. He is obligated to the faculty who've supported him and spoken up against the plan. I'm sure he knows the board is going to go ahead with Jordan's plan."

That ended the preparation for the hearing the next day.

Paul English, chair of the Geography Department, and David DeLaura from the English Department addressed the board, opposing the dismantling of their college.

Former Dean Silber spoke for almost an hour in opposition. His presentation centered around his argument that the divisions of knowledge should not be placed in separate boxes on an organization chart. He used flip charts to illustrate his point by showing the divisions of knowledge as overlapping circles, saying they should be seen in a three-dimensional relationship. He argued for the unitary nature of knowledge and against vertical hierarchies that would reduce essential horizontal contacts and relationships.

President Frank Harrison of UT Arlington was the only administrator to join President Jordan to speak in favor of the plan. Harrison testified that arts and sciences on his campus had been in separate colleges for years and had presented no impediments to interdepartmental relations and sharing of knowledge.

The hearing was completed before noon, and the board broke for lunch.

At lunch, I happened to sit at a table with a number of students. They did not know who I was and spoke freely, ignoring me altogether. In my obscure role I had at least the benefit of anonymity if not near invisibility.

Jeff Jones, the bearded student body president, and a girl arrived late to join us at the table, and several students pressed him hard, asking, "Jeff, where the hell were you? We needed you at the hearing. Silber was all alone. We kept looking for you. Where were you?"

Jones grinned and gestured with his thumb to the girl with him. "Milady here and I decided to sleep in. Guess we missed the fun, huh?"

One of the students told him the hearing was over and the regents were going to vote and go on to other business. He did not seem concerned.

Late that afternoon the reorganization plan was approved 9–0 by the board.

I was satisfied with the resolution of the controversy. The college was too big, had too many of the total faculty, and handled too many of the core academic and support courses for all degrees in the university in one administrative unit. There was too much power and money concentrated in one person supposedly subordinate to the president. Arts and sciences, all in one college at UT Austin, exceeded in size at least 90 percent of the colleges and universities of the world.

After adoption of the plan, Vice Chairman Jack Josey moved a vote of confidence in President Jordan and Chancellor LeMaistre. It carried unanimously.

Hurricane Celia hit Corpus Christi and Port Aransas three days later, wreaking havoc over the area and causing in excess of half a billion dollars in damage. Back on the campus in Austin the sardonic comment was, "God had the right idea, but his timing was off."

Even after the regents' approval of Jordan's reorganization plan for arts and sciences, disagreement and opposition continued on campus. President Jordan immediately changed the subject and focused on how to control enrollments, a subject popular with the faculty.

A federal court ruling came out against the university, holding that *The Rag*, the radical off-campus paper, could not be prohibited by the regents from being sold on campus.

One faint hope remained to keep the arts and sciences reorganization plan from final approval. The proposal had to be approved by the higher education Coordinating Board. When a committee of that board met, again Paul English and David DeLaura, joined by Vartan Gregorian, the history professor and prominent campus organizer, spoke against the plan. President Jordan and I made the presentation on behalf of the university.

State representative Frances "Sissy" Farenthold of Corpus Christi characterized the Coordinating Board hearing as having an "air of finality."

And, indeed, when the Coordinating Board met on October 19 at the Stephen F. Austin Hotel, the board did give final approval, after receiving assurances that the university would consider modifications in the organization if they were found necessary based on experience with the new plan.

After the Coordinating Board action I invited Paul English and Vartan Gregorian to join me for a drink at a bar on Seventh Street across from the hotel. They had known they were fighting a losing battle, and I went out of my way to show there was nothing personal in the differences we were arguing over. We had all been on the losing side on occasion and knew how each other felt. If we could not exactly part friends, we separated on good speaking terms.

There was rarely a rest period between fights over major issues. We moved directly from the arts and sciences issue into the enrollment control plan and the debate over whether the gay liberation movement would be permitted to register as a recognized student organization. In addition, there was strong opposition to a proposal being discussed by the regents to mandate a minimum teaching load for the faculty.

The Committee on Student Organizations, working with the Student Union, gave recognition to the gay liberation organization, and President Jordan immediately overruled the approval.

Erwin was irreconcilably opposed to recognizing this organization. His position, a view shared by many on the board, was, "We are not going to tell the parents of children coming to this campus that we have authorized a bunch of queers to organize to seduce their children into aberrational behavior."

Yet all of the lawyers on the staff told Erwin there was no way the university could win a lawsuit to keep the organization off the UT campus.

Erwin responded, "Well, I don't care. If we have to do it, we'll make the courts order us to do it. Everybody needs to know we're fighting this. Then we can at least tell the parents of our kiddos that we didn't just cave in or think it was a good idea. Let the courts take the heat."

On the enrollment control plan, the question turned on who do we exclude and how do we do it when we are getting far more applicants than the university can accept? President Jordan's plan called for setting a limit on how many first-year students would be admitted each year. Within that limit the university would automatically admit all students in the top quarter of the applicant pool. Those in the lower three quartiles would be selected on a purely random basis. This approach presented difficulties for some board members. Several wanted to admit students in rank order as academically qualified. All of the lesser qualified students would be denied admission.

Others, led by Erwin, did not want to favor only the brightest. Erwin gained support of other regents when he pointed out that in California only those in the top 12.5 percent of their high school graduating classes were accepted into the University of California institutions. He argued that this meant popular support for those schools was limited to less than 15 percent of the state voters. He saw this as a formula for political disaster and the loss of state funding.

Some regents were concerned about how to be certain the children of alumni and big donors got admitted. They could see how denying admission to certain young people might lead to the loss of support among some legislators and alumni parents and grandparents. At this point difficulties with special preferences became apparent. Less qualified students would be admitted on a preferential basis over better academically prepared students. At one point Regent John Peace threw up his hands and moved that we admit all students on a random basis, no preference for intelligence or grades or test scores, and no special admissions. Erwin was about to let the board vote on that when I rose to point out some problems with this approach.

I reminded the board that any university needed to be able to admit certain students selectively for special reasons that benefited the school. I wanted to avoid being too direct about the problem the board was about to create. I pointed out, for example, that the university might need an oboe player to fill an important and unique slot in the orchestra. They still did not see what I was driving at because someone said the orchestra would just have to take its chances. Then I went directly to the point. I said a university needed to be able to admit some students for the football team.

They got it. The idea of a random across-the-board lottery selection for everybody was discarded.

Then Chairman Erwin argued that after setting aside slots for certain special students, random selection for all the rest would be a good idea. He said we should not automatically admit students falling in the top quartile. He said the country needed more C students; they were the kind of people who made this country great. Besides, he said, look at the mess they are having on all the University of California campuses. Those campuses were letting in only students who fell in the smartest 12.5 percent of high school students. The troublemakers, by definition, had to be those A and B students. He argued again that universities needed more C students who would go out after graduation and make the university look good and later become especially grateful and contributing alumni.

Some board members were beginning to nod their heads in agreement. Because no one else was willing to take up the argument with Erwin, I again rose to speak. I said something along the lines that performance in high school courses had been found to be a reliable predictor of perseverance and performance in college. Grades were an indicator of how much students learn and how motivated they are to work hard. Standardized tests also help predict how successful students will be in college. I said something about graduate schools across the country admitting only students with the highest grades and test scores and that admitting lower performing undergraduate applicants over brighter students would be detrimental to the reputation of the university. I argued a position diametrically opposed to Erwin's idea that C students were the backbone of the country.

Disagreeing with the chairman was not something a person in total self-possession undertook to do, especially in public. Erwin kept coming back to his basic point that C students would make the university a better place. And he got general laughter when he warmed to his argument and said he was certain C students made better business administration majors.

"Or lawyers," a regent chimed in.

As Erwin rebutted my points, he kept shuffling through the pile of papers lying scattered in front of him.

Something was going on in the room that I could not miss. People started moving away from me. Two people sitting near where I was standing got up and moved to other parts of the room. There were many raised eyebrows, and looks of disapproval were exchanged about what I was doing. It was clear that some there thought I had lost my mind.

Finally Erwin brought the discussion to a close and I could sit down. And the board approved President Jordan's plan to give first preference to those in the top quarter of their graduating classes with a lottery for all the rest.

During the break just before we all went downstairs for lunch, everyone seemed to be avoiding me. No one came over to talk with me. I had made myself a pariah by not simply letting Erwin's arguments go unopposed.

It was at that point that Erwin showed how sensitive he could be on occasion. He was aware of what had happened and came over to me during the break and draped his arm across my shoulder. He said, "Professor, I want you to sit with me at lunch today."

With that gesture and me next to him at the meal after our recent disagreement, Erwin sent an unmistakable message to everybody that I had not just committed professional suicide.

Almost immediately after the regents and the administration had finally agreed on how to limit enrollments at the Austin campus, an inevitable consequence arose. Individuals who acted aggressively on behalf of the interests of the university in important matters and a few alumni who were major contributors suddenly found that their children or grandchildren could not enter the university from which these proud alumni had graduated if they had not been high achievers in high school. It became essential to find a way to modify the procedures to avoid offending these avid supporters.

This was a new challenge, but the president's staff labored mightily and refined a plan already in existence to admit marginally qualified or even clearly unqualified applicants. They would be admitted conditionally. The conditions were that the student would have to take classes when enrollments on the campus were at their lowest for the academic year, that is, during the summer. An unqualified student would have to take twelve credit hours of certain prescribed courses over the two summer sessions, and if by the fall semester the student had maintained a C average in those courses, regular admission to the university would be granted.

It was a smart and reasonable solution to the new problem. We all knew that almost all poorly qualified students who tried to do this would drop out or fail to meet the requirements to perform at the university level. Making reasonable grades in the fast-paced and tightly packed summer courses with classes meeting daily was not something an entering freshman could easily accomplish. And those who could survive were probably going to be capable of staying to graduate.

Another positive aspect of the proposal was that in the past some wise alumnus had decided to label their organization the "UT Ex-Students Association," not the *Alumni* Association. This meant that even those students who flunked out as having been conditionally admitted would qualify to join all former students, graduates, and dropouts alike as ex-students.

Although the plan was described as the conditional admissions program, the Austin administrators insisted on calling it the Provisional Admissions Program. Or very fittingly, PAP. Webster's defines the word as a soft food for infants or invalids, political patronage, or something lacking solid value or substance. And so, pap it was.

Events in the mill began to grind to a conclusion. The entire System Administration began moving from the Tower building on the main campus to the restored old post office buildings between

Sixth and Seventh Streets on Lavaca Street downtown. Part of the staff moved temporarily to the old Commodore Perry Hotel building at Eighth and Brazos. This move off campus was the first step of the System and the regents to become a true agency overseeing the entire system of schools and to reduce its previously primary function of overseeing the management of the UT Austin campus.

Lieutenant Governor Ben Barnes moved the tuition revenue funding bill forward. He described the plan to have the legislature far into the future replace tuition used for construction as similar to "buying a refrigerator and paying for it on the installment plan." He explained that the tuition revenue pledged to retire bonds would be replaced later in small amounts every two years. Thus the plan for building new campuses across the state that was probably unconstitutional began to move toward authorization.

Governor Smith replaced three members of the Board of Regents. One of the three new members was former first lady and UT graduate Lady Bird Johnson.

John Silber was appointed president of Boston University. President Jordan's press statement read, "In Dr. Silber Boston University will have an articulate spokesman and an effective advocate. I wish him well."

Chairman Erwin's statement read, "Dr. Silber leaves Austin with our best wishes for his every success in his new position in Boston."

The temporary move of the System offices to the Commodore Perry Hotel entailed one unusual episode. Every office had its own bathroom as we adapted the hotel rooms to our uses. Plywood over the bathtubs provided a good base for filing cabinets. One morning in January several of us noticed a number of very attractive, sharply dressed young women passing back and forth in the hallway and looking in the open doors with puzzlement. Finally I went out and asked a couple of them if I could be of help.

One of the girls answered, "Well, we've worked here before. We've just come up from Galveston. With the legislature about to start we're up here looking for work. You see, this has always been the 'favors floor' of the lobbyists when the legislature meets."

I explained what was going on with the floor at this time and they left.

That evening I had to meet Erwin for an item of business at the Quorum Club and while I waited for him I told this story to Nick Kralj, one of Erwin's young drinking buddies who happened to be from Galveston. When Erwin showed up, Kralj repeated and embellished the story and then said, "Frank, do you realize how fitting that is, for all the people who work for you to be on the whores' floor of the Commodore Perry Hotel?"

He did not find it amusing.

Erwin could be cruel and ruthless, and yet he could be sensitive and considerate enough to ask me to join him at lunch to show my arguing with him at the board meeting should not harm me in the eyes of my colleagues. His gesture of goodwill was much appreciated.

Yet I was so obnoxious at times I don't know how he put up with me. A few days after that generous demonstration, he came by my office and sat down.

Obviously in a good mood, he grinned and said,

"Perfessor, did you see me going through my papers while we were arguing about C students being good for a university? Well, I was letting you ramble on and get yourself in deeper and deeper because I was going to pull the rug right out from under you. I had an editorial there on the table I was looking for that supported everything I had been saying. If I'd found that I would have shot you down with it."

And how did I respond to the fun he was having? I said, "No, Frank, don't tell me you were going to use an *editorial* to support your position. That's just somebody's opinion."

No wonder he got up and left without another word.

CHAPTER 16

Erwin Takes a Spill

In looking back I don't know whether Erwin ever sensed that he needed anybody to push back against what he proposed to do or to advise him on statements he planned to make. He appeared to be entirely independent in his decision making and actions, and he rarely sought advice. That is not to say he did not sometimes try out his ideas before he went forward with a plan. But even then he did not so much run his proposals past others to solicit advice or seek opinions for improvement as to revel in the fun of rehearsing them before a small appreciative audience.

Now that John Silber had been removed as dean, there were a few faculty departures.

Erwin found departing faculty members who had been loyal supporters of Silber to be easy targets for personal attack. From his experience professors would respond ineffectively, giving him a chance for a cheap shot.

Following approval of the reorganization plan, President Jordan called on the departments under the new divisions to elect representatives to serve on a search committee for the new provost to be the head of the three new divisions of the old College of Arts and Sciences. Immediately Vartan Gregorian from the history department resigned when the faculty elected him to the committee, explaining he had been fervently opposed to the division of the college from the beginning and that it would be "inappropriate and highly hypocritical" for him to serve on a committee implementing its dismemberment.

Three new deans were appointed, and Stanley Ross, a historian, took the position of provost as the arts and sciences departments began to coalesce into their new colleges.

After several professors resigned from the faculty to protest Silber's firing and the division of the college, there were threats that others would leave the university.

Erwin could not resist issuing a statement: "My only comment is that if any person employed by the university wishes to resign, all he need do is quit playing games in the newspapers and submit his written resignation to the president of UT Austin and I am sure his resignation will be promptly accepted."

Considering that Erwin was eager to help Bryce Jordan become the permanent president of UT, he was proceeding in a most unconstructive way.

To my way of thinking, Erwin was choosing exactly the wrong way to smooth the transition to the new organization. He had won. I felt he should stand down and not pick at the scabs of healing that were beginning to form. Faculty should not be continually reminded that this had been rammed down their throats and that anybody who still spoke up was going to be berated for it.

Early in 1971, Roger Shattuck, an internationally recognized scholar and author of the highly praised *The Banquet Years* about Paris at the turn of the twentieth century, announced he was resigning to take a year off to complete some writing. He said his decision to make the break with the university involved many considerations but that his decision was precipitated by "the trend of events on this campus."

That was all Shattuck said. Nothing more critical, just "the trend of events on this campus."

Erwin came by my office and proudly handed me the press release he planned to issue. It was another of Erwin's diatribes, and it was clear he was happy to be on the attack again after a couple of weeks of quiet on the campus over the holiday break. I sensed what he sought from me was keen enthusiasm for his carefully crafted press statement. It was another of his attacks on what he called "expatriate professors." I was probably not the first person he had shared it with. I felt certain no one had tried to dissuade him from issuing it.

Just over a month earlier William Arrowsmith had resigned from the Classics Department. In his letter of resignation he had attacked Erwin's tyranny. He said the university had become the "personal property of one man."

Erwin had immediately fired back, "Apparently, when Arrowsmith learned that his lucrative playhouse had been exposed, he chose to find another job." Erwin cited the payment of $3,600 paid for a summer course (a fairly significant summer salary in 1970) with only thirteen undergraduates enrolled. He said Arrowsmith had been able to do this through the "connivance of certain high administrative officials who no longer hold administrative positions at the university."

Arrowsmith responded, "Not since the late Huey Long has there been a politician who could so befuddle the public with calculated distortion." He went on to explain how Erwin had mis-represented his teaching load, pointing out that in the previous semester he had taught six classes with 160 students. Arrowsmith said that to try to smear him, Erwin had chosen the semester when he had been on assignment with the U.S. State Department.

A month after Arrowsmith's resignation, another classics pro-fessor, D. S. Carne-Ross, also resigned and called Erwin "a disaster as chairman of the board of regents. Ever since he sacked Silber I have been convinced the university is done for."

Of course Erwin could not sit still for Carne-Ross's attack. In his retort he said, "Carne-Ross was scheduled this month to begin teaching nineteen students three hours a week and was to receive a salary of $3,222 per month from the State of Texas. When that bird nest on the ground was recently discovered, he resigned without notice."

His statement went on, "Carne-Ross is nothing but a co-conspirator with Arrowsmith in releasing separate but carefully spaced vicious attacks on the university. Many people did not real-ize that Arrowsmith had not resided in Texas since May of 1970 when he sent his venomous letter from Vermont last month. Now his associate Carne-Ross mails his venomous letter from Maine. . . . Enough of these attacks by the expatriate professors."

Carne-Ross retorted, "I thought he could have done better." And he continued, "At a time when higher education is in trouble, it does not make sense to let great power accumulate in the hands of a man like Erwin, who shows no signs of knowing what a university should be. . . . I used to be proud of the university. Now I would be ashamed to stay."

Then another classics professor announced he was leaving. John Silber had been appointed president of Boston University. However, Silber left without attacking Erwin or the university.

The exchanges among Arrowsmith, Carne-Ross, and Erwin triggered strong responses and rebuttals challenging Erwin's statements on remuneration and teaching loads as misleading and not factual. All of this was harmful to Bryce Jordan's chances of ever being favorably considered for the Austin presidency.

Now came Roger Shattuck's resignation, and I had in my hand the statement Erwin was eager to release. As I read it I realized how much he was enjoying these confrontations, and I knew he thought he could easily win in another fight with a departing professor.

I was troubled as well by the way his continuing battle with faculty members was being conducted. He was using the official university press office to issue all his press statements. An instrument of the university was being used against a piece of that university.

I told Erwin I thought he should not issue his statement. Silber was now gone from Texas. The controversy over the arts and sciences college was playing out, and the faculty was moving on to other issues.

I told him we needed to remember the good things Shattuck had done for the university. He had served on the search committee for the provost. After the Coordinating Board approved our plan to divide arts and sciences, he had said it was now more important than ever for him to stay on the committee and see that a respected provost was appointed. He had always been loyal to the university. He did not resign from the provost search committee as others had done, even though he, too, had been strongly opposed to dividing the College of Arts and Sciences. I reminded Erwin that Shattuck had been on our faculty for fifteen years. He had an international reputation.

I even mentioned that Shattuck was known as one of "Harry's boys," among the stars that Ransom had recruited.

I advised Erwin he ought to let Shattuck depart quietly. I told him I thought his statement would just open recent wounds. I said I thought what he was planning to say was likely to be received badly on the campus.

Erwin was extremely unhappy that I did not share his enthusiasm for this new attack on his principal detractors among the faculty. He snatched away his press release and said Shattuck was just another privileged faculty member leaving out of loyalty to John Silber.

Finally I asked, "Why can't you just let him go in peace?"

He shot back, "It's no fun to hate somebody if you can't hate 'em in public."

So he issued his statement. It said, "Roger Shattuck is another member of the Arrowsmith-Carne-Ross clique which was living high on the hog until their lucrative playhouse was discovered early last summer."

It went on, "During the last school year, Mr. Shattuck did not teach a single UT student, but spent the entire year in France, and for that vacation period he was paid $10,000 out of state tax funds, with the approval of certain high administrative officials who no longer hold administrative offices."

Upon his resignation Shattuck earlier had said he did not want to add to his comments when resigning but would let his colleagues comment on his leaving. But after Erwin's statement Shattuck did release an additional short comment. And it was especially effective for its masterful understatement. Shattuck said, "I don't want to respond to the unfortunate tone of Mr. Erwin's statement. The information he supplies is distorted. I very much regret that he sees fit to imply that the Research Institute of his own university misuses state funds in order to send professors on vacations."

The Research Institute was the source of the $10,000 grant for his research in Paris. In fact, the grant had been approved by Graduate Dean Gordon Whaley, Dean Silber, and President Hackerman, and the $10,000 had been substantially less than the usual such research grant.

Shattuck added that he had confidence that those "steadfast in their principles . . . will ultimately prevail in restoring integrity of leadership and high purpose at this university."

I was so proud of Roger and how he handled himself. I was elated by how Erwin was at last pulled up short. Roger's nuanced statement was the perfect response to Erwin's bombastic excess.

And in this case the defense of the faculty member was not just local. The dean of humanities at Stanford said of Erwin's statement, "That is the most benighted, bigoted, asinine charge I've ever heard."

Alfred Kazin, the New York literary critic, spoke out in support of Shattuck.

Willie Morris, editor of *Harper's Magazine* and author of *North Toward Home*, a book largely dedicated to his time on the UT campus, lamented what was happening at UT. He said, "It's very saddening that an institution that so many of us love is now in the hands of some of the most uncivilized wealth in America."

And, not to be left out, even John Silber got his licks in when he said, "Since Roger's award was openly and loudly acclaimed, it is strange that Mr. Erwin should speak of 'discovering' it—it was never a secret."

Even a regent parted company with Erwin. Jenkins Garrett of Fort Worth said Erwin spoke for himself only. Garrett said he was unaware of any "discovery."

There were calls for an apology from Erwin to Shattuck, and Dean Whaley and President Jordan had to step forward and defend the University Research Institute as a legitimate and representative body of the university, responsibly allocating research funds to the faculty.

These responses to Erwin's statement were like body blows, and they were unrelenting, day after day. He made no further ripostes.

Now chastised and his rollicking time over, he came by my office several days later and said he had been wrong and that he did not intend to take any more parting shots at additional faculty who decided to leave or to follow Silber to Boston.

When, a little over a month later, another classics professor, Thomas Gould, resigned to move to Yale, Erwin remained silent, even though Gould did make remarks about excessive board intrusion into the affairs of the university.

Erwin also remained silent when Sigmund Koch, a psychology professor chairing Comparative Studies, resigned shortly thereafter with a long public statement attributing his leaving to the Silber-Erwin fight of the previous year.

The game Erwin had been playing with the faculty was a clear case of excessive board intrusion into university affairs. Departing faculty should not have had to suffer assaults on their leaving or see their past services to the institution demeaned in public. The university was being damaged by Erwin interjecting personal vendettas and board politics into normal events and activities.

Let us assume that on occasion a governing board might identify an issue on campus that faculty members and administrators had overlooked or avoided. In such cases I do not feel it is inappropriate for regents or trustees to ask that the issue be studied and findings and recommendation be brought to the board for consideration. Openness, transparency, and inclusiveness should guide everybody's efforts toward building a consensus on such an issue.

I do believe the arts and sciences issue at UT Austin was a matter identified by the board of regents that needed to be addressed. But it was not handled well, and the ultimate resolution was too much prescribed by the chairman of the board, with him outright rejecting recommendations from advisory committees that were a standard practice to ensure inclusiveness.

An issue such as the arts and sciences problem raised from time to time by a board would not be inappropriate, and I would not label that excessive board intrusion. But when over an extended period of time there is a continuing series of issues and their solutions decided and forced on faculty, students, and administrators by a board, legislators, or a governor, that becomes political intrusion.

Universities have been one of the longest surviving institutions in human civilization. This life span has not been extended because there have been frequent outside redirection and mandates and authoritarian management to make the university more congruent with changes in society or political majorities. Quite the contrary. The university, the organized erudite culture that extends knowledge and understanding and passes them on, is able to make its contribution because it is separate from the society of which it is a part. When society intrudes to remove the uniqueness of the university to make it fit more neatly into society, it will no longer be able to make its inestimable contribution.

Universities have survived hundreds of years in part because they do not change easily to chase fads or chimera. Society, to garner the benefits of great universities, must exercise forbearance, patience, and tolerance. Forbearance because they must be elitist to be great. Patience because they are not easy to change. Tolerance because they must at times be critics of the very society that charters and supports them.

Consequently, repeated incidents of political intrusion damage a university and derail its course toward improvement and continued independence. If its mission is altered to make it an instrument directed by politicians or corporations, directly or through its governing board, then a university ceases to be an independent institution of higher learning and becomes a mere political or economic tool of those in power.

Evidence of political intrusion exists when regents impose one political point of view and censure another, insist on uniformity of opinion, require that those who speak out must be dismissed, and dictate what can and cannot be taught and what materials or ideas are proscribed. And such intrusion occurs when regents and politicians look on their university as a plaything they can manipulate to demonstrate their power or for their entertainment.

Of all of Frank Erwin's intrusions at UT Austin, I believe his greatest stigma was his playing games with departing faculty for his own entertainment and to aggrandize himself at their expense for his imagined admiring audience. No argument, he was misusing his university—and drawing on the resources of the university to do it.

In a timely manner a new political issue emerged. Should the Board of Regents permit the *Daily Texan* to continue publishing? But at least Erwin bit his tongue again when Charles Parrish from the government department quit and spoke out on the need for an independent student newspaper.

After his sortie against Roger Shattuck had backfired on him, Erwin was downcast and clearly feeling sorry for himself. As he left my office that day he said, "You think I don't know how hated I am on the campus? You think I don't know what they're saying out there? Well, let me tell you. They're saying, 'What we need is a faculty member dying of cancer who's good with guns.'"

He did stay in touch with his campus.

CHAPTER 17

Hiring a President

The search for a new president continued. In November 1970, after five months, the search committee said it had narrowed its search to five individuals from over a hundred candidates. But there was no release of the names, and they remained secret within the committee.

About this same time a movement began among some faculty members to request the chancellor and the regents to permit President ad Interim Bryce Jordan to be considered as a candidate for the permanent position. Pressures grew as it became known that Jordan was being considered for president at North Texas State University, Arizona State University, and one of the University of Michigan campuses.

Jordan very much wanted to be the new permanent UT Austin president. But for reasons never known to me, the regents at the May 29 meeting in El Paso had made him president ad interim with the condition he could not be a candidate for the permanent job. The faculty, ever distrustful of the regents, concluded that Jordan was nonetheless campaigning for the position. As a consequence, they weighed all he did to determine whether he was tailoring his recommendations to fit the desires of the regents over his duty to serve the interests of the university.

A large part of Jordan's problem was that he was in an impossible position much of the time. For example, after careful study of the options about how to divide the College of Arts and Sciences, Jordan submitted his proposal to Chancellor LeMaistre and immediately shared his plans with the faculty and student body. The student reaction was to editorialize against him for not having shared his plan with them *before* sending it to the chancellor. Of course this was a totally unrealistic demand, but it did not seem so to the students. President Jordan was crucified for doing what he had to do and got no credit for sharing his proposal with students and faculty at the same time he sent it to LeMaistre and the regents.

On another hot issue Jordan had had to try to implement the board's directive to prohibit the sale on campus of *The Rag*, the radical off-campus newspaper. And then the courts overruled the board's position. Jordan was labeled the enforcer.

To try to uphold the board policy prohibiting nonstudents from using the Chuck Wagon, a restaurant in the Student Union, Jordan had to work with the Austin police. When the police used mace and excessive force in removing nonstudents from the restaurant, Jordan was blamed.

Jordan was able to do little about how the faculty viewed him as Erwin launched into his prolonged attacks on "expatriate professors."

And the Board of Regents made it clear to Jordan that the university would never declare a moratorium of any kind on classes in protest of the Vietnam War. UT was not ever going to be closed on the demand of students or faculty. For Jordan this was a "nonnegotiable" directive that put him in direct opposition to students and faculty against the war.

Jordan had tough marching orders.

Late 1970, not yet six months into my job as vice chancellor, I personally was headed in two directions between Erwin and the University of Texas. I became convinced that on occasion what Erwin wanted for his university was not in the best interests of the school. Since the El Paso meeting, Erwin had changed his mind about Jordan and was working hard to make him the permanent president. I had strong feelings that this would be extremely damaging to the university. I simply felt that under the circumstances Jordan faced and with his occasional pandering to the board, he was the wrong person for the position.

In Jordan's pursuit of the position, it did appear at times that he was shaping his recommendations and actions to curry favor with the board. He seemed to take harsh positions regarding student protestors and campus disorder without full regard for how students and faculty might react. It did appear to many bystanders that his actions were crafted to gain favor with the board.

Considering the era it was hard to say Jordan was wrong. This was a time when boards, legislatures, and governors across the country looked for administrators who would stand up more forthrightly against student protests. Jordan made his choice: he was going to stand firmly with the board against student dissent. From one point of view this was highly commendable; from another, it was sycophancy.

Immediately after Jordan had been appointed president ad interim, Luke Thompson, assistant managing editor, summed up this view in the *Daily Texan*: "Jordan has plenty of courage to stand up to demonstrators, but not to stand up to the Board of Regents."

Yet it was true. Jordan did at times take positions when it seemed he might have gone the other way or found a softer approach. One for which he earned the justified resentment of the student leaders was over student fees. While vice president for student affairs he had staunchly opposed giving the total student body a choice over which portions of the student activities fee they wanted to pay. That is, he stood firmly behind the required "blanket tax" that every student paid upon registration, the income from which was used for various student activities. The blanket tax permitted the student government to exercise authority over how to spend the aggregated income from the student activities fee that all students had to pay at registration. With this money student government had real clout.

But then as president ad interim, Jordan reversed his position and recommended that the fee be broken into pieces to permit students to choose which activities and programs they wanted to pay for. This undermined the governance of the student body and was seen as an effort by Jordan to gain favor with the regents.

As these machinations were taking place on the campus, most of the faculty went about their academic pursuits as normally as they could. They did their research and presented papers and published articles and books. They consulted and served on state and national committees and advised governments and businesses. They taught their subject matter and tried to set aside what was going on in the administration of the university. They epitomized what Clark Kerr, the recently fired president of the University of California, had observed ten years earlier about faculty: "They are loyal to their field first, their department next, then their college and last to their university."

So it would be inaccurate to say the faculty was truly up in arms about anything at this time other than more and more of them were coming around to criticize the war in Vietnam. Although many tried to stand aside or remain on the sidelines, they could not avoid seeing what was happening to the country and to the nation's universities. They had to witness everyday events on campuses and comments by colleagues, students, political leaders, and administrators and regents as well as see graphic reports on the evening news of growing casualties in Vietnam. Although many of them tried to remain aloof or stay out of the fray, that became increasingly difficult, and more and more of them came to take positions or at least to find their views changing about what was proper and what was not regarding how UT was going about its business in these difficult times.

The end result was that Jordan was not accepted as the bona fide leader of the campus by a large segment of the faculty, more of whom were becoming increasingly vocal or at least more concerned about issues of the day. And circumstances only got worse for Jordan's chances of being accepted by the faculty and students. He had fired John Silber, who, although not universally liked, was popular with many and was seen as having been martyred.

What the UT community wanted was someone who would put the school back on course toward academic preeminence. They wanted a respected president who would be independent and speak for the university as a whole and thereby rebuild academic credibility for a campus that clearly was seen to fall more and more under the political control of the state through the Board of Regents and Erwin. Fair or not, Jordan's personal ambitions were hurt in that many on campus saw him as Erwin's stooge. It was a difficult stigma to overcome.

Even though I had only taught one undergraduate course at UT, I had numerous contacts on campus. When I first came back to Austin to join the Coordinating Board in 1966, my wife and I had been included in the "newcomers club" at the University of Texas. Over the years many of my contacts and friends in Austin were at the University of Texas. And through my defense of dividing the

College of Arts and Sciences before the Coordinating Board, I had come to know faculty from both sides of the issue. And frankly, the people on the opposing side turned out to be far more interesting than those who stepped forward to speak in favor of the division of the college.

Consequently, in the fall of 1970 I was acutely aware of faculty opinions about President ad Interim Jordan and his presumed ambitions to become their permanent president. Because there was little Jordan could have done to rehabilitate his image with the faculty, he became a victim of the times and the circumstances. Every foray Erwin made into campus affairs weakened support for Jordan. This became so obvious that Erwin even made a calculated effort to try to help Jordan appear independent of him. He openly criticized Jordan, which was duly reported in the *Daily Texan*. But Jordan's image as someone standing up to Erwin did not take.

One morning Regent Joe Kilgore, chair of the board's Academic Affairs Committee, with whom I worked closely, let me in on a decision that had been made in secret by the board.

That morning in his law office Kilgore put aside the material we needed to discuss. He began, "I agreed to something several months ago I regret I ever got into. I would give anything if I could take back a commitment I made." He hesitated whether he was going to tell me more, and then he went on,

"I agreed in a closed meeting with all of the other regents that we were ready to make Bryce UT's permanent president. Right then. We told him in Houston we were ready to make him president right there, on the spot, to disregard the presidential search underway, despite all the flack that would cause us. We were ready to chuck our rules and not wait any longer on the search committee.

"Bryce surprised all of us by saying he could not take the job under those circumstances. We knew he wanted it. But he said there was no way he could be effective if he was just imposed on the faculty by the regents. The faculty wouldn't accept him, he said, and it would be bad for the university to do it that way.

"Then we all pledged our vote to him anyway. We told him if he wouldn't take the job right then, we would wait for the search committee to give us their recommendations to choose from. Then we would pick him. We told him all he had to do was get his name included on that list from the search committee and the job was his."

This was news to me. I did not reveal my personal feelings nor comment. I just let Kilgore go on.

He added, "Now I've got a problem. I'm beginning to get worried that Bryce will be on that list of candidates. Since we pledged our support to him I have been watching the campus, and I've been watching him real close for months now. I've been paying attention to the kind of stuff he brings us. Whether he's doing it intentionally or not, Bryce looks more and more like a pawn of Erwin. I wish I'd never told Bryce in front of all the other members of the board that I'd support him for president. If he's our next president I think we are going to lose traction. We need somebody who can recruit like Ransom did. We'll slow down getting good faculty—or keeping the good ones. We're already losing good faculty. I'm really worried. I've given my word and there is no way I can refuse to vote for him now if he's on that list. I will have to."

It was probably about a month or six weeks later that I went to Kilgore's office to brief him on the agenda he would have to present at the next board meeting. After my briefing he said, "Remember what I told you last time we talked? I've done a little quiet probing and I'm not by myself."

I knew that as a former U.S. congressman, Kilgore felt acutely how unretractable a promised vote or pledge, once given, had to be.

The search committee finally finished its work and submitted three names to the chancellor and the regents on December 4, 1970. Jordan's name was not on the list. Within the next few days Joe Kilgore called and said he was breathing easier; he was off the hook. He did not elaborate; I knew what he was referring to.

Then a few days later I got a call to come to the chancellor's office. LeMaistre was alone when I went in. He told me he had just gotten off the phone with Chairman Frank Erwin and Vice Chairman John Peace. He said they had told him they had talked to other members of the board and they were sorely disappointed that Bryce Jordan's good work had not been at least acknowledged by the search committee. They were disappointed that he had been totally ignored and passed over. They felt that in recognition of Jordan's months of hard work for the university, he should at least be included in the list of candidates.

LeMaistre told me he had just been instructed to convene the presidential search committee the next day and explain they should consider Jordan a candidate. Then he was to make the case for why

Jordan should be added to the list the committee had submitted earlier. LeMaistre was to point out how the committee was slighting the man who had over many difficult months carried the responsibilities as president ad interim. LeMaistre's assignment was to figure out how to get the committee to add Jordan's name to their list.

From the way LeMaistre was telling me this, it was clearly not a job he wanted to do. He had held firmly to the position set by the regents in El Paso and had always said Jordan was not eligible to be considered for the permanent position. He knew from his own long campus experience how sacrosanct were the rights of presidential search committees. He lamented how onerous this task was going to be. But he had to do it.

I was almost too emotionally involved to react to this terrible duty the board chairman and vice chairman had laid on him. I must not have seemed to be of much use. I had no advice I could give him except to commiserate. I did tell him that I thought Jordan's appointment would be a mistake for the university. He nodded, whether in agreement or just acknowledging what I had said. And I could not betray my knowledge that the regents were no longer unanimously behind the directions LeMaistre had been given by Erwin and Peace.

Back in my office I shut my door and indulged the funk this news put me in. In taking on the job of acting president, Jordan could not have stepped into a more highly charged situation, and his chances of doing a job acceptable to the faculty and students had been poisoned from the outset. I felt certain that LeMaistre knew the board had pledged to appoint Jordan if his name was among the names submitted by the search committee. But I could not tell him I knew that. I felt sure LeMaistre knew the consequences if he did manage to get the committee to add Jordan's name to their list.

Although LeMaistre had talked with both Erwin and Peace, I felt certain that Erwin had pushed Peace into joining him in pressing LeMaistre with this assignment. I wondered how many other members they had actually talked with. They knew the other members would have to honor their vote for Jordan if his name was on the committee's list. Erwin had all nine pledged, irrevocable votes of the regents in his pocket, and he knew it.

I did truly believe the board finding a way to appoint Jordan president would result in immediate and long-term damage to the university. And the more I thought about the outcome of the search committee doing what LeMaistre was going to represent to them as a mere gesture of courtesy and recognition, the more convinced I became that some way had to be found to be certain Jordan's name was not added to their list.

The search committee was made up of bright and perceptive members, and they probably would see the full danger of putting Jordan's name on their list of recommended candidates, even if they did not know what I knew about the nine votes pledged to him by the board. But would they in the end decide to add his name?

I gave some thought to why LeMaistre had called me in to talk to me about the instructions he had just been given. This was the first time he had met with me alone on any topic. Was he just telling me because he had to tell someone? Did he just need someone to think out loud with? Or was he telling me for other reasons? He had been very open with me in saying he was uncomfortable having to do what Regents Erwin and Peace had asked him to do. He would never have said that to me if he had not trusted me not to pass this on to Erwin. Was there something more behind why he had told me this?

I made my decision. I picked up the phone and called Vartan Gregorian in the history department, a member of the search committee. I knew he had played a major role in the work of the committee, proposing names and pushing certain candidates. His active role on the committee followed naturally from his multiple involvements and appointments. And I had gotten to know him when we were on opposite sides of the arts and sciences issue.

I told Gregorian I needed to talk with him. He said, "Well, you know where I am. Come on out."

I said I would prefer not to meet him on the campus. He said, "Name the bar. I'll meet you there."

I explained I did not want to meet him where we might possibly be seen together that day. He invited me to come to his house that evening and we could talk.

Because he had by chance bought my home when I had sold it, thinking at the time I was moving to a new job in Arlington, I knew the neighborhood well. Ironically, this was also the former home of Page Keeton, the law school dean and the search committee's preferred candidate for president.

After dark I went over and parked up the street and walked down to Gregorian's house.

In his study I explained to him why LeMaistre had convened the search committee for the next morning. Gregorian listened and did not comment.

When I was finished, I said, "Vartan, I have just placed in your hands not just my job, but my entire career. If the regents ever found out about what I just told you I will never work in higher education again."

With a wave of his hand Gregorian tossed away my remarks. He said, "I have already forgotten where I got this information. No one will ever know you were here tonight. Rest easy. Forget it. We never talked."

Subsequently Gregorian moved to the University of Pennsylvania, where he rose to become provost. From there he became the charismatic president of the New York Public Library after turning down numerous university search committees pursuing new presidents. Following his subsequent presidency of Brown University, he was selected president of the Carnegie Corporation of New York, unquestionably the premier foundation dedicated to furthering education. But in 1970 he was merely a history professor.

Just as Gregorian and I finished our conversation, the doorbell rang. He went to look through the blinds. He said, "It's Mohammad Jazayery. He knows everybody, probably you too. I'll stall him at the front door for a minute. You know the way out through the garage."

I went home and spent a restless night. I had made no careful analysis of principles involved in this situation. What I had done was based on my instinctive reaction to what was about to happen and how it might affect the university. It was not fair; it was not right.

The next morning Chancellor LeMaistre met with the search committee. They listened politely to his presentation and then went into closed session and decided not to add Bryce Jordan's name to their list. I like to believe the committee would have acted as they did had I not gone to see Gregorian.

This left the regents to exercise their option of choosing among the three candidates recommended by the presidential search committee. I say the regents would make the choice, although the appointment was, by the regents' rules, to be made by the chancellor. With the close involvement of the board in university matters, there was no way LeMaistre would or could make this appointment without it, in effect, being a choice made by the regents.

When the regents and staff examined the list of candidates recommended by the search committee, Frank Erwin and Don Walker led some of us to impute to the committee a strategy to manipulate the board to appoint the single candidate the committee wanted from their list of three. Erwin and Walker, as well as a few others, thought they could see the committee's strategy by the characteristics of the particular three candidates on the list.

In looking over the list, it could fairly well be assumed that one of the candidates would be clearly unacceptable to the regents because he was one of the few college administrators in the country who in 1970 had publicly stated his opposition to U.S. involvement in the war in Vietnam. This candidate was John E. Cantlon, provost and vice president for academic affairs at Michigan State University. Tragically, his young son, a U.S. Marine enlisted man, had been killed in 1966 in Vietnam.

The second candidate, Stephen Spurr, vice president and graduate dean at the University of Michigan, had, it could also be assumed, been included for another strategic reason. It was well known that Spurr had been offered several other significant university presidencies and had turned them down, saying he had a better job in Michigan. Couldn't it then be assumed the committee had included Spurr because the committee felt quite certain he would turn down the Austin presidency as well, especially in view of national publicity about the board's interference in campus matters?

This strategy by the committee would leave as the only viable candidate the committee's third person, the candidate whom Erwin and Walker assumed the committee really wanted, the individual the board would be forced to appoint as president, the dean of the UT Law School, Page Keeton.

Erwin saw all this as a plot directed against him personally. Such an underlying strategy, imputed to the search committee, must have sprung from Erwin's projectionism shared by others in the UT System Administration. Because Erwin practiced manipulation so freely, he could recognize when the search committee was doing it to him. It all sounded quite rational, even quite probable. I bought into it. It looked like a checkmate move to me.

If the committee could force the regents to appoint Dean Keeton president, they would achieve a double victory: they would gain a progressive, outspoken, liberal-leaning president, and they would force the appointment of a person they knew was despised, even hated, by Frank Erwin.

Erwin and Keeton had a history of intense rivalry and animosity. Aside from his dislike of Keeton's politics, Erwin had crossed swords with Keeton a couple of years earlier on an issue on which they were both totally inflexible. Erwin had challenged Dean Keeton on the dean's admissions policies for the Law School. Keeton's position, which he had stated frequently and eloquently, was that to build a law school with a national reputation it was essential to be able to admit a substantial number of out-of-state students with high scores and outstanding college records from nationally recognized colleges and universities. In pursuit of his goal, Keeton defended 20 percent as a reasonable portion of each entering class that should be allocated to out-of-state students.

Erwin took the opposing position. He said he was hearing from Texas parents whose children had been denied admission because non-Texas students had been admitted in their place. Erwin stated at every opportunity that the university should give preference to the children of the citizens of Texas, those paying the taxes supporting the costs of the Law School. He wanted the percentage of out-of-state students cut significantly as a fixed university policy, and Dean Keeton refused.

To settle the issue with finality, Erwin chose to employ his usual heavy-handed approach. He often summed up his position to opponents by saying, "You do what you're big enough to do, and we'll do what we're big enough to do." In this case Erwin had a bill introduced in the state legislature to limit by statute the percentage of out-of-state students admitted to the Law School. That would settle the dean's position once and for all.

Dean Keeton went to work surreptitiously to oppose the bill through contacting his alumni. The state legislature was heavily populated by UT Law School graduates. And because the UT Law School had been one of the few law schools in the state for many decades, Keeton's school had graduated most of the lawyers in the state, a significant number of whom had acquired positions of wealth, prestige, and influence in the state. Keeton persuaded some of them to call their fellow graduates in the legislature about Erwin's "bad ole bill" designed to damage their law school.

Erwin's bill failed to get out of committee. And to add to Erwin's searing loss was his public defeat in his kingdom, the place where he was most accustomed to having his way. And he had no doubt about who had killed his bill. This defeat in the legislature alone was sufficient to cause Erwin to say that Page Keeton would become president of UT Austin over his dead body.

In the months after the committee submitted the required three names, a concerted effort began on campus to steamroll Keeton into the presidency. A petition for Keeton signed by 250 faculty members was submitted to Chancellor LeMaistre. Booths were set up around campus to enlist students supporting Keeton as their candidate. The student paper delayed endorsing one of the three candidates but gave heavy coverage to the efforts underway in Keeton's behalf, including a story on Keeton saying he would accept the presidency if offered to him. The paper then printed Keeton's eloquent vision for the campus. Finally, late in February, the paper ran a profile of Stephen Spurr and John Cantlon, the other candidates.

The *Daily Texan* then endorsed Keeton for the job. The latest report on support for Keeton's appointment was that five thousand had signed the student petition.

Chancellor LeMaistre took me with him to the University of Michigan, where we talked with Stephen Spurr to try to interest him in the job in Austin and to convince him to come to Texas to visit the campus and meet with the faculty. Spurr subsequently agreed to come to Dallas on Sunday morning, February 21, to meet with the new chairman, John Peace, regents Frank Erwin, Joe Nelson, and Dan Williams, and Chancellor LeMaistre. We all met in Dan Williams's Republic National Bank Tower. After several hours of discussion, questioning, and negotiating, the regents offered Spurr the presidency—and to everyone's relief and the surprise of some, he agreed to take it.

I overheard some private grousing between a few of the regents that they wished they had been given a more dynamic candidate, but their only real choice was to accept Spurr or reject all the candidates and reopen the search. The search had already dragged on for almost a year, and the regents knew well the turmoil they would perpetrate on the campus if they refused all of the candidates recommended by the search committee. And in the face of the extensive support growing on campus for Page Keeton, to turn down the entire list was to invite explosive faculty and student resistance and demonstrations. With all the pent-up disappointment and resentments from past neglect and condescension, the campus was a tinderbox.

Once agreement was reached with Stephen Spurr in Dallas, Erwin suggested we all fly down to Austin that Sunday afternoon and hold a press conference, with Steve Spurr taking questions from the media. Spurr readily agreed, and the chancellor and his press adviser, Mike Quinn, immediately got on the phones and started making arrangement with the press and radio and television stations.

I interrupted Chancellor LeMaistre to suggest that somebody needed to call Page Keeton about the decision just made, and he asked me to handle this.

As the regents and others mulled around, killing time while others were making arrangements for the press conference, I went to a phone and started dialing.

Erwin came over and asked, "Who are you calling?"

I told him I was calling Dean Keeton to let him know what was happening.

Erwin exploded, "What the hell for? Let the son of a bitch read it in the papers."

And as I sat and continued dialing and the call went through he stood over me, glowering at me over his half-moon glasses. As I spoke with Keeton, Erwin spun and stalked away in disgust.

I was not about to put down the phone while Erwin glared at me. Keeton deserved respectful treatment. He should not have to extemporize a response when the press called, as they inevitably would. He needed time to break the news of the disappointment to his family, friends, and supporters.

I could tell from our brief conversation that Keeton very much appreciated my call. He contained his disappointment.

So many things could have gone wrong with the search and the appointment of the new president that I felt we had dodged a number of bullets to have gotten through to this stage. Stephen Spurr was a most credible and distinguished scholar and administrator. We had made a good solid appointment and I felt relieved it was now over.

Beginning with the press conference in Austin that afternoon after he had accepted the job, Steve Spurr showed promising political skills even before stepping into the presidency. He was asked why he had been willing to accept the Austin presidency after turning down so many other offers. He said he was not willing to accept a presidency at a second- or third-level university. Nor was he interested in a first-rate university that was in a deteriorating condition. He wanted to go to a first-rate university that was capable of greatness where he might contribute to that academic undertaking. UT Austin fully met those qualifications. He stayed away from specific controversial topics and said he did not plan to become a second president while Bryce Jordan was finishing up his term.

With the *Daily Texan* so embroiled in controversy with the Board of Regents, one reporter wanted to know where Spurr stood on freedom of speech for student papers. Spurr responded coyly that he had been a student paper editor as an undergraduate. He was all for freedom of the press and called himself "an old newspaper man myself."

At the time I was encouraged by one thing in particular. I felt the board of regents had in this case behaved admirably. Although a number of regents did not like the protracted and seemingly interminable search and vetting and interviewing of candidates by the search committee, they stood by the procedure set out in their own Rules and Regulations on how the committee would be constituted and how the search for a new president would be conducted.

I feel certain if Erwin could have had his way, he would have cast aside the constraining board rule and had the board appoint Jordan permanent president regardless of the havoc this would have caused on campus. That he had not been able to get the board to do his will on this spoke well of a majority of the board in the restraint they placed on Erwin in their task of selecting a new UT Austin president.

CHAPTER 18

The Bauer House: No Bauhaus

The day after the *Daily Texan* announced President Spurr's appointment at the end of February 1971 and the issue of finding a new president was finally put to bed after months of vicissitudes, a new issue broke on the student paper's front page.

Erwin had maintained a continuing battle with the *Daily Texan*. But then an especially nasty fight began between the paper and Erwin about a home for the chancellor and his family. It began with a gift to the UT System from W.H. Bauer of stock to be sold and used to build a home for the chancellor.

Over lunch, Graves Landrum, vice chancellor for operations, took me out to see the house and large lot that had been bought for the new home. It was to be remodeled for the chancellor. Landrum told me that the house itself was in terrible shape, and it would probably be cheaper to level it and build an entirely new one.

Then, according to Landrum, over the months costs kept going up from the original estimate of $225,000, after it became clear the structure was too far gone to be remodeled. The decision was made to raze the old house and build a new one. Landrum said the contractor, like all builders, was probably taking advantage of every verbal change order to jack up the costs and to extend the time for completion.

In any event, the new home was begun and Erwin himself had become intimately involved in the work, frequently arriving and giving instructions on the site. After LeMaistre was appointed to succeed Ransom as chancellor, Erwin arrived one day and told the supervisor of construction to tear out a section of the third floor that was already nearing completion and rebuild it to accommodate "the chancellor and his wife and four children." The chancellor's home became a three-story, five-bedroom house with a four-car garage and a separate two-bedroom guesthouse adjoined by a bathhouse beside a pool. In addition, Erwin had settled on Arthur Watson, an extremely costly interior decorator. Purchases were coming from as far away as New York City for furnishing the home, especially those items bought for the downstairs reception and entertaining areas, rooms that were to be used in the future for receiving and cultivating wealthy donors and influential supporters of the university system.

Then a group of law students led by Ted Siff probed into the costs and overruns and sources of funds for the house. They asked whether the board had actually authorized, according to state law, certain decisions Erwin was making about the house. This was the news story that broke in the *Texan* in early 1971. Then there followed a drumbeat of stories about the facility. Day after day they raised more questions about legalities and how the project was being paid for.

The students had struck fertile ground. They questioned the cost-plus-fixed-fees arrangements with the contractor. The initial responses from the UT System were mixed. The spokesmen said some work was being done by university employees and some by the construction company. It turned out that the site foreman was on the payroll of the university but was the son of the owner of the construction company doing the work. As to why the project had not been put out for bids, the official response was that this was the only firm in town able to do the work. Other contractors immediately refuted this statement.

To the claim there were no state funds involved in the project, the students found from board minutes that $163,000 of state funds had in fact been used. Bauer, who provided the initial money for a chancellor's home, had given stock worth $119,000. Lester Palmer, speaking for the facilities and construction office, said the original cost was estimated to be $189,000.

With continuing inconsistencies and with architects, contractors, and interior decorators acting secretive and refusing to answer questions, the student paper kept the story alive for weeks. The Austin paper picked up the story, and other media around the state began to find the story of interest as well.

Then Erwin shocked everyone when he admitted the full cost figure was $907,700.23. At that the students wanted to know where the funds were coming from. Finally after several weeks Erwin stated that the bulk of the costs for the now notorious "Bauer House" was covered by a private donor.

That only whetted the appetite of the investigators for more details. Who was the donor? How much was the donor covering of the nearly $1 million that Erwin had agreed the renovations had cost?

Erwin finally relented and said he had a contribution of $600,000 specifically for the Bauer House renovations from a foundation that wanted to remain anonymous. He explained the contribution had been made on the condition the donor would never be known.

This, in turn, led to expressions of disbelief that there really was such a donor willing to give that kind of money anonymously. Who was it? Where was the contribution recorded? Was the money in the bank? And they would not give up.

The state senate appointed a special subcommittee under Senator Mike McKool, a liberal member from Dallas. McKool's committee learned from the builder that his agreement was not even in writing but was entirely verbal. The director of planning confirmed to the subcommittee that there was no written contract. The subcommittee called Erwin and Deputy Chancellor Don Walker to testify. Each time they were queried they refused to give the name of the donor.

At one hearing Erwin was finally driven to say, "This thing seems to have gone sour from the first. All I want is out."

And he did relent in part and agreed that the costs had run up far more than he had realized.

He said he had accepted the donation to apply to the costs of the house on the condition of never publicly saying who had given it. He said, "I can't take the people's money and do what I told them I wouldn't do."

But he found a way to strike back. He lamented that the coverage by the *Daily Texan* was hurting the university. He contended that the job would have been completed quietly "without cost to the state" if the Legal Research Project at the Law School and the student paper had not stirred up the trouble over the house.

The subcommittee chair insisted on learning who was contributing the $600,000, and a few days later Erwin recommended to the Board of Regents that they give back the money to the donor. The motion carried unanimously.

Even though Erwin by this time was no longer chairman, he spoke for the board and said, "Unfortunately, the public furor created by a group of self-appointed state auditors over at the law school and at the *Daily Texan* have made it impossible for us to accept this gift."

The board said unfortunately other financial sources, such as interest earned on deposits, would now have to be used to cover the costs. But no state funds would be applied to the Bauer House.

The students were not to be bested or forced to take blame unfairly. They pointed out that the students had documented nineteen charges of illegalities against the Board of Regents. They said their work should ensure that this kind of thing did not happen again.

Erwin called this his worst ordeal as a regent since he had been appointed.

Some months later after Erwin had cooled down on the Bauer House, I risked pursuing a sub-rosa story I had heard.

"Frank," I said, "there is a story going around that after you got the board to direct you to return the Bauer House donation, you had a session one night over drinks at the Forty Acres Club about the donor's check."

I had his interest. I went on, "The story is that you took a check out of your wallet and tore it in small pieces and burned them in an ashtray and said, 'Gentlemen, that was a check for $600,000. I made a promise never to say who gave it to me. You just saw me keep my word.'"

Erwin was clearly satisfied I had this story, but he acted displeased and said gruffly, "Somebody's talkin' out of school."

Then I said, "There is something else I picked up on the QT. I understand that the check was signed by Gene McDermott on the condition that you would never, ever let his wife know he had given it to you."

McDermott was one of the three founders of Texas Instruments.

To that point I could tell that Erwin had seemed pleased this story was making the rounds, but now he was most unhappy. He leaned forward and snapped, "Where did you get that?"

"I forget. I just wanted to see what you would say. I forget who I heard it from."

Very severely he said, "You *better* forget you ever heard that. And don't you ever repeat that. I mean it. I don't want that getting around. Nobody knows who signed that check but me."

Was Erwin as upset as he appeared to be, or was this an act? If I had heard this story was it because he had spread it around himself?

If I had to wager, I would say the story about McDermott was true.

Erwin, to my knowledge, never showed any interest in elective office. But other elected officials must have been watching him, wondering if he might change his mind. He would have made a formidable candidate, but his disinclination to compromise would have made it difficult for him to be elected. He always said bluntly, and even abrasively, what was on his mind. He was easily defined and his positions were well known.

At a dinner party in Houston one evening, Erwin had been expounding on one of his outrageous political views. When he finished, John Connally said, "You know, Frank, you should run for public office. You could run the cheapest campaign in history. I can see it now. You declare your candidacy in the morning. By sunset the entire state would divide itself into two implacably opposite camps. No amount of campaigning would ever change how a single voter feels about you."

CHAPTER 19

The Unraveling Begins

After Spurr came to Austin, he proceeded to take charge on the campus with new appointments to his staff and filling vacancies in the faculty. The fact that a true academician had been appointed and that he moved to take hold of pending issues did a lot to settle the campus and calm some of the continuing conflicts.

But Spurr also soon began to meddle in some affairs that he should have left alone. For example, he decided the food served at the receptions before the football games was too elaborate and expensive, and he cut the budget and directed that simpler, cheaper food be provided. Erwin was so furious at the poor quality of food at the next reception that he ordered Henrietta Jacobsen, who handled, among many other things, social events for the UT System and the regents, to call a caterer and get additional food delivered immediately. He and other regents were not going to economize hosting people the regents were milking for large contributions and important public favors.

Then President Spurr began cutting people off the invitation list for the football receptions. At the receptions he saw large crowds of people and thousands of dollars for liquor and the buffet. He could not possibly have known who some of these people were in Texas politics or Texas society and business. He should have taken the time to find out.

Joe Kilgore called me one day fuming mad with the new president. He said, "I worked almost two years to get Judge So-and-so and his wife on that invitation list, and now Spurr has cut him off. We'll see about that."

Football at UT Austin permeated the campus to almost every corner. The pregame receptions served their own important purposes, but the games themselves, the rankings of teams, the circus-like festivities surrounding the games filled the thoughts and drove the energies of much of the campus throughout each fall up through the bowl games. Football was said to be a religion, and it truly was, in the sense that if you were not an enthusiast and conversant with the latest developments relating to the team, their placement, and their prospects, you were looked on as the nonbeliever in any small southern town.

And the predominance of football on the campus only reflected the predominance of the Austin team nationally. In 1969 the UT football team had prevailed over Arkansas 15-14 after being behind by 14 points and went on to defeat Notre Dame in the Cotton Bowl 21-17. The team was ranked number one in the nation by the football polls and was given the number-one imprimatur by none other than President Richard Nixon himself.

Year after year the UT football team had been champion of the Southwest Conference, thereby gaining the highest honor then available to the conference champion, the right to play in the New Year's Day Cotton Bowl game. In fact, under Coach Darrell Royal, UT would win eleven conference titles and be declared the national football champion twice. Before he retired, Royal's UT teams had won 167 games and 16 of 20 bowl games. The string of thirty undefeated games and the national championships came in large measure from perfecting a new offensive lineup that presented to the quarterback multiple options of attack. The new offense, devised by Emory Bellard, an assistant coach at UT, was called the wishbone.

The setup behind the line was the quarterback directly behind the center with the fullback behind him and two halfbacks behind and to the sides of the fullback, resulting in a Y in the backfield, hence the label "wishbone." With the snap of the ball the quarterback could run either direction, hand off to the fullback behind him, or lateral the ball to one of the halfbacks if the defenders were coming after him. Or he could drop back and pass while being defended by his backfield teammates.

It was a very hard offensive lineup to defend against. It was dangerous to focus on the quarterback because at the last second he could lateral to the halfback right behind him. One defense was to send a defender past the quarterback and take out the halfback behind him, eliminating the option of the lateral. But then that left the quarterback to keep the ball and run it himself.

The secret to making the wishbone work was good ball handling, quick reading of the defensive response, and choosing among the best options remaining when the quarterback saw how the defense was responding. The options could be enhanced through a lot of faking and deception to make the defense unsure of who actually had the ball in the multiple options being played out or who maybe still had the ball. The success of running the wishbone depended on split-second timing. Every moment of delay by the defense in reading which option the quarterback was going to go with, or which option he might have already executed, resulted in extra yardage for the offense.

Any deception about who actually had the ball contributed to momentary delays in the defense reading the play. Consequently, the bright orange that had been used for decades for the football team's jerseys gave way to a new color. It was discovered that historically the true color for the Longhorns had been burnt orange all along, the single color in the spectrum closest to the color of a football.

But back on campus an issue was pending that would give Spurr serious problems with the regents.

On a spring day in 1971, Erwin came into my office in high spirits, with his happiest exclamation, "God has delivered another of my enemies into my hands."

He had a new opportunity for revenge. He said, "Who would ever believe the charter for the *Daily Texan* would run out on my watch? Who would believe that when their goddamned charter had to be renewed they'd have to come to me, after what they've done to me all these years. I'm going to get my pound of flesh."

It is certain Andy Yemma, the *Texan* editor, and his colleagues at the paper could not imagine a worse fate than to have the future of their paper rest in the hands of Frank Erwin. The decision in 1921 to seek a corporate charter not in perpetuity but for fifty years must have seemed completely innocuous at the time. That remote decision now, at this critical moment in the paper's relations with the Board of Regents, placed the paper at the mercy of its worst enemy. At stake was how the *Daily Texan* would be reorganized and managed in the future.

Erwin had actually said to Tim Donahue, a student member of the Texas Student Publications (TSP) board, what he told me in my office. He was "going to get the *Texan*" for having crucified him for five years.

The Bauer House episode had especially tormented him. He was not one to surrender or back down. For him to admit in a legislative hearing "All I want is out" was most unusual for Erwin. I believe in his work on the Bauer House he had, in fact, usurped authority that he had not run past the board, and the paper had exposed to his colleagues on the board and to the legislature the extent of his freewheeling and inept dealings. He had been embarrassed and forced to explain himself and his actions in public. He was not going to forget it.

A number of critical issues were on the table for negotiations: whether the *Daily Texan* would be rechartered in perpetuity or for ten years, what the regents might do with the paper's $500,000 in accumulated assets, what kind of control would be exerted over the paper and its editorial policies in the future, would the editor continue to be elected by the student body or be appointed, and if appointed, by whom? And because the paper was under the TSP board, how was that board to be made up? Would students now be relegated to a minority of the eleven TSP positions? Who would appoint the faculty members to the TSP board? Was the Board of Regents serious about requiring all student members of the TSP board to be journalism majors rather than be selected from the student body as a whole?

These were some of the imponderables of major consequence to the kind of paper the *Daily Texan* could be in the future.

And as if to underscore the importance of free press in society, less than a month before the *Texan* charter was to expire, the *New York Times* and the *Washington Post* had printed the classified Pentagon Papers about the Vietnam War, leading to extensive court fights about freedom of the press.

The conflict on campus intensified when students tried to make an end run around the Board of Regents to get the secretary of state to approve a new charter. They filed an amended charter with that office on their own, ignoring the requirement that they go through the Board of Regents. Politics seemed to favor the students when the secretary of state decided to accept the students' proposed charter.

At that, Erwin blasted the secretary of state, accusing him of making an "obvious play for the eighteen-year-old vote" to further his own political career.

The regents then cut the funding for the *Texan* and through the attorney general's office began their move to take over the paper's half million dollars in assets. Even under an extension of the charter granted by the secretary of state the paper was no longer a nonprofit corporation. The machinations by both sides intensified.

Then an immediate crisis developed over how the paper was to be financed. The student government wanted the Board of Regents to require students to pay for the paper as part of their "blanket tax" collected by the university at the time of registration each semester. When the regents refused to do this, the students, through the courts, tried to force the regents to do so. The students lost, and finally the two sides had to work out a temporary compromise. The regents agreed that summer to let the current *Daily Texan*'s board members continue for another nine months while negotiations continued, and the *Texan* agreed to provide $100,000 from the paper's assets to support continued publication.

But even in reaching compromise there was sniping. Erwin could not resist sarcastically congratulating the attorney representing the students for collecting $16,000 in fees for giving away $100,000 and dissolving the student corporation.

The students were incensed; they accused Erwin of being a bad loser. Erwin's refusal to compromise was the sole reason the paper was obligated to spend the $16,000 in legal fees.

In the meantime the long-term issues with the *Daily Texan* still remained unresolved.

That fall the paper's board adopted a set of operating procedures different from the set the Board of Regents had agreed to as part of the earlier compromise settlement. President Spurr had to enforce the compromise agreement, and he disapproved the new student operating procedures. Predictably, Spurr was then attacked and maligned by the student paper.

Then, in an effort to regain some credibility with the students, President Spurr decided to recommend that a small student charge be added to the blanket tax to support the paper beginning with the spring semester.

Up to this point John Peace, the new chairman of the Board of Regents, and Erwin, as Peace's designated negotiator, had been dealing directly with students and faculty about the paper. Now President Spurr had suddenly intervened and preempted the negotiations, using one of the bargaining chips the regents had been holding for further trading and negotiations.

The next day John Peace called me angrier than I had ever heard this quiet, slow-talking, soft-spoken man. He exclaimed, "I always knew that Spurr guy was not smart enough to be president. You and LeMaistre fed him the answers to what we asked him in Dallas so we'd appoint him. Well, now you can just prop him up for the next two years till we can fire that son of a bitch."

In fact, Stephen Spurr survived until September 1974, three more years. Then the board did fire him while he was recovering from heart surgery in Houston.

What made the regents, meaning Erwin principally, so unhappy with Spurr was that he had not become an instrument for them to use to run the campus. Spurr was caught in the middle. Some students were unhappy with him for taking the job and depriving them of their candidate, Page Keeton. They were displeased with him for not being a stronger spokesman with the board, and the regents were dissatisfied with him for not putting the lid on student dissent and demonstrations on campus. The faculty was not helpful to Spurr as they continued to wait to see how he would turn out. And in those encounters where he was able to stand up to the regents or wait them out on some improper proposal or otherwise prevent encroachment into campus matters, he had to do so quietly, and he got no credit or recognition for his efforts. Spurr's major defeats were in public, whereas his major victories were won in private and could not be publicized to build a base of credibility with the faculty and students. What faculty and students did not know hurt him.

Upon receiving Spurr's recommendation for funding the *Daily Texan* with mandatory student fees, Chancellor LeMaistre stood with the regents and refused to forward it to the board. Even this effort by Spurr on behalf of the students went for naught.

I was not consulted or involved as this controversy played out. I was not needed. The negotiations were being handled directly by Chairman Peace through Erwin and the chancellor.

Yet I did stick my nose in and, of course, I got cuffed for it.

In April 1971, Vartan Gregorian, the history department activist and outspoken opponent to the division of arts and sciences, and Bob

Binder, the new student body president, organized an appreciation dinner for the *Daily Texan,* using the paper's fiftieth anniversary for the celebration. Their plan was to stage an event to heighten awareness of the situation facing the *Texan* and Erwin's attacks on the paper.

Invitations to attend the dinner on April 29 at the Villa Capri Restaurant arrived in the chancellor's and vice chancellors' offices. The regents also received invitations.

From snide remarks about the event, it was clear no one from the UT System was planning to attend. Not attending was sort of a patriotic duty; it became a demonstration of loyalty to Erwin. He had made clear there would be no amnesty for the way the paper had treated him. People read the message he was sending: do not attend.

I attended. When I arrived that evening, Gregorian came over to the back table where I was sitting unobtrusively and said, "Ken, I am so glad to see you here. You are the only person from the administration here. Let me find you a place at the head table."

I may have been dumb, but I wasn't crazy.

I said, "For God's sake, Vartan, I'm putting my job on the line just to be here. Forget it. I am perfectly fine right here."

It was a marvelous evening with a number of former editors there, including Ronnie Dugger, Nancy McMeans Richey, and others. There were comments on what a tough spot Andy Yemma, the current editor, was in, trying to report faithfully on issues critical of the regents while balancing the need not to goad them excessively. Because his term was running out with the end of the semester, Yemma read to the crowd his final editorial for the *Texan* to be published the next day. Congratulatory telegrams and commendations for everything the paper had done over the years were read, including one from John Silber.

With John Henry Faulk, the popular and famous comic and satirist whose career was ruined by Senator Joseph McCarthy in the 1950s, serving as MC, the program was highly entertaining with much ridicule, satire, and outrage coming across the podium. Liberal congressman Bob Eckhardt was the featured speaker, and a number of other politicians appeared in support of the *Texan,* notably three of the legislators who had served on committees grilling Erwin during his Bauer House ordeal.

Faulk got the greatest laugh of the night when he told his story about the East Texas patriot who said, "Ah'm all fer freedom a speech.

Always have been. Always will be. Ever'body oughta be free ta say whutever they believe. That's the 'merican way. All *Ah* wanta do is git rid of them damned dissenters."

Through his intelligence network, Don Walker learned the first thing the next morning that I had attended the dinner. He had in hand a list of people who had attended to give to Erwin when he arrived in Don's office.

Moments after he saw the list Erwin stormed into my office, shaking the list at me and demanding to know if it was true I had attended the dinner. Then he shouted, "Why the hell would you do that?"

I said, "Frank, you shouldn't be the only one around here who knows what the opposition is up to."

He glared at me and then turned and left without another word.

Things could always be worse. I might have been dumb enough to sit at the head table.

As predicted during the battle over dividing arts and sciences, there were a few faculty departures. Some leaving said they could no longer continue as dean or department chair or head of a center. Standish Meacham stepped down as chair of the history department, saying he could no longer act as "the university's advocate." Vartan Gregorian resigned to go to the University of Pennsylvania to accept a distinguished chair. After citing his reasons for leaving he said he did not want to stay and continue his activist role and become "an Armenian Don Quixote."

Even President Spurr acknowledged that some faculty believed "high echelons of university and state government involve themselves more directly in the academic decision process than is good for a university of the first rank."

William Arrowsmith let fire another salvo. He contended that governors in states like Texas, California, and New York were trying to take over higher education and the faculty needed to form a national coalition to protect academic freedom. To make his case he accused John Connally of having been behind the regents' efforts at UT to force faculty and administrators to resign. He said they had replaced administrators with "a bunch of thugs who wouldn't make successful Shinola salesmen."

Regent Joe Kilgore called his remarks "patently absurd."

John Silber said Arrowsmith was wrong; he said Erwin himself had led the purge, and he shouldn't be let off the hook so easily by passing the blame to Connally. Silber said Erwin's purge had been "90 percent out of arrogance and the love of raw power."

Erwin seemed to have run out of metaphors. Using his old phrase, he reminded everyone about Arrowsmith's "lucrative playhouse" that he had been forced to leave.

Personally, I felt Arrowsmith's line about thugs and Shinola salesmen hit close to home.

CHAPTER 20

Firing a President

One morning in 1971 my secretary came in to tell me I was wanted upstairs in Deputy Chancellor Walker's office.

When I arrived, Erwin was seated on the sofa. He asked, "Do you know where your boss is?"

I knew perfectly well where Chancellor LeMaistre was. He was in Dallas to meet with the president of UT Dallas and to remove him from his position.

As I said earlier I was personally headed off in two directions with Erwin and the University of Texas. In that earlier case I worked against Erwin's desires to place Bryce Jordan in the UT Austin presidency. In this case, the firing of a president, I was in complete accord with him. What Erwin wanted here was in the best interests of the University of Texas at Dallas.

Over a year earlier Chancellor LeMaistre and I had traveled to Washington numerous times to persuade a member of President Richard Nixon's cabinet to take the presidency of our new campus in Dallas. After numerous visits, our candidate agreed to take the job but only on the condition that we would not announce his appointment until he was ready to leave his government post. He explained that he did not want to become a "lame duck" in his position in Washington, but he would be willing to come to Dallas from time to time to become familiar with the new university and faculty and to provide leadership to the new institution. This would prepare him to assume the presidency immediately upon leaving Washington.

The small faculty at UT Dallas under Frank Johnson's interim presidency was happy to learn who their new leader would be. In addition, business leaders in Dallas, who were fully behind the new University of Texas in their city, were glad to meet and discuss with the new president the city's plans to support the school. These spokesmen included the publishers of the city's major newspapers and the owners of the television stations, as well as key businessmen and real estate developers. No one in this large group ever announced or leaked the name of their new president, and he was able to come to Dallas over the months to meet and exchange views on prospects and plans for the new university.

Yet over these extended months our new candidate did not become fully engaged in his new job, and as more time passed he failed to provide the leadership and direction the new school needed. He continued to visit the city, but he was content to receive reports on activities and plans underway and did not grasp the initiative and take over as the leader of the institution as we and the faculty expected. LeMaistre and I were beginning to have our doubts about how committed our new president truly was. With him in the school's top position it was difficult for anyone else to establish the mission or provide the vision and initiate the forward motion needed for the new school to take off as we and everyone in Dallas wanted it to.

At one of our meetings with the new president, Frank Erwin unexpectedly showed up. He too had begun to press for firm plans for the school. We all wanted to know what new degree programs should be proposed as a basis for setting up an organizational structure and for hiring faculty and to plan for new buildings and laboratories. Nothing much seemed to be happening, and, independently of the staff at the school and in the System Administration, Erwin had noted the lack of movement and progress. At the meeting in Dallas he sat against the wall rather than at the conference table and said nothing, an unusual role for him.

My surmise was that some of the business leaders in Dallas had expressed their concerns and doubts to Erwin. Otherwise why would he suddenly take this special interest in UT Dallas? Certainly I had never mentioned my misgivings to him, and LeMaistre would not have, for this would have brought doubt to our vigorous efforts earlier to recruit the candidate. If anything, we were trying to prop the guy up and force some forward movement at the school.

On the plane back to Austin after the meeting in Dallas, Erwin commented, "I sort of wondered who that seedy guy was at the table. And then after about an hour I figured it out; he's our new president."

That was the beginning of the end. Over the next few months LeMaistre slowly came to the conclusion that he would have to remove our president before he had even been announced as taking the job. A date was set for our president's next visit from Washington, and LeMaistre would go to Dallas and do the dirty duty.

Now the date had arrived, and I was in Walker's office being asked by Erwin where Chancellor LeMaistre was. I answered, "He's in Dallas firing the president."

"No," Erwin replied. "Your boss developed an unavoidable conflict and has taken our plane to Corpus Christi for the day."

I was stunned. I knew that if we did not carry through on our plan to dismiss our designated president, all our alternatives looked bad. Although we had become disenchanted with him, our candidate might decide he wanted to go ahead and announce his appointment. Or his name might get leaked. Or he might hear of our dissatisfaction with him and announce his appointment to preempt our option to fire him. Or we might just continue to drift in this limbo we were in. It had become clear that he was going to have to make a vigorous uphill climb to be successful in the job. It was very possible he would have to be removed at some point even if he came on board right away. From all aspects and considering the alternative futures, the sooner we got the issue resolved the better.

I told Erwin that in that case I would go to Dallas and do the job. He was surprised and asked me just how I proposed to do that. I told him I needed to think about it and I would tell him in thirty minutes.

In half an hour I was back with two letters, A and B. I handed the first letter to Erwin and he read it without expression and handed it to Walker without comment.

Letter A said that our designated president needed to know that he had lost the confidence of the Board of Regents and would have to work hard to regain it, but if we could publicly announce his appointment immediately and if he could be on the job full time within two months, Chancellor LeMaistre and I would do everything we could to assist him to regain the confidence of the board.

Walker exploded when he read the letter. He shouted, "What the hell is this? You said you were going to fire the guy. This gives him the perfect out to stay in the job."

Erwin held out his hand and said quietly, "Wait a minute. I think he's holding another letter."

I started to explain that I felt obligated to give the guy a chance, that we had pledged to help him, and so on, but Frank waved me off, snapping his fingers, and motioned for my second letter.

Letter B was shorter. It said merely that because our candidate had been holding our letter offering him the presidency for eight months and had not yet signed and returned it, we were withdrawing the offer.

When Walker read this letter, he said, "Well, that's more like it."

Erwin said, "Eight damned months. And never signed the letter? Hell, I didn't know that."

I said that I proposed to explain the situation fully to our man and, depending on how he reacted, I would decide which letter to give him. I took them back and put one letter in each breast pocket of my coat.

Walker said, "I wouldn't give him any choice. Just withdraw the offer."

Erwin said, "Do what you think you have to do. If you need me I'll be having dinner at the Green Pastures."

I went to my office and wrote down the telephone number of the south Austin restaurant and took a plane to Dallas.

When I arrived back in my office the next afternoon Erwin dropped in and asked, "Well, what did that silly son of a bitch decide to do?"

I reported, "He was furious at all of us. We didn't even finish dinner before I dropped it on him. He didn't believe I could have been sent to tell him he was out of favor with the board and that his only choice was to take the job right now or give it up. He refused to believe it. I kept reminding him he had every opportunity to put things straight. He could keep the position, but he needed to know where he stood and we needed to know where we stood and all that. He still wouldn't listen. He would not believe that I could've been sent to tell him this. He hardly knew who I was; I had sat in on our meetings he had attended, but he didn't know what position I held or what I did. He said if LeMaistre had wanted to tell him this or fire him, he would have done it himself. He wouldn't have sent me. Finally I gave up and asked him if he would like to talk to you and he said, 'You're damned right I do.'

"So we went up to his room and that's when I got you on the phone. I stepped out in the hall to give him privacy to talk with you.

"In a little while he came out. He was composed by then and said, 'I am going to sue you sons-a-bitches for this. This is unbelievable.'

"Then I told him suing us and going public was entirely his decision, and his decision alone. We had not made public his appointment, and we never would make public what had occurred. Suing us was entirely his choice. I did remind him that he had never signed and returned our offer letter sent to him eight months before.

"He started to get angry again and said he would get a lawyer and we'd hear from him.

"Then I added that in a lawsuit we would have to make public that we knew that while he had been holding our offer letter for eight months, he had interviewed for another presidency in Massachusetts."

Erwin exclaimed, "That dipshit. You never told me that. If I'd known that we would've fired the son of a bitch. What else?"

I shrugged. "I handed him my letter withdrawing our offer. That was it."

Then I added, "Oh. Except that he called some of the faculty members last night and told them he'd been fired. They went apoplectic apparently and called each other and got in touch with LeMaistre. So he flew up early this morning and while I sat on the sidelines, holding the bloody hatchet, he began to sweet-talk them into understanding that this was all in their best interests.

"Mickey was just amazing to listen to. He was at his absolute best. He told them they needed to understand that the man had simply not turned out to be the leader we all knew they needed for their new university. He got them to nodding their heads. He explained to them that the man had never signed the letter accepting the offer and that because he hadn't, we could not be sure he would stand by his promise to join us later. The guy was holding us in limbo. We couldn't really say we had a president. He commended them for keeping the appointment quiet among ourselves; we had all kept his appointment from going public, and there would be no black eye for him or the school about this if they all kept their mouths shut. Then LeMaistre promised them they would have a major role in selecting a new president, somebody we would be sure had the full confidence of the Board of Regents and would move their school forward."

Erwin stopped at the door on the way out and turned and said, "Son of a bitch! I had no idea he was two-timing us. I guess you know, don't you, that he was playing you and LeMaistre for suckers. He had our offer as his hole card while he shopped around for a better deal. I would've fired that son of a bitch."

Did I feel used? No. I had not done this because Erwin wanted it done. His wanting it done fit the circumstances that Chancellor LeMaistre and I had already come to recognize. The man was a bad fit for the job as president of UT Dallas. We were in the midst of trying to figure out what we were going to do about the situation after we had gone to such great lengths to recruit him when Erwin interjected himself. He just hastened us along to find our way out.

What Erwin did not know was how troubled and terrible I had felt about myself right after I had fired the man. As I looked at myself in the mirror in my room afterward, I had really mixed feelings. I had done what needed to be done. And I felt I had passed some kind of test that had required me to be stronger than I thought I could be. But those feelings were a teaspoon of saccharine mixed with a quart of bile over what I had just done to another human being.

A few months later the story came to a happy ending. The search committee for UT Dallas discovered Bryce Jordan, learned of his strong support with the regents, and recommended him to become their new president. The Board of Regents appointed Jordan to the position in March 1971, at the same board meeting when the regents formally made Stephen Spurr president of UT Austin.

CHAPTER 21

Frank Erwin's Boswell ad Interim

I was surprised one day in the spring of 1971 when Erwin took a chair in my office and began, "Did I ever tell you how we busted that dumb ass son of a bitch Manny DeBusk as chairman of the Coordinating Board?"

Gubernatorial appointments to state boards are required under the state constitution to be confirmed by the senate. The senatorial confirmation process is for nominees to be interrogated by a senate committee and then, normally, to be recommended to the full senate for approval. In the committee hearing a nominee is usually presented or perhaps "sponsored" by the nominee's senator. On occasion there will be objections to confirming a candidate nominated by the governor. A courtesy rule in the senate permits a member to find a nominee from his district personally objectionable. A nominee declared to be objectionable by his own senator will, as a courtesy, be rejected or "busted" by the senate.

Manuel DeBusk was a Dallas lawyer appointed by Governor Preston Smith to chair the Coordinating Board for higher education. Smith had appointed DeBusk between legislative sessions, and his confirmation could not be submitted for senate confirmation until the legislature convened again. In the meantime, until confirmed or rejected by the senate, DeBusk would serve as chair of the Coordinating Board.

Some of the most telling revelations about Erwin's political strategies and machinations came from his own lips. The stories showed not just what he accomplished but how he went about it and what was in his mind as he did it. This was one of those stories that illustrated the extent of his ruthlessness and cruelty, as well as his ability to have his way in the legislature. It was vintage Erwin getting his revenge.

Erwin sat with one leg crossed with his ankle on the other knee. With his wrist on his raised knee, he swung his glasses in that hand as he went on with his tale. "I made up my mind we were going to have to bust that dipshit when he started lecturing the Coordinating Board about their responsibilities on their recommendations to the legislature. The CB was getting ready to recommend the funding needed for higher education for the next legislative session. And the calculations the staff came up with were way above what DeBusk wanted to hear. He decided they had to be cut back.

"Well, I was at that meeting because I was going to be pushing for increases for UT and I wanted to hear what kind of support the Coordinating Board was going to give us. So what do I hear? This dumb ass starts in lecturing the board and the universities on how they need to do their part to hold back the growth of the consumer price index. I could not believe my ears. Instead of Texas following what was happening across the country with the consumer price index, we were supposed to turn the corner for the whole country and slow it down by reducing appropriations for higher education. I had never heard anything so asinine in my life. I decided right then I was going to bust that dumb son of a bitch.

"Then he pulled that stunt about trying to limit our enrollments. And he follows that with a resolution telling us how to handle protests. He wouldn't shut up; he kept sounding off on stuff that was none of his business. Can you believe it? He even made my enemies in the senate mad at him, Oscar Mauzy and that son of a bitch Babe Schwartz."

A. R. "Babe" Schwartz was a senator from Galveston who had earned Erwin's undying animosity by opposing his senate confirmation to the Board of Regents in 1963 and again in 1969. Oscar Mauzy was a liberal-leaning senator from Dallas. Erwin professed to dislike him heartily but he frequently had drinks with him as they harangued each other over their opposing views.

Erwin continued, "So here is how we busted that dumb ass. To get ready for when Manny DeBusk came up for confirmation in the Senate, I went to see Ike Harris, DeBusk's senate sponsor from Dallas, and I told him I'd like him to find DeBusk personally objectionable. That would make him unacceptable and the senate would bust him. Ike said he would prefer not to have to say bad things about Manny on the floor of the senate, even if he was a dumb ass. After all, he was one of his constituents. It was not smart to make an enemy of anybody he didn't have to.

"So we came up with another way to do it. I went around and got enough votes from the rest of the senate to kill DeBusk's confirmation. I was sure I had the votes, but nothing is ever certain in politics. So here's how we made dead certain Manny would not be confirmed. When Ben Barnes told the secretary of the senate to start the roll call on DeBusk's confirmation, Ike would stand right in front of the podium where all the other senators could see him, but when Betty King called his name, he would not answer, and the roll call would go on. Everybody would know that Ike was withholding his vote to see if Manny would be busted without his having to find him objectionable. If Manny was not voted down by the end of the roll call, then Betty would call the roll again for those who had not answered the first time. When she got to Ike, if it looked like Manny was going to be approved, Ike agreed he would find him personally objectionable and his confirmation would fail. We had that dipshit double covered."

Erwin was obviously enjoying himself. He went on, "But that wasn't good enough. I really wanted to embarrass him and that idiot governor, Preston Smith. I waited until the Coordinating Board was about to have a meeting. They had one scheduled in Corpus Christi, so I waited that day for Manny and everybody to get on the road to Corpus, and then I went to Barnes and told him it was time. So we busted Manny's ass the day of the meeting in Corpus while he's on his way. I wish I could've seen his face. Preston had to appoint another chairman that afternoon so the board would have a presiding officer."

The week before, coming out of a discussion before a legislative committee, I had said to Erwin, "I couldn't believe what you just told those committee members. You worked so hard last session to get that issue of funding for patients in medical schools settled. Now you just opened it up again like you're ready to start all over

with new negotiations. Aren't you running the risk of losing everything you won in the last session? I don't understand why you
would risk doing that."

Erwin replied, "Look, in politics you have to have something to
trade. Otherwise nobody will talk to you. You got to be able to
make deals. I just put that on the table so they'll think I'm willing
to trade on it. I'm not about to give anything up, but who knows?
Something better might come along and change my mind."

I said, "You know, Frank, you need a Boswell."

He grimaced and shook his head, obviously rejecting the idea.

But within a week Erwin began to drop by my office just to chat
as he never had before. Maybe he knew I had been making notes.

On another occasion Erwin told me how the Texas Tech Medical
School got approved. He said he had had to cut a deal with Governor
Smith. He said, "We both knew we had to go beyond, 'You don't
kill my bill and I won't kill yours.' We already knew we could do
that to each other. We had to do better than that. So I went to Preston
and I agreed to help him get his medical school for Lubbock if he
would agree to sign off on our new medical school in Houston. We
would both work to pass each other's bills."

I said, "But you've always despised Preston Smith."

"Look, in politics you work with anybody who can help you. If
you're above dealing with your enemies, you've just eliminated a
big bunch of people. You're going to miss lots of opportunities. There
are times your enemies can help you the most. You know where they
are. They don't waffle on you; they just keep on hating you. You
know what they want. So you know what to trade. And sometimes
you get to know the sons-a-bitches better than your friends because
you have to spend so much time fighting with 'em."

Then he went on, "Did I ever tell you how that dumb ass Preston
Smith got elected governor? Everybody thought Connally was going
to run for another term. I mean everybody; Connally had everything
going his way and he was immensely popular. So Smith, while he's
lieutenant governor, goes around and asks every politico he can
corner if they will support him for governor if Connally *doesn't* run
again. And, knowing it was an empty pledge and, thinking that it
might help them with something they might need from the lieutenant
governor, they'd say, 'Sure, Preston, you've got my support—if
Connally doesn't run.' Nobody knows but Smith how many of these
people he gets lined up behind him as the second choice for governor

because he doesn't tell anybody, and I can assure you, nobody goes around braggin' about having pledged to support Preston Smith for governor. And then Connally decides not to run. And Preston calls in his pledges.

"But it was more than that. Smith had been laying his groundwork for his runs for statewide offices from way back. Get this: he used to write a letter to every defeated candidate after an election. A couple of candidates who lost showed me their letters. He would tell all those losers what a wonderful service they had rendered to American democracy by being willing to run for office and other bullshit. And then he wrote another letter to congratulate every person who got elected. He had both sides thinking he was a great statesman. And he was just a Lubbock dumb ass all the time."

Without a pause he continued, "You remember the embarrassment he caused all of us at that luncheon before the Cotton Bowl game with Notre Dame? When Preston was asked to say a few words of welcome to the guests from up north, he actually referred to coach Ara Parseghian as 'Coach PARsigan.' PARsigan, PARsigan, three times he mispronounces the name of one of the most famous coaches in the world. We all wanted to crawl under the table. I think some of their people thought our governor was mocking their coach and their team. Only we knew Smith was dumb enough to do it out of complete stupidity.

"But then Parseghian got him back good. Ara stood up and said, 'Thank you for those nice words of welcome, Governor Schmidt.' The place went wild laughing and applauding. And Preston never got it. What an idiot."

One afternoon Erwin came in saying, "Well, God just delivered another one of my enemies into my hands. Maybe you don't remember the fights I had with Don Kennard in the senate over UT Dallas."

Kennard had been the senator from Fort Worth and he was beholden to no one and afraid of even fewer. Erwin began describing his difficulties with Kennard.

"He's been fighting me all the way. First he opposed us taking over the Southwest Center for Advanced Studies from the Texas Instruments honchos, Jonsson and Green and McDermott. Then he fought us on bringing UT Dallas into the System in '69. Then when we tried to get the school set up to take freshmen and sophomores rather than just juniors and seniors, he filibustered that bill to death.

And it got personal; he made out I was some kind of villain behind the scenes because I was trying to help that school.

"Well, God just delivered him into my hands. I found out Dean Gronouski over at the LBJ School had actually hired him as an adjunct professor. What the hell could he teach anybody? Well, I just went to see Gronouski and put an end to that."

Still in his euphoric mood at taking away Don Kennard's job, Erwin said, "God has delivered all my enemies into my hands except that son of a bitch Babe Schwartz. And his time will come."

Erwin then said, "Truly, God has delivered my enemies into my hands. I'll give you an example. I was at the university when the Board of Regents fired Homer Rainey in 1944 as president because he wouldn't fire Bob Montgomery and Clarence Ayers in the economics department."

Montgomery and Ayers were two of the most outstanding and popular faculty members on campus. The two professors were both hated by the conservative business community for their unwavering criticisms of business fraud and government favoritism.

Erwin continued his story about President Rainey. "There was uproar across the state. Chapters of ex-students from all over sent in resolutions condemning the board. Most of the press was up in arms, and at UT the faculty and students were protesting against regents messin' with university business. What I have tried to keep quiet is that I was one of the students who organized a protest march on the capitol. We got a coffin and wrote "Academic Freedom Is Dead" on the sides and carried it to the capitol with the Longhorn Band marching with us playing Chopin's funeral march. There were about five thousand students with us that day.

"Bet you didn't know I was a student protester, did you? But I want you to keep that between us.

"Anyway, here's the point. After it was all over and Rainey stayed fired and the campus settled down again, Dean Burdine called me to his office. He threatened to expel me for participating in the protest march and organizing the students. It was a close call. He could have destroyed my whole future. He finally agreed to let me stay and finish my degree.

"So guess what, after I became chairman of the board, a committee came to me and wanted to name a building after Burdine. See what I mean about God delivering my enemies into my hands?"

I said, "But, Frank, surely you didn't . . ."

"Hell, you know I didn't. There's a Burdine Hall. But I sure did make that committee sweat before I would agree."

To this day I don't know why Erwin told me that story about organizing the march on the capitol protesting Rainey's firing or about Burdine threatening to expel him. Later I found he had told the same story to others as well. It was demonstrably false. At the time Rainey was fired in 1944 Erwin had been in the navy since 1942 and was stationed in Norfolk, Virginia. Erwin himself left the evidence—a letter he wrote from Norfolk that was published in the November 21, 1944, issue of the *Daily Texan* just weeks after the events surrounding Rainey's firing.

On another occasion when we were talking about the problems we were having with one of the presidents and wondering if he would be able to survive, Erwin intoned, "For God's sake, let us sit upon the ground and tell sad tales about the death of kings. Some have died in war, some were poisoned. Some were murdered . . ."

Richard Gibson, the UT System lawyer, was with me on that occasion. We sat there agape.

And Erwin said, "Well, don't look so astonished. I did go to college, you know."

In trying to recover I turned to tease Gibson and I said to Erwin, "I was down in the legal office the other day and Gibson and all the lawyers were scurrying around about something. They all looked dead serious, some big crisis. Gibson still won't tell me what was up. You know what had 'em tied in knots?"

Erwin grimaced and said, "You don't want to know. Hard to believe. You know down in Houston at the Dental School the students study their anatomy dissecting indigent dead people. Like over at the Medical School. The Dental School gets bodies from the morgue and local undertakers. Maybe you've never thought about this, I never had. But think about it. At the Dental School they don't need to dissect the whole body, like at the med school. So they cut off the heads and cremate the rest of the bodies. Then each dental student gets his own head to work with. Sounds terrible, but it makes sense, for a dental school.

"So here's what happened. A man dies and remains unclaimed for a long time in the freezer at some funeral home. It turns out he's poor and nobody wants him. So this undertaker calls the Dental School and tells them he has another corpse for them if they want to come and get it. So they get the body and treat it like they do all the others.

"Then a couple a days later the undertaker calls and says, 'Hey, you know that body I sent over the other day? Well, turns out he's from some big Indian tribe over in Alabama and they want to pay to have his body shipped over there so they can bury him in their tribal mound or something. Have you still got him?'

"So our man at the Dental School says, not exactly; he only has the head now. Then the undertaker beats around the bush about how profitable this Indian's body could be for him—and you can see what's coming. He finally asks if maybe along with the head the Dental School might have another body he could have, you know, not the whole thing, just the part they don't need.

"Well, the best we can say is people who work around corpses all the time get hardened to this kind of thing and maybe they can understand how this kind of thing could happen. Anyway this man who works for us has lousy judgment, and he actually tells the undertaker to send his hearse on over. He can accommodate him.

"So the undertaker sews the head on the body and ships it in a sealed coffin to the tribe in Alabama with strict instructions; the casket is not to be opened under any circumstances.

"Well, you know those Indians; they probably got out their tomahawks and chopped the lid open and they weren't fooled for one minute. White man speak with forked tongue. Guess we got a dozen lawsuits out of that."

One afternoon, Erwin came by in a more subdued tone than usual. He told me, "I was having drinks with three students over at the Quorum Club last night. We were talking Kappa Sig business. Something interesting happened. I'd beat those boys down pretty bad on something we were arguing about. So they're all three sittin' there sort of dejected and quiet, and I realize I need to ease off. So I said something like, 'Just because we can't agree doesn't mean you have to be reticent about telling me what you think.'

"And this one boy sort of mumbles to himself, 'Reticent, reticent.'

"Hell, I thought he was mocking me, so I ask him sort of rough like what the hell he means and he acts embarrassed, but then he says, 'I've read that word a couple of times, but I've never heard it before. I always thought it was *reTIcent.*'

"The other two guys laughed at him. But you know, it hit me right then: that young man is what our university is all about. We're going to send that boy out into the world to do some kind of important work. Right now he's paying attention, like that kid was listening to me, and this is our chance to give him what he's goin' to need.

"Think of all the rough edges we need to polish off and everything he needs to learn about how the world works and all the other stuff we need to cram into him."

"And," I said, "the self-confidence he's going to need."

"What? Yeah, well, that too. That's what the university is all about."

"How did it happen with you, Frank?" I asked. "I mean where did the self-confidence come from? When did it start?"

"Oh, hell, I don't know," he answered. Then he growled, "Did you hear a single goddamn word of what I just told you?"

Every time I got a story from him, I had to ask myself just how skewed it might be. But certainly not all his tales could be said to be self-serving. Some of them showed him petulant or vindictive or just plain mean. But he would tell them to me anyway.

CHAPTER 22

Politics and the Legislature

Most legislators we dealt with were personable and reasonable and conscientious people. Getting elected usually requires a person to be sympathetic, outgoing, approachable, and receptive to suggestions. But there were always a difficult and disagreeable few to deal with. Some legislators, through longevity and intelligence and political savvy, had come to wield disproportionate power in relation to their colleagues.

All of them, good and bad, traded favors, cut deals, incurred obligations, and searched out ways to leverage each other and state agency heads. That was the nature of politics. Most of them plied their trade for honorable purposes; some also looked for ways to feather their own nests.

Legislators with real authority were perhaps best characterized by Bill Heatly from Paducah, a very small north Texas town located just south of the Red River where the eastern edge of the panhandle turns north toward the Oklahoma panhandle. As chairman of the House Appropriations Committee, Heatly showed his disdain for the governor's budget by using it as a doorstop in his office.

He and Senator A. M. Aiken, chairman of the Senate Finance Committee, dictated the financial matters of the state. They decided how money would be allocated and which bills and programs got funded and which did not. What few items they could not control through their own committees, they could deal with in the budget conference committee when they reconciled the differing versions of the money bills from the two houses. With this power they also held important influence over the votes of every other member in the legislature who wanted to pass a bill or see a program funded.

During the 1960s and 1970s, universities did not fare well in the allocation of state funds. This was in part because higher education did not receive dedicated funds like highways and public schools. In addition, the state was still in the process of shifting political power from the rural areas to the urban centers. Rural representatives had always been skeptical of the financial needs of colleges and universities, and they were generally more conservative than urban legislators in their willingness to pass new taxes.

In addition, the budgets for higher education, along with those for the schools for the deaf, blind, and handicapped, were considered late in the budgeting process. This meant that routinely their needs were considered after monies had been largely used up or even overly obligated for other programs. This gave rise to one of Erwin's oft-quoted lines: "The state budget is built on the backs of the lame, the blind, the halt, and the ignorant."

Then finally within the scraping together of the higher education appropriations each session, the very last item to be funded was research. Erwin saved some of his bargaining chips to try to secure some of the crumbs still left for faculty research. Some sessions he did better than others, but research continued to be underfunded year after year. Legislators, especially Heatly, simply could not understand why faculty needed to spend time on research; it only diverted them from what they were being paid to do, that is, to teach students. Erwin valiantly tried to explain the need for supporting research, but Heatly was a hard man to convince; any increased research funding Erwin got would entail some kind of tradeoffs he would have to make with Heatly.

One technique Erwin used was to work hard to obtain funds beyond what was actually needed in some area such as building maintenance or administrative costs. Then after long bargaining and much lamenting about the loss of essential support in those areas, Erwin would reluctantly agree to trade these if Heatly would give him a like amount in research funds.

Heatly was a grouch of an old man, short and overweight, who had represented the district around Paducah for untold years. He was opposed to new ideas, change, or innovation of any kind. These always turned out to cost money.

He did not seek to be recognized or honored. He was a hard man to flatter because he suspected everyone of being insincere. Anyone nice to him did so for the sole purpose of trying to get money out of him. He rarely committed himself to anything quickly. His famous lines were "I'll think about it," and "I'll have to get back to you on that" or "I'm not informed on that."

Nonetheless, Erwin's day-by-day efforts and personal involvement to obtain more money for UT Austin each session had an enormous effect. And much of the result was due to the cajoling and personal attention he lavished on Chairman Heatly and Senator Aiken. When Erwin was criticized for the disproportionate extra money he was getting for UT Austin, his response was "A rising tide lifts all boats."

And that was true, due to the legislature using a formula system to fund higher education. Although the formulas were not followed exactly, they were extensively used because the universities had participated in developing them as the best approach to an equitable distribution of appropriations among the many different kinds and sizes of colleges and universities. As Erwin won higher appropriations for UT Austin in one formula area, for example faculty salaries, similar increases were made across the board to help all the universities.

Erwin, due to his continuing promotion of UT's budget, became an expert in most of the schools, agencies, and universities that made up the UT System. In the 1971 session, Erwin decided that he would, as part of his grand finale before giving up the board chairmanship to John Peace, present the entire budget for all of the UT System, describing needs, justifying requests, and answering all questions from the committee members. Here was another opportunity for him to perform and command the limelight. Indeed, it was a tour de force and a spectacle to behold for the few who could appreciate what he was doing.

With his influence he could arrange the scheduling of hearings of the committees. So this year he had the hearings before the senate and house committees set for the same evening, back to back, to make his presentations even more impressive.

In contrast to the presidents of other universities making presentations with their coterie of staff beside them, he sat at the hearing table alone and did not consult with anyone on any questions put to him, laying out the requests of all the schools and drawing on his knowledge about their budgets to respond to all inquiries put to him. His comprehensive command and his confidence dazzled everyone present.

As he finished his long presentation before the Senate Finance Committee, he rose with the entourage of all the institutional representatives and System staff behind him in the hearing room and marched across to the house side of the capitol.

By the time we had reached the rotunda and were coming to the House hearing room, I had pointed out to several of Erwin's closest financial advisers an obvious mistake he had made in his presentation, expecting someone to tell him so he would not repeat it before the House committee. No one would do it. One said, "You tell him; I'm sure not going to." Another said, "It's not that important."

Finally I caught up to Erwin and told him myself about the error. He said, "My god, Heatly would have been all over me on that. Why don't people tell me stuff like this?"

After the hearings were completed, the negotiating continued for several months. Following a particularly stressful night listening to what Heatly and the House Appropriations Committee were about to do to the Galveston Medical Branch, Erwin pulled Frank Graydon, the UT System budget director, and me aside and told us to meet him back at our offices. When we arrived, he directed Graydon to come up with figures on how many beds we would have to close under the cuts that Heatly insisted on making in the hospital for the poor people of Texas at the Galveston Medical Branch. The charity hospital in Galveston had served for years as the hospital of last compassion for seriously ill indigent patients from anywhere in the state. It also served as the principal teaching hospital for the Galveston Medical Branch.

Erwin assigned me to help Graydon come up with the figures. We worked a good part of the night pulling together what he wanted.

Erwin then took the data Graydon had prepared and made it public. He also called President Truman Blocker at the Galveston Medical Branch and told him he wanted thirty beds closed in the public hospital.

The ploy worked. The appropriations for the hospital were restored. The thirty beds were reopened.

I learned from Hermas Miller, one of Heatly's trusted assistants, the consequences of Erwin's strategy.

Hermas told me he got a call one afternoon from Heatly, who told him he wanted them to drive to Galveston that evening. Hermas said he was given no idea of what Heatly was planning to do on their trip. He said they stayed, as was Heatly's wont, at one of the cheapest motels in the area, rooms so bad, Hermas told me, that you did not dare put your bare feet on the floor in the dark. When you turned on the lights, huge roaches scurried under the bed and furniture. They ate a terrible meal at a greasy spoon café and then, without comment, went to bed. Hermas said he was awakened at 2 A.M. by the phone. It was Heatly. He said, "Get dressed and meet me at the car. We're going to count beds tonight."

It was widely known that when Erwin was in the capitol and the senate was in session, he would often commandeer Lieutenant Governor Ben Barnes's office. From there he would make phone calls, draft bills or amendments, swap favors, and meet with UT staff and others helping him with legislation. He did this as though it was a right of possession, with never a sign of apology or explanation. He just breezed past the secretaries and assistants through the door with his entourage following, and Barnes's aides accepted his use of the lieutenant governor's office as though he, too, had been elected to share it.

Any lobbyist who wanted to speak with a member of either house could go to the lobby outside the House or senate and send in a message by a page. Unless, of course, he was a former member, in which case he had access to the chamber floor. After the message was delivered, if the senator or House member wanted to speak with you and felt he could leave the floor, he would come out for a consultation. Not Erwin. He had access to the back halls behind each House where he could meet in private with a member. And any legislator he wished to see would accommodate him.

When in the House or senate galleries, Erwin nearly always chose a seat in one of the corners at the bottom of the U, assuming we are looking down on the gallery from above and the dais is at the center of the open end of the U. From either of the bottom corners he could look directly down on the podium where the presiding officer stood at the dais and from where he could see the largest section of the floor and participants below. I never saw him sit in a seat at the top of the U, that is, above the dais, looking down on the back of the presiding officer. He might move from his corner seat in the U to one on the long sides if he wanted to look down on a particular legislator or he wanted to let that legislator know that he was watching him.

One evening I was anticipating giving my testimony against a bill, and as my turn came I became more and more eager to do so. I had worked for days to polish my statement. Erwin passed a note to me. It read, "Are you sure you want to speak? We clearly have the votes right now."

I got the message and, when called on I said I had decided not to testify. The chair asked if there was any objection to sending the bill to a subcommittee that the chair would appoint later. There was no objection. Everybody knew he would never appoint the subcommittee. The bill would die. Just what we wanted.

To emphasize the point he made that night, Erwin explained to a group over drinks one night, "What some people don't get is that legislators don't hold hearings to let people get up and talk. They hold hearings to decide to pass a bill to the floor, or vote it down, or find some other way to kill it without embarrassing the sponsor. You work over the members before they meet because you want to get the committee to do what you want it to do. Then you go to the hearing and just sit there to let them know you are watching to see they do what they told you they'd do. Don't get up if you don't have to. If you do talk and you see you've got the votes, shut up and sit down."

One obnoxious legislator had gained a position on the House Appropriations Committee. In that position he arrogated to himself status, authority, and power. And he used his committee appointment to humble anyone who did not recognize his august position.

Each fall one of the UT football receptions was dedicated to honoring members of the state legislature and heads of major state agencies with whom the university might have dealings. It was held in the new art building and museum north and just across the street from the stadium.

While hundreds of people walked by and as dozens upon dozens of dignitaries approached to enter the art museum, this particular legislator chose to use this as an occasion to show how important he was. He drove up right in front of the museum. He rolled down his window and began loudly to order the policemen to remove the barriers blocking an area along the curb. He demanded to be permitted to park right there. And he began to push against the barriers with his car as the police were trying to stop him. He shouted to them that he was on the appropriations committee and an important member of the legislature and demanded that they immediately move the barriers if they knew what was good for the university. As they were not moving the sawhorses fast enough to suit him, he continued to push ahead against the barriers with his car, all the while honking his horn and shouting for them to hurry up. He parked and magisterially entered the reception.

This stellar legislator continued to exploit his position on the appropriations committee and was never reluctant to make threats to have his way. President Bryce Jordan called me one day to describe a problem that had come up. He needed to discuss a touchy political issue. He described how, in an effort to smooth things in the legislature, this legislator's brother-in-law had been appointed a proctor in the new Jester Center dormitory. As proctor, he had been given a rent-free apartment on one of the upper floors. Jordan described what the young man had managed to accomplish in his position as proctor. He had moved a pool table from the student recreation area into his suite and was charging students to use it. In a very suspicious move he had made an arrangement with a laundry company and was restricting students to using only that laundry service. And he had moved his girlfriend into his apartment. To top it off, Jordan's staff had discovered that the young man's activities had kept him so busy that he had had to drop all his courses and at present was not even enrolled at UT.

Jordan was concerned about the repercussions if they booted the kid out of the dormitory. I advised him to go ahead and do it. My reasoning was that this was not going to remain an issue known only to us. I started to paint a picture of what the *Daily Texan* would do with a story like this and how we would be made to look like we were part of a scheme to favor a relative of a legislator when Bryce stopped me and said he agreed. He was calling to let us know what he was about to do and to warn us to be ready to stand by him when the representative came after the university.

Of course, the guy was furious and said he could see nothing wrong with his relative's arrangements. He exclaimed to Bryce, "He's going to marry the girl!"

One thing we all learned early was to be deferential to legislators regardless of how obnoxious and overbearing they might be. No administrator in any state agency is ever equal to a legislator. The people who can deal most effectively with an obstreperous and difficult legislator are other legislators. And our friend had apparently done much to invite their retribution.

This is the story as told to me. During a slow day in the legislature, a large delegation of schoolteachers was present in the gallery observing progress on a bill of concern to them. One of the legislative colleagues of our august member decided to send him a note supposedly from one of the attractive teachers up in the gallery watching them go about their business. The note described how this young lady had never been in the legislature before and how impressed she was to watch him as her representative. She had been watching ecstatically for hours. The jokester and a few friends on the house floor watched as he was brought the note by a page and as he read it and stood and looked around the gallery, obviously wondering which of the young ladies had written it.

In a little while the legislator received another note from the lady, telling him she was disappointed he had not been participating in the business on the floor as she watched him and talked to her friends about him. She wondered if he might do her a favor and go to one of the microphones and make some remarks. It would make her so proud.

Those in the know had to contain their mirth as he quickly went to the back mike to comment on the bill on the floor. In short order the word began to spread around the chamber what was happening. Several members caucused to determine what they should do next. They came up with a capstone message. The young lady explained in her next note how she was so enchanted with what he was doing and the progress on their education bill that she had called her superintendent and gotten permission to stay for another day. She wondered if he might like to meet her. If he would, perhaps he could give her a message. Perhaps he could stand up and comb his hair.

Their victim read the note and jumped to his feet and began vigorously combing his hair and continued to do so to the delight of his colleagues in the house for an extended time and then sat down, looking back as pages brought notes into the chamber, obviously waiting for a further message.

CHAPTER 23

My Credentials Questioned

It was not unexpected that my qualifications as vice chancellor for academic affairs would be challenged. My credentials would have been scrutinized even more severely, and rightly so, had I been appointed to an academic position on a campus rather than as a functionary in the bureaucracy at the UT System. My appointment would have been inconceivable had the position been one requiring faculty nominations, reviews, and recommendations. It was only because the System Administration was a quasi state agency that I could be advanced to a high position with such limited faculty experience. My appointment was possible because the Board of Regents was then interceding in administrative matters so extensively that they could make their own appointments to the System offices. Under sound administrative practices, a vice chancellor should have been appointed not by the regents but by the chancellor because vice chancellors serve as his staff and subordinates. But due to the unusual circumstances of Mickey LeMaistre's appointment in El Paso as chancellor designate, he had not been consulted about filling the vice chancellor position.

I did not feel adequate to the position I held. I clearly was not qualified, and I knew it. If I was going to try to hold the position, I had to hope I might learn fast enough to be able to do the job.

As I dealt with administrators on the campuses, I did not feel inadequate. It was when I met with faculty and department chairs or deans that I kept wondering what they really thought about having to deal with someone with so little familiarity with a university campus and so little experience in academia. When conversation flowed smoothly, I wondered if they were just being polite; when business got done, I thought perhaps I really was performing satisfactorily in the position.

In any event, obscure and distant as we were from the campuses making up the UT System, we on the staff were largely unknown, not visible, and seemingly unimportant to most of the faculty and students on the campuses across the state. Only on the Austin campus did there seem to be much awareness of the influence we System administrators might have. In hindsight I suspect that the nature of my job and my approach to it also mitigated against any outrage that someone with so little university experience should hold such a high rank in academic planning. We initiated very little at the System level and spent the great bulk of our time responding to proposals originating on the campuses. Our job was primarily to review, polish, and present campus materials in a consistent format that could be readily understood and acted on by the Board of Regents. Our most substantive contribution was to manage the timing of when issues should go to the board and to be supersensitive to the politics of the regents and the legislature as matters came to us from the campuses.

Indeed, there were legitimate reasons for calling into question my preparation and qualifications for the post I held. And the most direct request for me to justify why I should hold the position of vice chancellor came in the fall of 1971 from Ronnie Dugger. A former editor of the *Daily Texan,* Dugger had been the first editor of the *Texas Observer* and, as a result, largely the creator of that journal. His personal and journalistic integrity won him the continuing support of several liberal thinkers and businesspeople in the state. His insistence on complete editorial freedom to take on any issues or public figure defined the mission of the *Observer* and garnered the continuing support that was the basis for its ongoing survival. Dugger had made the journal into one of the few liberal, exposé-oriented, investigative reporting magazines in the state among an almost uniformly conservative press community. Dugger had published articles in national journals, and in 1971 he was writing *Our Invaded Universities,* published in 1974.

His inquiry, on personal letterhead to me at my home address, read as follows:

- -

1017 West Thirty-First Street
Austin, Texas 78705

August 28, 1971

Dear Dr. Ashworth,

I am now in a long writing about UT. It has been a matter now and again with unpleasantness mixed in, and among representations made to me has been the contention that you should not be the Vice-Chancellor for Academic Programs (if I have that title not right, I hope you will so advise me). The main point advanced against you is the contention that you received your Ph.D. only in 1969 and prior to your appointment had tutored one course; in other words, that you have next to no experience, yourself, in the classroom. I do not like the incumbency on me to ask you in effect to respond to this matter, but it seems the straightforward way to proceed in a matter obviously of moment in the University's life. I hope that I may hear from you at your convenience.

Sincerely,
/S/
Ronnie Dugger

Dr. Kenneth Ashworth
2100 Griswold
Austin, Texas

P.S. Should you choose to drop me a letter, I assure you that I would not quote you in such a matter, rather simply feeling free to dismiss, on the basis of your letter, these points advanced against your holding your present post, or at any rate to put into the scale, as an act on my own responsibility, the considerations that work against the points made to me.

After the initial shock of being called out by a person of Ronnie Dugger's repute, I had to consider how I would respond. The contentions he presented were well founded, and my holding the vice chancellor position was difficult to defend. All I could say was that I, in fact, had management skills and had accumulated ten years of practical experience in public administration and organizational politics at the federal, state, and local levels. But it was undeniable that this background did not qualify me to hold my top-level position over academic matters in the UT System Administration.

Upon closer reading of Dugger's letter, I concluded from his phrasing that he was perhaps uncomfortable in having to ask me to respond to these contentions. My wife Sonia and I were active in the liberal arm of local Democratic Party politics, although we did not advertise the fact. Through this and Sonia's volunteer work and because of the kinds of friends we had in the economics, political science, and history faculties, we were not seen as the typical occupants of positions in a Frank Erwin administration. Sonia was very active with the League of Women Voters and a literacy group working in East Austin. Among our best friends were liberal Democrats such as Dave and Ann Richards, Mary Beth and John Rogers, Lester and Janet Reed, B. J. and Bob Fernea, Toni and Bob Palter, Dan and Mary Morgan, Mary Lee Claiborne, Dagmar and Bob Hamilton, Janice May, Barbara and Millard Ruud, and Cliff and Barbara Grubbs.

Through Dugger's research for his book he was certain to have talked with faculty members with whom I was in touch even if we did find ourselves on opposite sides on some university issues. I considered it possible that through some of these mutual acquaintances he knew of my political leanings. Perhaps the awkwardness of the wording of Dugger's letter was due to a reluctance to have to ask about the credentials of the one person inside the administration who might have sympathies anywhere near his own. But as he said, he had the facts before him and the allegations about my credentials.

I did not feel Dugger was wrong to pursue the matter. If he felt any ambivalence in asking me the questions, I likewise felt some regret in the way I chose to respond to him. I was under no obligation to plait the rope he could choose to use to hang me. If he was looking for ammunition to traduce Erwin's team of cronies "invading the University of Texas" I might need to be sacrificed. I would not put that choice in Dugger's hands. So I answered him as follows.

- -

September 20, 1971

4507 Balcones Drive
Austin, Texas 78731

Dear Mr. Dugger,

I am now in the continuing process of evaluating journalism in Texas. It has been a matter now and again with unpleasantness mixed in, and from time to time the contention unfortunately has been made that you leave something to be desired as an objective journalist. The main points advanced against you are the contention that you often are not accurate in your facts, that you editorialize in your news articles, that you are willing to accept the limited criteria set by other persons in judging an individual's qualifications to carry public responsibility, that you seek information on a person's qualification in limited and unusual ways, and that you have worked only for the *Daily Texan* and the *Texas Observer* and written a few articles for magazines; in other words, that your experience and objectivity are limited. I do not like the incumbency on me in effect to evaluate myself, when that is the job of others, in order to respond to your letter of August 28, and it seems the straightforward way to proceed in this matter is to answer in this way.

Sincerely,

/S/

Kenneth Ashworth

Mr. Ronnie Dugger
1017 West 31st Street
Austin, Texas

P.S. Should you choose to write an objective article about the University of Texas, I assure you that I would cite it often, simply feeling free to dismiss, on the basis of your article, those points advanced against your work as a journalist, or at any rate to put into the scale, as an act of my own responsibility, the considerations that work against the points made to me.

- -

In 1974, at Dugger's autographing party for his new book at Florence Rosengren's bookstore in San Antonio, he greeted me warmly with the comment, "As I recall we had an exchange of correspondence. What are you doing now?"

Of course, Dugger was on to something in the thesis of his book; the colleges and universities of this country were, in fact, coming increasingly under the control and direction of moneyed interests and being damaged by political intrusion.

CHAPTER 24

Sharpstown Fallout

B en Barnes, having risen rapidly to become speaker of the
Texas House at twenty-six and then to be elected lieutenant
governor, was seen as the bright, rising star in Texas—and hopefully
in national politics. Still in his twenties, Barnes was supported by
both Lyndon Johnson and John Connally. At a political meeting at
Dolph Briscoe's ranch in 1962 to plan Connally's run for governor,
Barnes and Erwin had met for the first time and formed a mutual
admiration society.

Barnes and Erwin were useful to each other. The younger man
was receiving much advice and counsel from an experienced practitioner. Erwin had been chairman of the Texas Democratic Party and
was close to most of the major players in Texas politics. It was common knowledge that Erwin used the lieutenant governor's office and
Barnes's political position to help gain his own way in the capitol.

But by late 1971 and early 1972 the election was not going well
for him. Barnes was now running for governor, the next step up the
ladder. During the 1971 legislative session, federal investigators
from the Securities and Exchange Commission (SEC) identified some
fraudulent financial deals involving members of the legislature
and their aides.

The indictment alleged that a banker, Frank Sharp, a wealthy
housing developer and owner of the Sharpstown State Bank and
the National Banker Life Insurance Company in Houston, needed

some special legislation to help him with a financial scheme. The Speaker of the House, Gus Mutscher, and several of his colleagues had gotten a bill passed that brought about an increase in the value of Frank Sharp's insurance company. As a reward, gifts of stocks and unsecured loans were made to those who had helped to pass the bill. Those who had pushed the bill along received loans from Sharp's bank that could be used to buy Sharp's insurance company stock. Then the stock, which had been pumped up by virtue of the special legislation, could be sold for large gains. It was a daisy chain of back scratching, and federal regulators from the SEC were onto it quickly.

Also caught up in the allegations and suspicions was Governor Preston Smith. He had been the beneficiary of unsecured loans even though he had vetoed the bill from the legislature to assist Frank Sharp's troubled conglomerate. The governor had to deny publicly that he had made any deal related to the Sharpstown scandal. Not a good thing to have to do just before the primary, to have to declare "I am not a crook."

Ben Barnes, in his campaign for governor, seemed to be clear of any involvement, but that did not stop the rumors and allegations. An energetic and blooming entrepreneur as well as politician, Barnes had many business dealings, all of which were now subject to scrutiny and damaging speculation. He had learned early the use of capital. The way to make money was to borrow, invest in an enterprise, make it a success, and pay back the loan. This entailed the constant moving around of money and securities. Now all his loans and transactions and stock sales and swaps were examined and questioned. It was never shown that Barnes was involved in any way in the scandal. Yet it all seemed suspicious to some and, in the midst of a political campaign, rivals made it appear suspicious to as many voters as possible. As the May primary approached, polls showed that the public tended to lump all of the state leadership together in the "Sharpstown Scandal," the Speaker, the lieutenant governor, and the governor.

Also in the run for governor in the Democratic primary was Frances Farenthold, an outspoken new House member from Corpus Christi, who was very popular with the young voters and students in the state. She was running a strong campaign and was doing well in the polls. She was highly critical of the Board of Regents for all the same reasons that Erwin had been under attack by the students. In fact during a special legislative session in 1972, Farenthold managed by a vote of 59 to 56 to get the House to adopt her resolution calling on Erwin to resign from the Board of Regents.

The fourth Democratic candidate was Dolph Briscoe, a former legislator and banker and rancher from Uvalde. He campaigned for honesty, openness, and economy in state government.

At that time the Republican primary and their likelihood of doing well in November were far less than they would come to be in later years. Texas at that time was still overwhelmingly Democratic, even though it was very much a two-party state; both parties, conservative and moderate, just happened to be inside the same political party at that time.

To make things worse for Smith and Barnes, Speaker Gus Mutscher and three others were indicted at the end of 1971, and, after already blighting the earlier campaigning, their trial now began in early March. This was right on the cusp of the primary election, not even two months away. Then in the middle of March, Mutscher and his compatriots were found guilty.

Polls for the governorship turned discouraging for Smith and Barnes. Both had entered the race thinking they would be the principal rivals for the job, and Smith was confident that as the incumbent with experience and maturity, he would prevail over the youngster moving up too quickly. But Farenthold and even Briscoe were shown in some polls running ahead of the governor and lieutenant governor.

In the midst of all this and just before the election, Alan Tanaguchi left the UT deanship of architecture to move to Rice University. He tried to leave quietly.

But Erwin would have none of that. He had remained silent as long as he could in the face of ongoing taunts from departing faculty. He had not forgotten that Tanaguchi was one of the two deans who refused to vote to support President ad Interim Jordan after he fired John Silber.

Erwin's remarks, made at a political rally for Ben Barnes, were widely reported. "All the people could leave in the history department and architecture school and it would be good. It would give us a chance to start over and develop some fine departments."

He went on to say that Tanaguchi had wanted to open a private architectural practice in downtown Austin and the regents had refused to permit it.

There could hardly be a more blatant example of political intrusion into the university than Erwin's attack during a campaign on a faculty member and dean of a college.

So Tanaguchi could not leave quietly after all. He called for the president and the chancellor to set the record straight about Erwin's caustic allegations and added, "The campus has deteriorated into a climate of distrust at the expense of quality education."

Because I had advised Erwin not to continue in his attacks on faculty and to let Roger Shattuck go in peace, did I attempt to advise him further as he was on a rant again? No. And he did not ask for my views—or show me any draft press releases.

I had to wonder how Barnes reacted to Erwin's comments about the history department and the architecture school. Such comments would be resented by any thinking alumnus. Did Barnes feel Erwin was being helpful to his election? Did he agree? Did he have any control over what Erwin said at a rally? Did Barnes have any control over whether Erwin should even appear as a supporter?

As for myself, the personal price I was paying to gain experience in the UT System Administration was getting very high. I did not have to wait long for the final development to push me on my way. For I had occasion to see how desperately Erwin was committed to getting Ben Barnes elected governor.

During some moments of leisure at a board meeting early that year, Truman Blocker, president of the Galveston Medical Branch and a plastic surgeon, was giving me a progress report on the deteriorating condition of our mutual friend, David Hunt, president of Galveston Community College. David was growing more melanomas that Blocker was harvesting, and it had reached the point where David was in his final year, maybe final months. It was a self-centered response on my part, considering the dire circumstances that David Hunt faced, but I mentioned to Blocker that I had a spot on my face that would not heal. Truman looked at it and told me to come to Galveston for a biopsy.

In March, when I was in Galveston for this procedure, Erwin and I were both very much surprised to encounter each other there. He did not ask why I was there, and he didn't tell me why he was there.

On biopsy my excision was found to be precancerous, nothing to worry about.

By the next time I saw Dr. Blocker, Dolph Briscoe had won the primary election, which was tantamount to being elected governor because the Democrats had prevailed in every statewide general election since the Civil War. At that time I casually commented to Blocker on the coincidence of running into Erwin while I had been in Galveston for my biopsy.

Blocker said, "Yeah, you don't know the half of it. That trip was all dirty politics. There we were in the run-up to the primary and Frank was down there trying to get me and my staff to tell him why Dolph Briscoe had come to Galveston a couple of years ago. Frank wanted to know what we'd treated him for. I told him that was confidential patient information and we couldn't tell him. He kept after us and tried to get us to confirm what he was looking for. He said he'd heard that Dolph had been treated for some kind of mental problem. He wanted to know if that was true. Had Briscoe had shock treatments? I don't know where he came up with that. It was sheer nonsense, but we wouldn't tell him anything. I knew better than to get into answering any of Frank's questions. You can't say 'no' to him and have it end there. We wouldn't talk and he finally gave up and left."

This really surprised me because toward the very end of the campaign I had seen a newspaper report referring to the possibility that Briscoe had been treated for a mental problem. Now, with Blocker's information, I knew the source of that report.

Judging from the hoopla later that summer over Senator Thomas Eagleton having been treated for depression and his forced withdrawal from the Democratic ticket as George McGovern's running mate, if such reports about Briscoe had gained wide circulation, it might have cost him the election.

This was when I decided it was time for me to start looking for another job. The UT System administration was a comfortable place to be if favoritism did not bother you, if you were content to feel secure and insulated by powerful people who knew how to circle the wagons and protect each other, if you enjoyed being associated with people of wealth and influence who carried them with a sense of entitlement.

It was the accrual of all too frequent events and circumstances that began to undercut my ability to feel true loyalty to the UT System administration. There was the exposé that found members of our administration like the deputy chancellor for financial affairs, Don Walker, were serving as paid members on the boards of banks where we deposited UT System funds. Questions were raised whether the university was getting the interest returns it might have gotten if there had been open bidding for those deposits. And then it turned out that a regent or two also served on those boards. Did we really have to wait for exposure of such conflicts of interest to develop rules on what was right and proper?

And I learned of the political intrusion of the Medical Association of San Antonio and Regent Joe Nelson representing the Texas Medical Association on the Board of Regents. They were up in arms when President Carter Pannill of the UT San Antonio Medical Center had sent university faculty and residents into the barrios of the city to give inoculations during a serious diphtheria epidemic. The M.D.s of San Antonio had been deprived of the income they could have made by giving those shots. This became part of the case against Pannill for his dismissal as being too liberal for the medical profession of Texas.

And there was the tenure situation in the government department with Janice May. After using her for years as an underpaid instructor, it was discovered that someone had neglected to dismiss her after six years of using her. Now that she was in her seventh year, AAUP rules required, even without a tenure review, that she be granted tenure. The outcry of opposition to promoting a woman into a tenured position and the hostility to her appointment fell below the dignity of a great university.

And why did it take so inordinately long for the University of Texas to find it possible to recruit black students to its athletic teams? But the university did put a magnanimous face on its concession to face a team in the UT stadium that had a black player. Wasn't it becoming embarrassing to be one of the few major universities still playing on national television with an all-white football team?

If I had felt conflicted two years earlier about my job with the UT System Administration, I had a new sense of discomfort. I had matured in my work and grown more sensitive to the extent of our interference in running UT Austin. Erwin was increasingly bold in his use of the offices and staff of the System Administration, even though he was no longer officially chairman of the board.

Harry Truman's sign on his desk in the Oval Office, "If you can't stand the heat, get out of the kitchen," often came to mind. Was I cut out for this? I reasoned that if I stayed in the kitchen I might be able to change the menu. But I began to wonder whether I was all that effective; maybe I was merely rationalizing my staying.

What were my options? I could not feel loyalty to the leadership and therefore serve comfortably or conscientiously. And disagreeing on policy or speaking out against proposed actions would just make me less acceptable to my work colleagues and more suspect and ineffective. There was not much that I could shirk or neglect in my work that would not end up simply hurting some of the schools whose requests I was sending forward for board action. I didn't have a lot of choices. So I began to wonder why I was hanging around when I felt so uncomfortable with actions I couldn't agree with or stop or modify.

After seeing the extremes that Erwin was capable of with his visit to Truman Blocker's medical staff at Galveston to try to blacken Dolph Briscoe's name, I began actively to look at options. Quietly I interviewed with Paul Hardin and his faculty for the provost and vice president position at SMU and for the presidency at the University of Louisville. It was time to leave, but little did I know that I was about to hasten my departure through a major political blunder.

CHAPTER 25

Presidents Old and New

By 1972 John Peace from San Antonio was chairman of the Board of Regents but Erwin, with two years yet to serve on the board, remained the major spokesman for the regents and the UT System in Austin. Although Erwin focused most of his attention on the affairs of UT Austin, he continued to monitor what was happening on other UT campuses.

On one occasion Erwin told me how he had saved the state money by forcing the presidents of the medical schools to alter their curricula to shorten the M.D. degree to three years from four. He complained about the trouble he had had with Charlie Sprague as president at the Southwest Medical School in Dallas because he refused to give in to Erwin. Sprague's argument against the change was that it did not save the state much money and only increased the number of physicians insignificantly. Sprague pointed out there was only a one-year gain in graduates, a onetime saving, and then the number of M.D.s graduated by the schools went back to the number admitted each year, as before. And the price for shortening the medical degree to three years was to lower the quality of graduates. Erwin was angry that Sprague would not give in to his orders.

He said, "Do you realize I have replaced or moved every president in the UT System since I've been on this board? Except Blocker at Galveston, and Sprague, that son of bitch, and I should have gotten him too. He wouldn't carry out orders."

"But, Frank," I said, "in a couple of years all the other medical schools went back to the four-year curriculum."

"That's not the point. He would not cooperate when I needed him to."

Problems at UT El Paso (UTEP) in 1972 attracted Erwin's attention. He nursed a continuing concern about the effectiveness of the president, Joe Smiley, feeling he was far too soft on student organizations and protestors.

Joe Smiley had been president of UT Austin in the early 1960s and before that president at UTEP. Then he had left Texas, becoming president of the University of Colorado. When Joe was forced to move from Colorado in 1969, Harry Ransom, while he was still chancellor, brought Smiley back as president at the University of Texas at El Paso. Smiley's appointment was well received due to his academic reputation and former association with the Austin and El Paso campuses. A well-recognized scholar in French literature, in 1967 he had been awarded the chevalier of the French Legion of Honor. Smiley was a national figure in higher education, and his appointment brought prestige to the UT System and the El Paso campus.

Smiley was tolerant and open minded, ready to think the best of others until they wronged him or showed their incivility or boorishness. And even then, he was reluctant to make an issue of confrontations or cause unpleasantness. He had learned in his years of experience that often cases of unpleasantness left unattended disappeared of their own accord. These were not attributes of leadership that Erwin appreciated.

In fact, there were a number of indicators that Joe Smiley might have lost motivation and did tend to let things drift on his campus. He had come from the old tradition before the new student revolution when the president was just one academic among equals and not expected to act aggressively without careful consultation with the faculty. New conditions unquestionably required more prompt and assertive leadership.

Smiley continued his practice of avoiding and evading controversy with faculty and alumni, and especially with students in those years of their distemper. At times there was more railing about the Vietnam War, desegregation, and civil rights on his campus than in Austin.

It seemed every dissident group in the country had a branch or chapter at UTEP: CORE, the Congress for Racial Equality;

SDS, Students for a Democratic Society; MALDEF, the Mexican American Legal Defense and Educational Fund; MAYO, the Mexican American Youth Organization; and MEChA, Movimiento Estudiantil Chicano de Aztlán, a group calling for all Chicanos to unite and reclaim the land of their birth, that is, Mexico and the American Southwest. There was also SNCC, considered at the time among the most notorious of them all, the Student Nonviolent Coordinating Committee, pronounced "snick." Stokely Carmichael led it until he was replaced by H. Rap Brown, who changed the organization's name to the Student National Coordinating Committee and made a clear change in direction, no longer eschewing violence.

Also suspect in the eyes of much of the Anglo establishment in those years was La Mesa Directiva, an Hispanic organization intent on aggressively promoting higher enrollments and the advancement of Hispanics, Chicanos, Latinos, or Mexican Americans, whichever of these labels they should agree to use for themselves.

By the time President Smiley had arrived at UTEP, most of these student organizations had long been in residence there and had been active in war demonstrations, freedom rides, voter registration activities, the marches on Selma, Washington, and Birmingham, and other efforts to oppose the war and extend civil rights and minority representation. What these organizations were doing on the El Paso campus was entirely congruent with their practices elsewhere. They were using the university as a citadel from which to sally forth and attack or criticize institutions of society standing in the way of progress.

Back in Austin, Don Walker as deputy chancellor for administration continued to pander to Erwin's prejudices against anyone not wholeheartedly behind clamping down on student protests and standing firmly against student demands for change. Because the police on the campuses reported to the business officers, who, in turn, reported to Walker, the deputy chancellor had an intelligence network that enabled him to know more about what was going on at the campuses than their presidents often did. This even included Walker knowing on occasion who on the faculty was advising which student organizations and who was having affairs and with whom. Walker learned that one of Smiley's vice presidents had one of the finest collections of pornography north of the Rio Grande, in early days when such a library was both prized and still rare.

When Smiley was asked if he knew this about his vice president, he responded, typically, "That's interesting. I didn't even know he had a pornograph."

That was the end of it. Joe commented no further.

Walker reported to Erwin on Smiley's inability to control events on his campus. Smiley permitted one of the national student groups to hold a national meeting on his campus. The group was so grateful to find some university, any university, to provide them facilities for their meeting that the leaders quickly agreed to President Smiley's condition that their meetings be open to the campus, the public, and the press.

However, upon the arrival of large numbers of non-UTEP students on Smiley's campus, the organization shut the doors to their meetings and permitted no one but members inside. Without access to the meetings, the assumption was they were busily planning their next 'bomb-throwing' attacks on civil society. Smiley's efforts to persuade the students to open their meetings were ineffectual. For his efforts he gained the animosity of the left and added to the displeasure from the right that he had incurred by permitting the group to meet on his campus in the first place.

In addition to Smiley's faculty and student problems, his campus also suffered from embarrassing scandals in athletics. One had resulted from the track coach recruiting African runners for his team, which went on to distinguish itself and to incur the wrath of competing coaches from other universities in their conference.

These were the kind of reports Walker was making to Erwin to gradually erode Smiley's reputation. There was little I could do to help Joe when he seemed intent on not helping himself.

While all this continued to unfold in El Paso, developments in San Antonio were not going well for John Peace either. San Antonio was Peace's town and his political base with the Democratic Party.

Arleigh Templeton, the new president, styled himself as the savant of higher education. He worked to make himself highly visible as a new power on the scene. His arrogance about bringing higher education to the largest city in the United States without a public university did not set well with the presidents of the several Catholic and independent universities long present in the city and their many graduates and supporters. Moreover, Templeton kept his academic plans for the new University of Texas at San Antonio entirely to himself. I felt certain he had not yet formulated an academic plan for his school.

He instead focused on planning for the physical plant for the new campus to be built on the far northwest side of the city. Community leaders and the newspapers began to ask where President Templeton was planning to take the new university. In his numerous public presentations around town, Templeton continued to convey his overbearing style and his view that he had arrived to bring higher learning to a benighted San Antonio. And when he did occasionally mention the kinds of degree programs he was planning to introduce, the local universities saw them as duplicating their offerings. They increasingly came to see him as a rival and competitor for their students rather than a colleague.

But for President Templeton, all this was simply background noise compared to the differences growing between him and John Peace. As chairman of the Board of Regents, Peace considered this new university to be his legacy to his city. For all his clout as chairman of the board and having taken matters into his own hands, Peace had been late in getting a president appointed for his university. Now that he had a president, he wanted the new university to start to make its mark and to open as quickly as possible. But Templeton dragged his feet.

The new campus would be built about ten miles from downtown on the outskirts of the city and out beyond the new UT medical school. O'Neal Ford was the architect for the new campus, and Ford and his staff worked primarily with the architectural and engineering office from the UT System administration in Austin. Although Ford and his colleagues listened patiently to Templeton's blustering pronouncements to them, they proceeded very much on their own.

When it became clear that the new campus could not possibly open before late 1973, or more realistically in 1974, it caused open conflict between the president and the board chairman.

Peace wanted the school open as soon as possible, even if that meant starting in temporary leased facilities. Templeton saw any plan to open in temporary space as requiring fast hard work to plan, obtain facilities, publish a catalog, and recruit faculty to be ready for the first students. He saw it as a major investment of time and effort without the splash and glamour that an opening on the new campus would provide. And above all, Templeton knew that in January 1973 John Peace's term on the Board of Regents would expire, and he would no longer have to put up with Peace's pestering directions. Templeton held a very comfortable position with high visibility and prestige in the community requiring limited effort at the moment. He merely had to continue his dilatory behavior and things could only get better for him.

Peace continued to call me but less frequently. With the new president in place, there was little we could do from Austin to launch Templeton into action.

However, Peace did call about the vacancy in the presidency of his UT Medical School as a result of the board firing Carter Pannill. He lamented that he would be leaving the board soon and this presidency would still be vacant. Then he asked me how we might find somebody because medicine was a field neither of us knew much about.

I told him there was a president of another UT campus who had moved there from a medical school. Frank Harrison had held a couple of administrative positions at the Southwestern Medical School in Dallas and was now president at UT Arlington. Besides, he was uniquely qualified: he held both the Ph.D. and M.D. degrees. Peace knew Harrison, and I reminded him that he had been the only president who had volunteered to speak against John Silber before the Board of Regents on the division of the College of Arts and Sciences at UT Austin. He had courage.

In early November, the board announced that Frank Harrison would be moving to San Antonio to head the Medical School.

The impasse between Templeton and Peace continued, and as the months of 1972 began to slip by, it became clear that Templeton was going to have his way. Peace's university was not going to open in temporary facilities in 1973, and Peace's influence at the new university would soon end.

In early November, Joe Smiley announced his retirement to return to teaching.

With the imminent replacement of Smiley, I made a trip to El Paso in late November to meet with faculty leaders to reassure them about the search process. They felt themselves at the mercy of the Board of Regents and that a president would unilaterally be imposed on them without consultation. At the end of the meeting I confirmed there would be a bona fide search for a new president and that we would honor the prescribed process of getting evaluation and recommendations from faculty members and others in the community before we made an appointment.

The next day Erwin came by my office and wanted to know what I had been doing in El Paso. I found it interesting that he knew so quickly I had been out there. But I knew the source of his information. When I told him what I had been doing, I had no idea whether he agreed, approved, or disapproved. This was often the case.

Early in December, a Hispanic FBI agent told me that he had been attending school at UTEP under cover and had been at several meetings with some student groups. He said he had been referred to me to make his report because he was being reassigned. He said he had come to the conclusion that unless we got somebody in charge of that campus with a firm hand, there was going to be serious trouble. He said there could be some bombings and somebody could get killed if we didn't get the campus under control.

Bells went off in my head. I remembered how Charles Whitman had talked with a counselor at the UT Austin health center and had told him that some days he felt like going up on the Tower and shooting people. The counselor had taken no action, and sixteen people had died and many more were shot when Whitman launched an attack on the campus from the UT Tower. This hot potato from El Paso had just been dropped in my hands.

I promptly reported the situation to Don Walker. He called Erwin in, and they listened to my report without comment. If he and Walker made a decision on what they planned to do, they did not tell me.

A week or so later Erwin came into my office and closed the door. He said, "I've got a story you're not going to believe."

He took a seat and proceeded, "I made a trip to El Paso yesterday to calm down some of our business supporters out there. I want them to know we have things under control with the problems we've had with the track coach and with Smiley's retirement. So by yesterday afternoon I've seen several of them and I'm in this banker's office, and out of the blue he says to me, 'You know, Frank, I really like that guy you've got picked to be the new UTEP president.'

"So how's that for a shocker? I played along. I didn't show anything and just nodded.

"So he goes on and says, 'He's been out here to talk to some of us several times.'

"Well, you can be sure that's news to me so I continue to play dumb. I tell him, yeah, we're keeping it quiet for right now. And he says, 'Yeah, I know. He told me about your plan, how you're going to wait till after John Peace goes off the board.'

"Now that really gets my attention and I'm still wondering who our new El Paso president's going to be. So I say, sure, John's term runs out in January so it won't be long till we can announce it. And this banker says, 'Yeah, he told me the plan is to wait till Peace is off the board so he can't have anything to do with selecting his successor in San Antonio when he moves out here. He says that way he can get his friend, Drex Vincent, the president over at Angelo State, put in his job in San Antonio.'

"So now I know who we are going to appoint as our new UTEP president. That son of a bitch Arleigh Templeton. And who we're going to appoint as his successor. He's been doing all that behind our backs, and Don and I didn't know a thing about it.

"So I stall for a while and tell him to keep all this quiet, and he says he will, of course, and I ask him if he's got a phone I can use. He gives me an office and I call Peace and tell him all this.

"There's this long quiet spell, and John says in his usual unflappable way [and Erwin imitated him], 'Wal, Ah guess we'll jest have ta call a meeting a the board and *fahr* that son of a bitch.'"

Erwin continued with his story. "So I tell him, 'Let's think about this, John. Why not put all our bad eggs in one basket and ship Arleigh off to El Paso? Then we'll find you a new president while you're still chairman, somebody who can get your school open next year.'

"John says that's fine; he just wants that disloyal son of a bitch out of San Antonio. After all, he made Arleigh his president. So Peace appointed me chairman of the search committee to do the job. And Perfessor, he put you on the search committee too. Come with me. We're going upstairs to meet and get this done right now."

When we met I made myself persona non grata because, despite the preordained outcome, I kept trying to make some kind of record that we had actually considered Templeton's credentials, experience, and qualifications for the new job. In part I was assuaging my guilt at failing to be able to deliver on my promise to the faculty at UTEP that they would be involved in our search. I had promised that, and here I was having to take a role to break that pledge by cramming Templeton down their throats.

After we finished our meeting and had voted unanimously to select Templeton for the job, Erwin said he wanted to get on with tying down the offer so he could tell Peace it was done. He wanted to know when we could get Templeton to Austin and make the reassignment.

Walker, through his expert intelligence system, knew Templeton was in town in a private hideaway and knew precisely where to reach him. An appointment was set for later that afternoon to have Chancellor LeMaistre offer Templeton the El Paso presidency.

At that meeting with Templeton we all anticipated wrapping up the matter quickly. LeMaistre explained our process and decision and waxed eloquent about how perfect Templeton would be for the job in El Paso. LeMaistre made his usual excellent sales pitch. Then he offered the job to Templeton.

To everyone's absolute astonishment Templeton said, "I don't know. I'm perfectly happy where I am. Why would I want to move to El Paso?"

Erwin got up and went to the window, where he stood looking down on the street below. Everyone sat in stunned silence.

As the silence continued, I finally said, "Arleigh's right. Why would he want to take on all that crap in El Paso? Jesus Christ himself couldn't straighten out the mess we've got out there."

What I was trying to do was lost on the other committee members. To them what I said just followed on the questions I had been asking in the committee meeting that they had interpreted as my effort to prevent Templeton's appointment. Walker and others on the committee looked at me like they'd like to toss me out of that third-floor window.

But Erwin caught on immediately. He spun around from the window and said, "No. Ken's right. Why would Arleigh take on this tough job just because we want him to? It's the worst job we have in the whole System. No. We need to start a nationwide search and see if we can find somebody strong enough to come to El Paso and deal with that mess out there."

Immediately Templeton said, "Now wait a minute, wait a minute. Maybe we need to talk about this."

Erwin, Walker, and Templeton went down the hall to Walker's office and talked, and Templeton negotiated a deal for himself. Erwin had accomplished the task John Peace had given him.

The UTEP faculty objected and complained about the imperious imposition of Templeton on them as president, both as to him as a person and the way it was done, but in the end they accepted it. What they expected would be done to them had, in fact, occurred.

I had been unable to deliver on my promise that the UTEP faculty would be consulted in the selection of their president, yet another reason for me to feel it was time for me to leave my position as vice chancellor.

It was now December, and the new legislative session would begin in a few weeks. The terms of three regents were expiring: John Peace, Joe Kilgore, and Frank Ikard. We had made the decision to move Arleigh Templeton to El Paso from San Antonio and Frank Harrison to the San Antonio Medical School.

John Peace, still chairman of the board, called me toward the middle of December and took some time to explain he was in a bad situation in San Antonio. His term on the board and his chairmanship would expire in a little over a month, and as things now stood, he was going to leave office with the principal presidency vacant in his own hometown. He asked me if there was anybody who might make a good president for UT San Antonio, somebody we might get on a month's notice. I told him there was an outstanding administrator at UT Austin who had served his time in administration and had good management skills and had shown he could get things done. I reminded him that he had seen Peter Flawn in action before the regents as UT's executive vice president. I told him I thought Peter might be primed to take on the UT San Antonio job. He grunted his enthusiasm for the idea.

CHAPTER 26

Politics Big and Small

By that point in my profession I had learned to practice what I came later in my career to call "subordinate leadership," the ability to influence people above me to get them to help me accomplish an objective I wanted. This was more than just doing good staff work to implement what a superior wanted done. It was a variation on doing what leaders do from the top but doing it from below to leaders. I was learning to find ways to lead a leader from a subordinate or lower position in the hierarchy of authority in order to influence a superior to undertake some enterprise or quest I wanted to pursue.

There were numerous policy positions that I recognized would be impossible for me to establish or even to influence substantially by speaking out myself. Similarly, there were decisions and actions that I believed were needed that I had no authority to take myself. So I set about trying to find ways to get people in positions of authority to take actions I thought desirable. It was not so much the practice of opportunism as it was finding ways to convince someone in authority that it would be beneficial for them to do something, whether to speak out or act or take a leadership position.

Sometimes it was no more than getting somebody in charge to provide a cue to subordinates that would free them up to act when they had been unsure of what the boss really wanted. Other times it amounted to finding a way to help a leader to do something he wanted to do when he did not have the time to put together the tactical moves necessary to make it happen. Sometimes it amounted to being aware of the propensities and wants of a leader and figuring out a way to play to those needs in the leader by proposing an action that would not have occurred to him. In these ways I could get a leader to help me to do what I sought to accomplish and at the same time have that leader satisfied with the recognition or reward he got for taking action or speaking out. I had done this even in my first job out of graduate school, and I had used it many times since.

In the three years I had worked at the UT System I had become dismayed by what I saw as continuous capitulation by the Coordinating Board on higher education. They were giving in to almost every whim and aspiration of the colleges and universities of the state. New duplicative degree programs and professional schools were being proposed by the universities and were being all too readily approved by the Coordinating Board.

A new kind of doctoral degree not requiring a dissertation was being promoted. New campuses were springing up across the state and being authorized and approved by that board. Universities were beginning to offer courses off campus, and many of the courses were being taught by "pickup" faculty hired at the local sites with no upholding of academic standards.

It was no longer any of my business in my new position that this was occurring. But it galled me to see this happening when it was the Coordinating Board's responsibility to hold the line and maintain standards and carry out the charge of the legislation that had created the board.

Out of my frustration I drafted a diatribe criticizing what was going on. I argued that the Coordinating Board needed to toughen its standards and stand up to local ambitions and pressures in the interest of maintaining quality and stopping the dilution of resources among more and more campuses. I knew if I released the statement it would get less reaction than a book falling off a shelf in an empty library. But I continued to polish and strengthen the statement.

One day in the fall of 1972 when Erwin was leaving town, I told him I would like to take him to the airport and talk with him about something. I gave the statement to him in the car and asked him if he would feel comfortable releasing it under his name. He read it as I drove.

When we arrived at the airport, he said, "I agree. This needs to be said. It's a good statement. But I'm not the one to say it. Everybody would say I was the pot calling the kettle black. Look how many new schools we've grabbed up. And now Tyler is pissing in their pants to get in the UT System. And let's face it: I've gotten most of our expansion by going around the Coordinating Board."

I pointed out that no one would pay any attention if I released the statement.

He acknowledged that was true and said, "You need to find somebody else."

I considered several other possible sponsors for the statement, and in the end I decided to talk with Wales Madden, a former UT regent and Panhandle businessman and lawyer. In 1972 he was serving on the Coordinating Board.

Madden looked at the statement and was immediately enthusiastic about using it. Although he had been party to some of the runaway approvals of degree programs and construction projects passed by the Coordinating Board, he was concerned that the board and staff were not doing their job. He said he and other board members might disagree with staff recommendations to approve more degree programs, but they didn't have the data or the time to build a case to override staff recommendations for approval.

Timing was good for him as his term on the Coordinating Board was about to expire. He asked to make a statement at the end of his last meeting as his swan song, and he read the criticisms of the board that I had prepared. When he finished, the entire audience stood and gave him a standing ovation. So many others shared our concerns about the board needing to tighten up its review and approval procedures, even those in the audience who were benefiting from running over the Coordinating Board.

Madden's criticism of his board was resented by a number of his colleagues and by the staff of the Coordinating Board, but parts of it were immediately picked up by newspapers across the state and reprinted with editorial endorsements.

A couple of months later I was visiting with Art Dilly, the chancellor's chief of staff, in his office, and at one point he reached over and lifted a sheaf of newspaper clippings and shook them at me.

He said, "See these? These are copies of editorials from all over the state endorsing Wales Madden's statement about over-expansion at the last meeting of the Coordinating Board. Erwin says with this kind of reaction it's going to be impossible to convince legislators to expand higher education. And Frank says that includes our plans to change the two-year status of our schools in Dallas and Odessa to add the freshman and sophomore years. Madden just shot down our plans to get that done the next session."

Dilly went on, "And that was done to us by our good friend, Wales Madden, who used to be on the Board of Regents. Who needs enemies when we've got friends like him?"

I found that most interesting. Erwin had said nothing to me about this, and, of course, he knew exactly where Madden's statement had come from; he had read it himself in my car.

Then just before the election in November 1972, I committed a blunder that Erwin found unpardonable.

In our regularly scheduled discussions to prepare for his role at board meetings, Regent Joe Kilgore and I would nearly always discuss state politics. His enthusiasm and confidence that Senator John Tower would be defeated by former Dallas federal judge "Barefoot" Harold Sanders were contagious. It looked as though at last, after eleven years, the Texas Democrats had finally found a candidate who could unseat Tower.

John Tower, a political science professor at Midwestern University, had initially been elected senator as the Republican candidate when the liberal branch of the Democratic Party decided to cross over and vote for Tower or to sit out the election as a way of defeating the reactionary Democratic candidate "Cowboy" William Blakley. Governor Price Daniel had appointed Blakley, a Dallas millionaire, to fill Lyndon Johnson's seat when Johnson became vice president. Blakley had become an embarrassment to the Democratic Party as he represented Texas in Washington. Some of the more progressive members of the Texas Democratic Party devised a high-risk plan to get rid of him.

One of Blakley's political sallies occurred when Robert Weaver, an African American, was appointed by President John Kennedy as head of the Housing and Home Finance Agency. During Dr. Weaver's confirmation hearings, Blakley thought he had Weaver on the run as a witness when he hesitated in answering one of the senator's questions. Blakley pressed Weaver, demanding an immediate answer to his question.

Blakley had glanced quickly at a note from an aide and asked Weaver, "Isn't it true that you wrote a book with a man named Jim Crow?" Now he was pressing for his answer.

When Weaver regained his composure, he answered, "Well, no, I never wrote a book with anyone named Jim Crow, but I do recognize the name."

The concern of the Texas Democrats was that if Blakley were elected to the Senate by the Democrats in the special election, he could never thereafter be defeated. It made more sense to elect a lightweight like John Tower, even if he was a Republican, to deny Blakley the seat. Their strategy was then to replace Tower with a more progressive Democrat in the regular election.

In 1972 the Democrats were facing Tower's third run for the Senate. He had won the special election in 1961 and reelection in 1966, and it appeared that "Barefoot" Sanders could be elected. There was much early rejoicing at the comeback of the Democratic Party with a more progressive candidate in the race.

Things were looking so bad for Tower that even he and his supporters were becoming discouraged. I witnessed evidence of this at the Washington Dulles Airport on a return flight to Austin. At this unusually designed airport, passengers enter a bus that is elevated to the entry level of the terminal, the bus compartment is lowered and driven to the plane away from the terminal, and the bus is again elevated to the door of the plane.

On this particular flight I happened to be standing behind Senator Tower and his wife as the driver began to position our bus to extend the ramps for us to enter the plane. We were standing at the front of the bus next to the driver and watching as he positioned the bus and the ramps.

John Tower's wife nudged him and nodded toward the driver of the bus. She said, "Well, John, you could always get a job driving one of these."

Joe Kilgore's enthusiasm for "Barefoot" Sanders's election was welcome news to me. When I received a call from the Democratic Party, I agreed to contribute. Then as I was about to hang up, the caller asked if they could use my name in a public advertisement listing people endorsing Sanders's election. I was hesitant, and then I threw care to the winds and said, yes, why not? It would be such a joy to be associated with the defeat of John Tower at long last.

I had considered Tower a pretender in the job of senator since 1962 when I had witnessed his performance one day in the Capitol in Washington just after his first election. I was in the Senate gallery to observe the debate on a bill I was monitoring when there was a roll call vote. I watched Tower leave his seat and go through the doors off the floor just as the roll call was getting close to his name. "Senator Tower," was called twice without him answering as I watched him peering through one of the small windows in the doors where he had just exited. Then the roll call of those who had not answered on the first call began. When Tower's name was called this time, he created his own little drama on the floor of the U.S. Senate as he flung open both swinging doors and strode into the chamber shouting, "Present."

The misjudgments and shortsightedness of my hasty decision to become politically involved became quickly evident.

A few days after John Tower was reelected, I was called to come up to Don Walker's office, where Erwin sat on the sofa and waved a clipping of the newspaper advertisement at me. He exclaimed, "What in the world possessed you to put your name in this ad?"

All I could say was, "I thought Sanders's election was a sure thing."

"There is *never* a sure thing in politics," he shot back.

Then he added with resignation, "Let's just hope they don't come after us on this."

I knew I had made a fatal mistake. I considered it fortunate that I had already begun to look for another job. Erwin had not said it, but if Tower's people called, he would have to fire me immediately to preserve the university's relations with the senator's office. But I knew also that even if they did not call, I had to leave.

Among my independent actions and opinions, my misjudgment in signing the political endorsement for Senator Tower's opponent had to be the final stupidity in Erwin's eyes. After that we consulted when we had to. I think he decided he had to make me inconsequential and he froze me out. Certainly he wanted me to have a low profile so as not to be identified by Tower's people.

In sum, Erwin came to see me in the end as worse than a nuisance, someone whom he could find no further use for and a burden to the UT System, someone whose mere presence could be harmful to his university. I had become a liability.

Erwin never told me it was time to go. I knew it without being told. I don't know that Erwin instructed Chancellor LeMaistre that he had to get rid of me, but I do believe he did. LeMaistre avoided every unpleasant encounter or confrontation possible, and he would not have come to me as he did had he not been instructed to do so.

In any event, I was not surprised when LeMaistre came to my office one afternoon and said, "Things are getting very bad here. I have already talked with Bill Knisely [vice chancellor for health affairs], and I wanted to talk with you."

LeMaistre continued, "We may all have to go. We need to be looking around. I may have to go myself. I want you to know that our whole operation is being questioned by the regents. I can't tell you what the future holds. You need to know that if I have to leave, you will need to make your own plans."

I had already begun to do so.

With Joe Kilgore leaving the board, Lady Bird Johnson, who had by 1973 served for two years on the board, was chosen to take his place as chair of the board's Academic Affairs Committee. Consequently, on January 22, 1973, Kilgore and I were set to brief Mrs. Johnson on her new duties. That afternoon he and I went up to the top floor of the new LBJ Library building to meet with her.

Just after stepping off the library elevator, to the left there is a replica of the Oval Office. In front of Kilgore and me were a couple of tourists who stood in the doorway to the Oval Office, where they had pressed a button to activate a recording of President Johnson's voice commenting on the significance of that office to the nation.

Turning to the right, Kilgore and I went into the room where we were to meet with Mrs. Johnson. As we sat on the sofa and waited for her to arrive, we could hear the president's recorded voice come on again and again as additional tourists visited the Oval Office outside and listened to the former president's briefing.

Kilgore and I knew President Johnson had suffered a second heart attack earlier in the year while visiting his daughter in Virginia. At that time Lady Bird had acknowledged that since retiring to Texas he had resumed smoking.

We commented to each other about another four years of Lady Bird's six-year appointment being a long time and how we doubted the president would survive her full term on the board.

We commented on what it would be like for the regents if he were to die during her appointment.

Mrs. Johnson joined us and spent a focused couple of hours with us going over what would be expected of her and the roles she would have to assume from Kilgore to chair his committee. As we finished and were gathering our papers, one of her assistants knocked on the door and told Lady Bird that her husband had had another heart attack at the ranch and was being flown to San Antonio for treatment. They were sending a helicopter for her.

Within a few hours the announcement came that President Lyndon B. Johnson had died.

CHAPTER 27

Sizing Up Frank Erwin

L eadership and decisions in the UT System and with the Board of Regents in those years came largely from Frank Erwin, firmly and without question while he was chairman and continuing even after John Peace took the chair. Erwin was careful not to displace or go around the authority of the new chairman, but he initiated much of what the board and staff did even after he was no longer chairman. Some of this he did after talking with Peace, but much of it he did on his own, knowing Peace's propensities and extrapolating them while continuing his own influence over individuals.

Frank Erwin and John Silber were much alike in several ways. Each had a vision of what the University of Texas at Austin should and could be, and each was willing to work assiduously to achieve his goal. They were both forceful and at times ruthless in pursuing their plans. In contrast to Harry Ransom, who never seemed to do anything for the university for self-aggrandizement, they both were using the university for personal purposes as well as to promote the progress of UT.

It did not take me long after John Silber left to come to the conclusion that the vision he had for the university, despite his using the school for personal advancement and to pursue political office, was more congruent with the functions and processes of a great institution than Erwin's vision for UT. Silber could tolerate, and often he even relished, conflict and confrontation. Erwin preferred to do, as he put it so often, what he was "big enough" to do, and he did not indulge in what he considered unnecessary public debate over differences of opinion as part of reaching a decision. Silber was a fencer; Erwin, a broad swordsman.

John Silber understood that a major role of a great university is to be a critic of society at large. Erwin begrudgingly tolerated the freedom of tenured faculty members to speak out on political, economic, social, and legal issues. He did not like it. In his view this hurt UT. He felt certain the school would be better off with the public and its elective officials if faculty members would just keep their mouths shut and not feel compelled to speak out on controversial issues. Erwin felt the faculty often bit the hand that fed them; Silber, I think, felt that was a duty of a top-flight faculty.

Contrary to popular belief, Erwin was not solely interested in concrete, walls, buildings, athletic facilities, the stadium, and the enforcement of peace and calm on the campuses. He knew a university had to have outstanding programs, top-quality faculty and laboratories and research facilities, and a great library. And he wanted to have leaders in place who knew how these things were garnered and aggregated. As inadequate as he may have considered Harry Ransom as a forceful leader when up against student protesters, he nonetheless recognized that Ransom somehow knew what would put UT on the list of nationally recognized institutions. As a result, he supported many of Ransom's endeavors, especially his acquisitions for the Humanities Research Center and the library. He granted Ransom much latitude. Efforts to constrain Ransom's expenditures by bringing them under the budget of the general library were initiated by President Spurr and later enforced rigorously under President Lorene Rogers.

What Erwin did not understand was that his well-publicized sallies into policymaking and administration were limiting the pool of leaders who would be willing to come to head up his university and its colleges. And continuing publicity about his role in the encroachment of the board into UT academic matters may have affected faculty recruitment as well. Of the six UT presidents since Stephen Spurr, only two were not from the Austin campus. Of the seven chancellors since Harry Ransom, only one was not from within the UT System.

By no means were Erwin's machinations simply, to use Silber's phrase, an exercise in "arrogance and the love of raw power."

His intent was to help the university, and often what he did was extremely beneficial and was done behind the scenes without personal recognition.

For example, while serving as the UT president, Logan Wilson saw a way to obtain more visibility in Washington for the school. He set out to arrange for more UT representation on science boards and review committees to raise the national recognition and rankings of the university.

Wilson, because he was not a scientist, asked Norman Hackerman, then department head of chemistry, if he would be willing to help him in the efforts being made to appoint President Wilson to the National Science Board. Hackerman readily agreed, and then he heard nothing more about it. A few months later Wilson explained to him that he had not been able to accept the appointment. There was a state law prohibiting any state employee from holding two positions of "honor and trust." Wilson would have had to give up his $18,000 a year salary to take the unpaid appointment to the National Science Board.

When Erwin came on the Board of Regents and Hackerman was being considered for president, Erwin told him that when Hackerman was made president of UT, he was planning to go to President Lyndon Johnson and get his support to appoint Hackerman to the National Science Board. Hackerman explained the difficulty that had prevented President Wilson from accepting such an appointment.

Erwin researched the matter and got around the prohibition by including in Hackerman's official appointment as president the requirement that one of his duties as president would be to serve on the National Science Board and to accept any other honorific appointments that came to him. Through help from the White House, Hackerman was appointed and was able to hold several positions of honor and trust simultaneously.

Hackerman explained to me that this helped him to serve the university. Even more importantly, the ability of the president to hold multiple positions of honor and trust was thereafter used as a precedent to permit faculty and other administrators to serve in similar positions.

No one monitored activities on the Austin campus as closely as Erwin. Even after the System Administration had moved off the campus and he had no office there, he returned to walk the campus and check firsthand what was going on.

One hot summer day Erwin came by my office with his suit coat on his fingers thrown over his shoulder and commanded breathlessly, "Come with me."

As I followed him up the stairs I saw that his shirt was soaked through with perspiration.

We entered Walker's office and Erwin threw his coat aside and flopped down on the sofa. He was still breathing hard. He said, "Guess what I just discovered. I decided I would climb up the ramp to the top of the new stadium addition to see how things are going to look from up there."

That explained his sweaty condition. The elevators in the new construction were not yet working. He had walked up the long ramp equivalent to an eight-story climb that would be used by the crowds on football afternoons when the stadium opened.

He continued his recitation, "From the top deck where the seats are going to be, the view will be magnificent. But, Don, you really ought to make that hike yourself—and take some of your architects and engineers with you. You'll find something they won't believe. Remember that air-conditioned overhang under the upper deck where the television people are supposed to cover our games and where our most distinguished visitors are going to watch? Well, I discovered something interesting. No one in that area will ever see a touchdown. Or televise one. Know why? Because the steel girders supporting the upper deck hang down so far that they block the view of the goalposts at both ends of the field."

Erwin supported appointments, promotions, and awards of tenure as recommended by the faculties and academic leaders. He occasionally chafed at some of the hiring that brought troublesome and voluble critics to the law school and the humanities. And when administrators showed they were not strong enough to stand up to internal and external critics, he could not and would not stand aside to see "his university" damaged or injured.

Once I asked Erwin, "Does it ever concern you that you might be weakening administrators by making decisions for them? Not everybody will stand up to you the way Singletary did."

His grin encouraged me to go on to be sure he got my point. "I'm saying maybe you take away some initiative, or people wait to see what you think before acting on their own, even on little things."

He replied, "You ever hear that old saw about when the emperor's in the field all his generals act like lieutenants? Hell, all I have to deal with is corporals."

Silber was strong headed as well, but he had more faith in the ability of a university to adapt to what was needed and retain what was fundamental even in the face of disorder. Both basked in the attention they received as a result of their policies and public statements.

What did the university lose as a result of Silber being fired and not becoming president upon Hackerman's departure for Rice? The university would have been led more contentiously than it was by the first presidents following Hackerman. Silber knew he was smarter than anybody else. As president he would have been voluble, assertive, and progressive, and he would have stood toe to toe with the chancellor and the System Administration and even the Board of Regents on issues he felt were fundamental to the interests of the school, even if they were controversial or unpopular.

Silber probably would have used the presidency as a spring-board into Texas politics, as he did in Massachusetts, where, from his presidency at Boston University, he ran for governor and was barely defeated. He exuded confidence and certainty and never lacked for words. His ability to state and hold his positions articulately carried him far. He might have been more successful in Texas.

Why do I believe this? In one of Silber's generous moments when he was probably motivated by the hope that he might educate me to his point of view, he gave me a copy of a talk he had given to the UT Faculty Senate about the history and functions of universities. I found it didactic and thought it must have seemed to some of the faculty presumptive of him to feel they needed to be educated on this subject. But it was a good talk. Silber truly had a strong and well-documented view of the uniqueness of universities and their role in society.

But Silber's interests extended beyond ordering and running UT Austin. Politics was in his blood. He could talk conservative and progressive at the same time. His speech in Dallas that alarmed Erwin was a perfect example. Maintain order but protect freedom of expression. Abhor chaos but tolerate intellectual ferment. Control student dissent but make it a learning experience. Deprecate student profanity but joke about it. Acknowledge student decline of religious belief but lament the loss. Acknowledge presidential timidity in dealing with disorder but make clear his readiness to be firm. Recognize universities as sometimes troublesome but plead for public support.

But turning to Erwin, who was the audience he performed for? He did not seem to need much extrinsic recognition or approval. It did not appear that he ever got or took advice from anyone outside the university, such as leaders in the Democratic Party or ex-president Lyndon Johnson or ex-governor John Connally. Although I'm sure he would have preferred to be loved by the faculty and students and appreciated for what he felt he did for them, he tempered his actions and statements only when forced to do so or when losing a battle. I never saw him pander to the university community to gain approval or recognition. In fact, he seemed to relish the fight even when he knew full well that his actions or views were going to be scorned on campus.

When I repeatedly witnessed his enthusiasm as he mobilized forces for a fight, I concluded he was driven in part by the sheer excitement of rallying his troops and issuing directions. He was exhilarated as he maneuvered an organization toward a goal he pursued. In putting together his strategies for action, he was organized, calculating, and rehearsed. Above all he loved to wield the baton that assembled the troops, set the pace, cued the players to their individual roles, and made the marchers move out in step. This applied whether he was working with the legislature, the UT System Administration, or the Board of Regents. And it applied to the positions he held in the Democratic Party as well. He loved gathering the troops. In these forays he always retained a major role for himself.

Yet he was accepting of defeat. He was far from indifferent to his losses, but when he was being counted out, he often showed no surprise that it was happening to him.

But when he was winning, he was relentless; he would show no mercy. He celebrated his victories. He may not have always been a poor loser, but he could be a sore winner. He never relaxed or sat still at a Longhorn football game or seemed to be enjoying himself until UT was ahead by at least four touchdowns and the game was in the final quarter. It was all less about the game and more about the winning. He never felt comfortable seeing the second team come on to get some playing time. Why take the risk? They might lose momentum. He went after politics and university business with the same unrelenting attitude.

I asked Erwin once why he was not at least willing to meet and talk with the other side.

He said, "Why bother? It'd just be a waste of time. All we'd do is get a better understanding of our disagreements."

Most of the time he was sophisticated and refined, but then he would be surprisingly crude. He could sit in his living room discussing the classics and listening blissfully to an operatic aria one evening and the next day use one of his favorite lines: "I've got his balls in the palm of my hand."

As to what intrinsic rewards he granted himself, I have no way of knowing. He was very private and never in my presence talked about personal wants, disappointments, or satisfactions. Although he did love to share his joy and satisfaction when God delivered another enemy into his hands.

He did speak unabashedly and even sentimentally about his love for the university. His greatest satisfaction in life was to see his enemies stumble or fall and to see his university move on to greatness, be it in athletics or academically.

His greatest failing was in his conviction that his university needed his protection. He did not understand that the university was fully capable of protecting itself. He simply underestimated the resiliency and strength of a great university to live with critics and dissidents. He failed to see that the value of the University of Texas to the state was so great that no one would be permitted to do great harm to it.

He felt the university needed to be steered; he did not understand that a great university finds its own way. Erwin often intervened too soon when an issue could have been left to mature and even succumb quietly without the university doing anything. He did not like to leave challenges unanswered and as a result got into some fights that never would have come to much if he had not gotten involved personally and made the issue front-page news. He was stubborn and once embarked on a course was a hard man to redirect. Once Erwin assumed the "hero role" to defend his university, it was hard for him to give it up. And the more he messed in the business of the university, the more he knew about it and the more challenging it became to him. This led him to get involved in matters toward the end of his term on the board that he would not have bothered with earlier.

Had Erwin ridden the students less hard and not insisted on more administrative constraints, would they have gotten out of hand?

I doubt it. The great majority of UT students were more conservative or at least less radical than students on other major campuses. And UT students did not lack the judgment or the ability to control the aberrant elements in their own ranks. Nor did they show any broad base of support for nonstudents trying to stir up serious troubles around the fringes of the campus.

Would fewer individuals have resigned or left UT for other positions if Erwin had been less disrespectful and reproving of the faculty? There might have been fewer who left, but as President Spurr was able to show, faculty retention was, in fact, very good during this period. At a press conference he announced that faculty resignations for 1972 had totaled eighteen, compared to an average for the previous four years of twenty-nine per year.

Would the legislature have cut funds to UT or otherwise have punished the school if Erwin had been less visible and had appeared to have less control of the campus in those years of turmoil? Unlikely, but maybe.

Would UT have received lower funding from the legislature without Erwin's active lobbying on behalf of the university? Definitely yes. His knowledge of needs and his ability to sell programs and ideas and to swap and trade on behalf of the school without question resulted in higher appropriations over the years. But whether in arguing for those funds Erwin really needed to carry with him the impression of a controlling and restraining overseer of student behavior and campus order is less clear.

Not many political movers and shakers have had three of his protégés run for governor in two states. Erwin was instrumental in talking Connally into coming back from secretary of the navy to run for governor. Then there were Ben Barnes and John Silber.

I have sometimes wondered whether Erwin ever considered working with both Barnes and Silber. He had been actively promoting Barnes for political advancement to governor or senator for years. The other he worked with successfully for several years because Silber obviously had his eyes set on the UT presidency. It was when Erwin suspected that Silber also might be looking at the same positions as Barnes that Erwin had to make a choice.

Did he ever consider backing two strong runners in two different races? Frankly, I don't think he ever considered Silber to be a viable political candidate, certainly not one he would support. He clearly closed the door on Silber's Texas political ambitions when he fired him and then went on an unremitting attack on those he labeled Silber's "expatriate professors."

The last time I talked with Erwin was in connection with the 1979 legislative session. He had mobilized his forces and the universities across the state to promote a constitutional amendment. The change would create a new fund for construction for the schools outside the UT System. The amendment also would authorize the schools that had been added to the University of Texas System to participate in the construction funds guaranteed by the Permanent University Fund, the so-called PUF. Up to this point in time only three schools in the UT System had been able to issue construction bonds that were paid off by the proceeds from investments of the PUF. They were UT Austin, the UT Medical Branch in Galveston, and the old School of Mines, later renamed UT El Paso. All the other UT schools had to obtain funds for construction from other sources, mostly state appropriations.

Those limitations on the use of the PUF had over the years accrued mightily to the benefit of UT Austin. The limit of indebtedness against the PUF for bonds for construction on the three campuses was set at 20 percent of the PUF total value. The first draw on the proceeds of the PUF investments was for the retirement of outstanding bond indebtedness against the PUF. The spendable proceeds of the PUF investments were called the Available University Fund, the AUF, and after those proceeds had been spent on meeting construction bond requirements, the entire remainder of the AUF could be spent for academic enrichment but only at the main campus, UT Austin. Over the years this had been the basis for UT matching outside grants and building its national and international reputation.

Erwin's proposed constitutional amendment not only added all the other UT universities and medical schools to share in the PUF construction funds, it did something far worse. To be able to issue additional construction bonds for those campus, the amendment also authorized the indebtedness ceiling against the PUF to be raised from 20 percent of its value to 30 percent.

By the time of our conversation almost a decade had passed since I had worked with Erwin at the UT System Administration. As commissioner of higher education, I had watched with dismay his plan to divide up the PUF. I had seen the compromises being made to bring it about. I called Erwin one morning and told him

I needed to talk with him. Even though it had been years since he had left the Board of Regents, he still called the shots on key legislative matters and had been appointed by the regents to help them in their political undertakings. Erwin sounded reluctant, but he agreed to see me and suggested I meet him at the Caucus Club on Red River that evening.

When I got there, he bought me a drink and motioned for me to follow him into a back part of the club that was not yet open. We sat at a table and he asked brusquely what I wanted.

I gave him the whole load of hay. I said, "Frank, I am really concerned about this constitutional amendment on the PUF funds. Here's how I see things playing out if it passes. You're going from three schools eligible under PUF to fourteen. The nine members of the Board of Regents will become a little senate dividing up the bonding capacity of the PUF among the fourteen campuses. Five cities bigger than Austin have schools in the System: El Paso, Houston, San Antonio, Dallas, and Fort Worth, if you count Arlington as part of Fort Worth. Those cities will lobby to get appointments to the Board of Regents to look after the interests of their cities. And the primary job of those regents will not be to look after UT Austin the way you have; it will be to see that their cities get their share of the construction bonds. They will care less and less about Austin being a university of the first class in the state and more and more about getting their share of the PUF for the schools in their cities. And with you increasing the bonding capacity against the PUF by 50 percent, that means the bonds the regents can issue will also increase the portion of the Available Fund obligated to pay off construction bonds. Then for academic enrichment and excellence, UT Austin will only get anything that's left over in the AUF after the bond payments are made. UT Austin will even have to compete against the other cities to get their share of the construction bonds. I think that amendment is the worst thing that could possibly happen to UT Austin. And it will pass because there are more schools and cities gaining by the amendment to spread the money around than by leaving the money concentrated at Austin."

Erwin was quiet for a long time as he stared at me and sipped from his drink. Then he said, "You may be right, but I had to decide what we could do to protect the PUF from being divided up and given to *all* the other schools in the state. You've heard Tech and the Lubbock senator saying they want their share, and the University of Houston wants the same. That son of a bitch, the speaker of the House, wants the PUF divided among all the schools so the legislature can reduce their appropriations. That's been going on for years. And the other schools in the UT System are always griping that UT Austin is the darling of the regents.

"I had to take a calculated risk about what was best for UT. This is a compromise, but it's better than having the whole PUF divided up and dished out across the state. Or to have it subtracted from appropriations for higher education. I've been fighting to keep the PUF for UT since before the '73 Constitutional Convention. I've been fighting this for over ten years. At least this way we keep it all just for the UT schools. That's why I supported a separate construction fund for the other schools, so we can keep the PUF to ourselves. And with oil prices going up, I'm hoping there will be a lot more to go around."

He went on, "You say the nine regents will become a little senate divvying up the PUF? Better, I say, than having the legislature spreading it around to everybody and using it to cut appropriations."

We talked some more about this and the legislative session.

He said, "Do you realize how hard I've had to fight for every dollar I ever got out of the legislature? Take those new campuses. The land didn't cost the state a nickel. Not a penny. And we had to fool them into thinking the students were paying for all those new buildings with tuition money. Most of 'em have never figured that out. And then there's research. It's like pulling teeth to get them to put money into that. And sabbaticals? Forget it. We're one of the few big universities in the country that doesn't fund sabbaticals. We have to do it sub rosa. The legislature is not our friend. Never has been. We are going to have to fight them forever to get the money they should be giving us."

He got in a more jovial mood. He actually smiled and chided me, "You know I made one bad mistake when I was drafting that bill for John Connally to set up the Coordinating Board. We should've put in a provision that requires the senate to confirm the appointment of the commissioner. In fact, we should've required reconfirmation every session. I would've busted your ass every two years if you messed with UT."

I laughed and responded, "Once would've been enough, Frank."

Then Erwin really surprised me. He said, "Ken, you really do love the university, don't you?"

I was totally nonplussed. I stammered something that of course I did. Maybe at times I had asked UT Austin to justify something they wanted to do. That was just part of my job as commissioner. That the state needed to maintain its two premier schools, UT Austin and A&M. Stuff like that.

He frowned when I mentioned A&M.

I did not stay long, but it was clear he was reluctant to let me go. He was a lonely man.

Erwin's question to me summed up our differences about how we thought about UT Austin. I saw what was coming down with the constitutional amendment as bad public policy. I was looking at the damage that was going to be done to UT and A&M as harmful to the state as well as to the schools. But he did all that he did out of true, heartfelt love for UT Austin.

After he left the Board of Regents, the drama of his presence was gone. No other regent could possibly be as colorful or at times as outrageous. Lloyd Lochridge, a prominent Austin lawyer, told me that when the Cambridge Tower was being built years earlier at the corner of Lavaca and Nineteenth Streets, he was retained by the Dallas firm developing the site. The developer described the problem they were having with their construction fence between the excavation work and the Kappa Sigma fraternity house adjoining their property. They told Lochridge that as fast as they would construct a fence, the fraternity boys would tear it down and throw the pieces in the excavated hole.

Lochridge said, "And then the client said to me, 'Oh, by the way, there is an older fellow up there with the boys. He seems to be giving directions while they're tearing down our fence. We want you to stop that for us.'"

Of course, the 'older fellow' was Frank Erwin. He was still loyal to his fraternity and dropped by to look after their interests and cause mischief.

After Erwin left the Board of Regents, the presidents at UT Austin and the System chancellors became more independent. They appointed their own subordinates and spent less time trying to figure out what the regents might want and more time selling and convincing the board of their needs to move UT Austin toward greater academic excellence. But it was not solely that the presidents had become stronger; the Austin campus became more manageable. The campus was far less polarized on political issues, and the faculties could settle into their true scholarly tasks and not have to fight to protect their turf against political encroachment.

Among all else that I learned from working near Frank Erwin in those years, nothing he taught me was so important as discovering that I had to fight to maintain my independence of judgment. And of this I can be absolutely certain: that was the one lesson Erwin never intended to teach me.

A short time after Robert Caro's tome came out, *The Power Broker: Robert Moses and the Fall of New York*, I asked Erwin if he had read it. He had.

Caro, in over a thousand pages, described how Moses used power through the Port Authority of New York and the multiple other positions he held to build numerous mammoth bridges, freeways, parks, beaches, and housing projects, often riding roughshod and uncompromisingly over opponents and supporters alike to have his way.

Without my having to ask, Erwin volunteered his opinion.

"Let me tell you something. Robert Moses was a great man. If he hadn't pushed people out of his way and run over people opposed to him, New York would be impossible to live in today. He knew what needed to be done, and he got the power and he used it. There was no way talking about it or being nice was going to get it done. The system was broke. The only way to get anything done in New York was to let Robert Moses do it."

I had seen in Caro's book what he had seen. How could he not like Robert Moses? He was describing himself.

CHAPTER 28

Loyalty to What?

Who did I think I was to arrogate to myself the right to work against Frank Erwin, a man appointed to two terms and twice confirmed by the Texas senate to represent the people of the state in leading the University of Texas? Who was I to presume that I could on occasion work underhandedly against Erwin, a man who had a firm vision of the university? Who was I, a mere subordinate, to dare to disagree with Erwin's best judgments and interpretations of events, a man who directed his every move to protect and enhance the future of the university he loved?

Fair questions of anyone having just read my confessions of disloyalty. Mere minion though I may have been, I had my own sense of what was not in the best interest of preserving and advancing excellence at UT. I felt I knew the positions that the faculty would have taken if they had been at the table participating and had been consulted on what Erwin was proposing. My recent protracted readings in the history and philosophy of higher education for my doctorate had prepared me to measure what Erwin proposed doing against standards of excellence and accepted forms of governance in the universities of Europe and the United States. Theory and history had been raised to potent awareness in my mind, and they placed high in guiding my thinking.

Yet my critics could answer, what difference should my views make when I disagreed or how knowledgeable I thought I was about the history of higher education? I had not been deputized to represent the faculty. Frank Erwin was in every way legitimately in charge of directing events and decisions at the university. Critics could say it was my duty to support him; if I couldn't bring myself to help him, I should have had the good sense to get out of his way.

Two opposing judgments might be rendered on my behavior. From one viewpoint I was guilty of shameful insubordination; from the other, I had taken necessary, even daring, action in the interests of the university and the faculty. But I was not looking for judgment from anybody beyond myself, and recognition of any kind would have been disastrous. What I did was private to me and shared only on the one occasion when I needed help from Gregorian.

As to responsibility or accountability for what was being done under Erwin's direction, in my lowly position I would never have been seen in any way as responsible or accountable. Yet I felt accountable and responsible. I was part of the team carrying out his policies and decisions.

On those rare occasions when I did oppose Erwin, I did not do so merely to disobey nor to fulfill some self-interest. I simply did not feel that my first loyalty was to Erwin and those supporting his actions and policies. Although never feeling any self-righteousness, I did feel the purposes and mission of the university were being undermined.

When I worked to ensure that Bryce Jordan's name did not get on the search committee's list of candidates for president, I felt the damage that would be done with his appointment would be permanent and immediate, and it could not be undone once he was appointed. I truly believed this, and my conclusions had been substantiated by Regent Joe Kilgore sharing his reservations with me. I felt sure Kilgore and I were correct.

Not that Jordan couldn't have been forced on the university by the regents as permanent president. He could have been made president because the regents, the System Administration, and the legislators, standing behind Erwin, would have backed Jordan regardless of the vehemence of the reaction on the campus. He could have survived. But the price of his taking the position would have been devastating to the campus.

Erwin had his views of what was right for UT, and I had mine. He could do far more than I about his views, but I was able, on occasion, to do what little I could.

As a matter of fact, most of the time I had no difficulty in implementing Erwin's plans. Most of the time I felt he was on the right course, even when I had reservations about the closed procedures he preferred to follow in reaching his decisions. Only occasionally did I work to undercut or try to slow down or ameliorate some position he proposed taking. In such rare cases where I did decide to interfere, I took each case as it came. I had a nagging feeling that if I didn't do it, who would? I never saw what I did as part of an overall plan to oppose him. In each case I made my decision almost instinctively. As I look back on what I did, I defend my actions as essential democratic insubordination.

So although I was less than enthusiastic about Erwin's orders or sometimes worked against his interests, how did he look on me? I think Erwin thought at first that I would be a useful tool to him if I could learn fast enough. A number of things I did and recommendations I made to him were fully congruent with his preferences. As he had said to Otis Singletary, I was not a complete idiot. I think this led him to believe I would be a useful member of the organization pursuing the welfare of the UT System and especially UT Austin, *as that welfare was envisioned by him.*

I have described situations when he deferred to me or my judgment, which could have happened only because he thought I was on board as part of his team or he thought my advice was worthwhile. Until I removed the president of UT Dallas, I think he had seen me as a mere functionary. Firing that president had impressed him, and he told me so. For a while he may have felt I showed promise. But there were too many missteps and then some palpable disagreements and an occasional personal initiative that I had not checked with him. And he was promptly informed about each of these, whether it was a quote in a newspaper he took exception to or something more overt such as my having drinks with faculty members who opposed the division of the College of Arts and Sciences. Someone was poisoning my interests with Erwin, and he began to have his doubts and then to lose confidence in me. Finally I removed all doubt of his ability to trust my judgment with my public endorsement of Senator John Tower's opponent.

But why hadn't he fired me after I went to the *Texan* dinner and after I gave him my smartass answer that he shouldn't be the only one knowing what the opposition was up to? He could have. It would have sent a message. I can't speculate on why he didn't. Yet at the time I had absolutely no sense that my job was in danger for attending that dinner.

How must I have been seen by those with whom I worked? To the presidents I was probably at times an obstacle between them and their desires to get their academic wants before the board in unadulterated form. Several of them sensed that I shared with them their reservations about the overreaching intrusion of the regents, and hence the System, into their campus affairs. On occasion they recognized that my proposed modifications or suggestions on timing for presenting their requests helped them to get what they wanted. Some appreciated my small help; others saw me as a hindrance and a filter between them and direct access to the board. Arleigh Templeton was one of the latter. He wanted to deal directly with the board and resented me or the chancellor or anyone on the staff interfering with him going straight to the top, directly to the regents.

Chancellor Charles A. LeMaistre, "Mickey," my boss in the hierarchy, was an anomaly to me. He could be absolutely marvelous, and then he could be his own worst enemy. He could sell anything and promote any idea. He could spin a line of reasoning and justifications that had you wondering what he was going to pull out of the hat next. But he hated confrontation. When under pressure, he would tell people what he thought they wanted to hear or what would make them feel good. This meant that reality got bent at times to fit the needs of the moment. Basically he was a kind man. When he had no choice and was pressed to the wall he could be tough, but I never saw him be outright mean; it was not his nature.

If he was an anomaly to me, I must have been a conundrum to him. First, he had not hired me. I had been appointed by the regents at the same time he had been elevated to chancellor. He did not provide me with much direction and used me very little as an assistant to support him. This was almost certainly in part a result of the way I had been appointed by the regents to work under him.

Moreover, within a month of my appointment as his vice chancellor, he had held that ill-fated meeting with the deans about dividing the College of Arts and Sciences. He had to have known that the letter Erwin forced him to send to the deans that afternoon, clarifying what he had meant to say, had to have resulted at least in part from my having reported to Erwin on what took place in the meeting.

LeMaistre also had to pick up the pieces after I fired the UT Dallas president. I am sure he must have decided I had done that on Erwin's orders, not that I might have done it of my own volition. As a consequence, LeMaistre must have come to see me as an Erwin "crony" or loyalist in a position in which I should have been totally subordinate to the chancellor. He would have been justified in feeling he could not trust me.

Yet he also came to know that I had my own differences with Erwin. He knew about my having attended the celebration for the fiftieth anniversary of the *Daily Texan* and Erwin's explosive reaction to that. He knew I maintained contacts with some faculty on the Austin campus who much of the time were opposed to what we recommended to the Board of Regents. Regent Dan Williams, as one of LeMaistre's closest friends and strongest supporters, must have told him he was certain I was leaking information to the Coordinating Board. At a minimum LeMaistre had to see me as too individualistic, independent, and unpredictable to be his reliable loyalist as part of his management team.

I think it was as a consequence of all this that he left me fairly free to determine my own positions on academic issues and submissions coming from the campuses to the UT System. Every one of my recommendations for board consideration I submitted to LeMaistre, and they were usually readily accepted. I did, in fact, try assiduously to work as a staff person subordinate under him as my boss, the chancellor. My views of loyalty to the boss as fundamental to the effective workings of an organization had been thoroughly ingrained from my earliest management experience.

But we parted in our own ways. When I submitted recommendations for him to forward to the board for action, it was understood that if the recommendations had to be explained or defended to the regents, it was my responsibility, not his. I think he knew I would tell him what I thought, but he may have never felt completely comfortable or confident that my differences would stop with my having voiced them to him.

Yet he confided in me about having to reconvene the presidential search committee to try to get them to add Bryce Jordan's name to the list of recommended candidates. Did he think I could help him? That I would? He had to have trusted me to tell me what he did that day.

But in all honesty, if I had been chancellor, I am not sure I would have wanted to have someone like me working for me.

When LeMaistre came to my office to tell me that he, as well as the vice chancellor for health affairs and I, might need to find new jobs, little did he know how accurately he was describing his own fate. Don Walker would frequently comment to me about how "my boss" (not *his*) was having difficulty keeping his different stories straight. How LeMaistre would tell different regents different versions of the same situation, not recognizing that regents talked to each other and compared stories. For example, one day Walker told me he had just talked with a new regent, Ambassador Ed Clark, and he mimicked Clark's drawl, saying, "Dahn, kin you tell me whah the chancellor *lahys* ta me?"

In just over a year Walker would have so poisoned the board on LeMaistre that he was moved out of the chancellor's job and into the presidency of the M.D. Anderson Cancer Institute in Houston. And Don Walker happened to be conveniently available to become chancellor.

Shortly after becoming chancellor, Walker arranged through Ed Clark, his principal supporter among the regents, to receive an honorary doctorate from Southwestern University in Georgetown. Walker then insisted that his staff address him as "Doctor Walker."

John Silber's scathing assessment of Erwin's remaining administrators and advisers, LeMaistre, Walker, Jordan, and me, that day he was fired in Don Weismann's office had been remarkably prescient.

As for my colleagues on the chancellor's staff, I was probably mostly a puzzlement. I did not fit the mold of what was expected of us as advisers and facilitators to the board. I must have appeared too dense to catch on or I seemed intentionally to ignore the cues from the board as to their desires. My recommendations were sometimes contrary to what the board had made clear were their preferences. Or from time to time my proposals were slightly off the mark of the regents' stated desires when my recommendations could so easily have been made to conform precisely to what they wanted. This resulted in whispered exchanges among some of the staff about me not being long for this world or jokes about how "our forces are in disarray." Another reaction was wonderment at times that I managed to survive at all after defending or justifying a position incongruent with where the board very obviously preferred to go. That I did not see as my foremost obligation in preparing recommendations to the board the need to determine first their wants and then conform to them made me unpredictable and therefore dangerous.

And, of course, there was the in-house intrigue required to keep Deputy Chancellor Walker informed about everything he might be able to use to gain favor with the board. Because I was not one of his informers and he could not make me into a tool supporting him, I was seen as uncooperative and therefore unreliable. I became someone his informers reported on. Anyone not carrying Walker's water and trying to make him look good and keeping him from a possible misstep he saw as threatening.

As to the board itself, I believe most of the regents saw me as loyal staff support, but clearly only that, support and staff, and definitely subordinate. They were experienced businessmen, lawyers, or physicians and had served on numerous corporate boards. They did not seem to resent or be troubled by recommendations and data that might run contrary to where their instincts or politics led them. They never showed any inability to sort out differing opinions and contrasting information. And they clearly knew they were in charge. Reports and views coming from a subordinate did not present an insurmountable obstacle to their doing whatever they decided to do. Staff recommendations did not so much close off choices the regents wanted to consider as provide information they used in arguing different options with each other.

Almost all of the academic items I prepared for the board were presented by the chair of the Academic Affairs Committee, headed during my tenure by Joe Kilgore. The fact that he, rather than a staff person, presented the material gave the recommendations more weight. And, of course, he never presented anything to the board he did not agree with, so the presidents and I had an advocate on the board to carry our water.

I never got the impression that individual regents were keeping a tally of how many "mistakes" their staff members made, how many times they overrode a staff member's recommendations, or whether an adviser groveled enough or pandered to their wants sufficiently. Yet I believe some of my colleagues kept their own tallies on each other and projected their own views onto the board in their efforts to anticipate actions to be taken by the regents.

It was that very procedure of open debate by the board that made Walker uncomfortable. Deliberative discussion and open debate made ambiguity and irresolution possible on issues brought before the board. The ideal board meeting in Walker's view was one in which the staff recommendations were received by the board, needed only perfunctory discussion, required no debate, and were adopted without modification. Walker's preference was that every issue be so thoroughly circumscribed that the only possibility for board action was to adopt what he recommended. All too often what was recommended was what Walker and Erwin had already decided on.

Within the resulting obsequious and groveling environment that permeated the System Administration, anyone not playing the game was a setup for backstabbing. Someone once applied the description of a legislative session to our offices and the Board of Regents, "It's like an Italian opera: a person gets up to sing, and someone stabs him in the back."

One example will illustrate what the environment was like. In 1972 the new UT Dallas president, Bryce Jordan, proposed adding a law school to his new campus. This proposal resulted immediately in two older, established public universities proposing to create new law schools in Dallas as well, Texas A&M University and North Texas State University in Denton. They both believed that if any university in the area deserved a new law school, each of them did, not this new school, UT Dallas.

It fell within my responsibilities to prepare the analysis of Bryce Jordan's proposal for presentation to the board. In my material for the board I drew from studies and data that showed Texas did not need a new law school to produce more lawyers because the public universities with law schools in Austin, Lubbock, and Houston were producing all the lawyers needed for the state. In addition, there were several private university law schools, one of which was in Dallas. Moreover, both of the public law schools in Houston and Lubbock were increasing the size of their entering classes. Based on my analysis I predicted that the state Coordinating Board would deny all three requests for a new law school. Therefore, I recommended that the UT System not send the UT Dallas proposal forward to the Coordinating Board.

Nonetheless, the regents approved the request from UT Dallas. My next duty was to deliver and justify the proposal for the new Dallas law school to the Coordinating Board, and I did so. No one at the Coordinating Board ever knew that I had, within the System Administration, recommended not forwarding the proposal.

The commissioner of higher education appointed a special committee of attorneys, chaired by Leon Jaworski, who would soon become the special investigator in the Watergate scandal, to evaluate the needs for new law schools in Texas. The committee brought in a strong report recommending disapproval of all requests for new law schools. And their report, unfortunately for me, was based on much of the same public material I had gathered and presented to the board about Bryce Jordan's initial proposal.

A few weeks later I received a call from Regent Dan Williams from Dallas. He was extremely angry and accused me of opposing the new law school in Dallas and of having fed the information I had provided to the Board of Regents to the Coordinating Board and Leon Jaworski to kill the request.

I replied, "Dan, you served on the Coordinating Board before you were a regent, and you know how they research their recommendations. They're not idiots over there. The material I gave to the regents is from public documents available to anybody who wants to find out if we need more lawyers in Texas. They were bound to come across the same stuff I found. In fact, they found a lot more reasons than I did for not approving any new schools."

He remained angry and said it looked very suspicious because some of the phrases were almost duplicates of what was in my report.

I told him I couldn't account for similarities in language, and he continued to press me about leaking my material to the Coordinating Board.

Finally I told him that he needed to clarify for me how I was doing my job and tell me if I was not doing it correctly. I said, "The regents pay me well in this position, and I assume you have me on the staff to provide you with information you haven't got the time to get together yourselves. I assume you pay me to provide you with stuff you need to know and not just tell you what you already know or what you want to hear. That's what I did on Bryce's proposal for a law school. If I am wrong about that then I need for the board to tell me how you want me to do my job differently."

He calmed down and said he guessed that was right. But he did not apologize about his initial accusations. I was sure he terminated his call still feeling I had been disloyal and had helped the Coordinating Board turn down his university's request.

The point here is that I knew immediately when he called and made his accusations what was going on. It was part of the setting in which we all functioned in the UT System. There was no way Dan Williams, as president of a major bank and insurance company and as a big Dallas civic leader, had obtained copies of the Jaworski report and my earlier report to the regents and then sat down and compared them "phrase for phrase." I had been set up with Dan Williams by someone intent on undercutting me personally. Several candidates came to mind.

In this milieu of byzantine sycophancy, what leadership did I provide? Very little. I was primarily a facilitator, a mere functionary to move materials along for approval or some action required at the System level or by the board. On occasion it was necessary to send some item we dealt with to another state agency such as the Coordinating Board or to a federal agency. These were little tasks I could do effectively.

But this was far from providing leadership. Most of what we did was to receive ideas and proposals originating on a campus and polish and package them for action by others. Initiative and leadership originated on the campuses, and we provided the lubrication to bring proposals from others to fruition. Very little original action began with us. But, in the life of any true university, that was, in fact, as it should be. The futures of universities should be determined more by what originates with their faculties than what comes down from some central office or governing board.

I certainly cannot claim to have become during those years in the UT System Administration a disenchanted innocent in my job. I did not simply awaken one morning to discover to my horror the scheming and maneuvering taking place inside the university. It was worse than I had anticipated. But I understood perfectly what Princeton president Woodrow Wilson had meant when he said, "I don't want you to suppose that when I was nominated for governor of New Jersey I emerged from academic seclusion, where nothing was known of politics."

I have related from those three years I spent with the UT System the most significant events and my role in some of them. I do not pretend to have played a laudable role; at times I played a less than admirable one, depending on which side of an issue the judgment rests. At times I played a devious role and certainly by some standards a disloyal one on more than one occasion. I carried out instructions from Erwin that were harmful to UT Austin. And usually I played an invisible or intentionally concealed role. Frankly, I was entirely happy with my obscurity.

I just happened to spend these three years during a particularly volatile time of political intrusion at the University of Texas. I fully recognized from the beginning the tiger I chose to ride, and I rode it with a purpose. I had ambition to rise in higher education. With vaulting ambition driving me, I found it possible to rationalize a lot of things. Only a fool or a self-righteous simpleton not familiar with life's limited chances would fail to see the opportunity to work in the UT System Administration as the ideal place to acquire valuable experience and to prepare for a future university career. Although I clearly knew I was not qualified to hold the position of vice chancellor for academic affairs when John Peace selected me for it, the opportunity was too appealing for me to refuse to give it a try. The option was to move instead to UT Arlington as vice president. Once I decided I was going to attempt to do the vice chancellor's job, unqualified as I might be, I was not going to go about it halfheartedly.

I benefited immensely from the experience I gained. I grew and matured in my interpersonal relations, particularly with my superiors in the organization. Above all, I gained self-confidence in my own judgment and acceded to opposing views less readily. I acquired a respect for openness and inclusivity that would take me far in my future work. It had been a tough learning environment, and it left me a stronger person.

On New Year's Day 1973, the Board of Regents met in a room under the Cotton Bowl stadium, where UT was playing for the fourth consecutive year. The regents appointed several new presidents: Arleigh Templeton for UT El Paso and Frank Harrison for the UT Medical School in San Antonio. They also appointed Peter Flawn president of UT San Antonio, and Flawn informed the regents that I had agreed to become his executive vice president.

As evidence of how essential I had been in the System offices, when Chancellor LeMaistre announced a month later my move to UT San Antonio, he stated that my position would not be filled immediately.

In assessing those three years, I tracked a career similar to that of Pliny the Younger. He chose to become engaged in Roman politics, and his timing was such that Domitian, one of the most corrupt and vicious of Roman emperors, was in power. Pliny's challenge was how to climb to success in the Roman system and not sacrifice honor. In looking back on my time with the UT System, I share Pliny's summation of his career under Domitian: "I have avoided shame but deserve no praise."

Conclusion

L ogan Wilson and Harry Ransom stand out in the modern era as having led those setting the University of Texas on the path to greatness from its modest beginnings, and their vision has defined the trajectory of the school ever since. Some may argue that Frank Erwin's strong hand during the troubled years of student disorder on campuses across the country was essential to keep the school on track and to protect UT from even greater interference from the state. But no one can deny that the more circumspect and hands-off approach of regents and chancellors since the 1970s has been of major benefit to the Austin campus. To the great good of the university, political interference, both partisan and bureaucratic, has, for the most part, been held in check.

This diminution of political intrusion explains in part why UT Austin prevailed in its quest for greatness and international recognition. Above all else in that advance, of course, has been the outstanding faculty gathered and retained by the departments and colleges over the decades. It was not manifest destiny that UT Austin should rise to greatness. Prominence has come to UT through its strong faculty. In turn, assembling a critical mass of faculty necessary to attract national and international recognition required the leadership, vision, and persistence from administrators, deans, and department chairs as well as support from regents.

But in a world where university rankings are based on reputation, the faculty and their academic leaders could not alone have raised the university in the estimation of those leaders in higher education who decide the rankings. It was essential that the regents and administrators be seen to understand their appropriate roles of funding, facilitating, and protecting the university in its quest for excellence—*and that they stay within those appropriate roles.*

Yet the garnering of scholars and nurturing of faculty to mark the name of the University of Texas would not have been possible without abundant resources. In the early years, as the school made its first moves toward eminence, the excess income from the oil and gas endowment, funds that could be spent only at UT Austin, provided the impetus used by Logan Wilson and Harry Ransom to kick-start the institution and sustain the ambitions of the departments and colleges of the campus.

There is no denying Frank Erwin had an impact on UT Austin. His strong-handed control and continual interference in the affairs of the university were ultimately surmounted by the school and over time did not prove as injurious as they had seemed likely to be in those difficult years. This in itself attests to the resiliency and strength of the university. Erwin did make helpful contributions through fighting with the legislature for essential funding, which he could not have acquired for the school had he not been able to consolidate his political clout. Where he mobilized outside support behind the university he was always helpful; where he interfered and intruded, he was often harmful.

It is difficult today to imagine that the University of Texas could ever have been a mere college on the prairie. It is at present without question one of the premier universities of the world with a number of programs and departments ranked among the top twenty and even the top ten in some fields. Its faculty, its research, its library, its funding level and resources, its graduate programs, and its physical and research facilities rival those of competing institutions across the globe. In arriving at its recognized place among the great institutions of higher learning, UT Austin had to displace and leave behind many other universities in rankings. Schools do not give up their place in the roll call of "greats" without stiff resistance. UT had to struggle mightily to surpass and climb over others to its present place of recognition.

Austin still sits on a river on a fault line separating the Hill Country from the plains that run flat to the Gulf, a setting clearly part of the prairies of midwestern and southwestern America. But it is no longer physical geography that defines the city and the University of Texas. The institution sits at the nexus on Interstate 35 between Dallas and San Antonio along a line of population and economic power that far exceeds those of the entire state less than half a century ago. Austin plays a major role in the triangular economic mega-region anchored by Houston, Dallas, and San Antonio, one of fewer than ten such mega-regions in the nation and among forty such economic and population concentrations in the world. These forty mega-regions of the world produce nine out of ten patents and two thirds of all global economic output. The Texas mega-region has benefited immeasurably from the presence of the University of Texas. While serving as a contributor through scientific discovery and technology transfer, the university has also provided educated and trained citizens and contributed to the broader cultural environment that is essential to attracting and holding bright professionals and their families. Arguably UT is the most important single participant in the innovation and progress of this entire mega-region.

After a tumultuous beginning that involved repeated intrusions of politics into campus affairs by governors, legislators, and regents, the extended period of stability at the University of Texas at Austin in recent decades has contributed incalculably to the continued progress of the institution. Karl Jaspers, the great twentieth-century philosopher, described the role of the university best when he said, "The calm that is allowed at the university exists so that we may experience the storm of world events in our hearts and thoughts in order to understand it. The university ought to be the place where there is the clearest consciousness of the age, where that which is uttermost attains clarity, be it that in one spot, at least, full consciousness of what is taking place is achieved, be it that this clarity, working out into the world, shall be of assistance."

I had a minuscule and short role during the long quest for distinction by the University of Texas. In those few years I served, I witnessed the damage that can be inflicted by interference from outside the university community. Let the lessons from that time guide the regents and chancellors and other leaders of the University of Texas in supporting its continuing pursuit of preeminence.

Index